After the Baby

After the Baby

Making Sense of Marriage
After Childbirth

∽

Rhonda Kruse Nordin

Foreword by Dwenda K. Gjerdingen, M.D.

Taylor Publishing Company
Dallas, Texas

Designed by Janis Owens

Published by Taylor Trade Publishing
1550 West Mockingbird Lane
Dallas, Texas 75235
www.taylorpub.com

Library of Congress Cataloging-in-Publication Data
Nordin, Rhonda Kruse.
    After the baby : making sense of marriage after childbirth / by
Rhonda Kruse Nordin.
        p.   cm.
    Includes bibliographical references and index.
    ISBN 0-87833-168-9
    1. Parenting—Psychological aspects. 2. Marriage. 3. Marital
conflict.
I. Title.
HQ755.8 .N675 2000
649'.1—dc21   99-056432

10 9 8 7 6 5 4 3 2 1

This book is dedicated with love and appreciation, to my dear husband Bruce, and to my sons Addison and Ian. Their love and encouragement have enabled me to indulge my passion and bring this book to fruition.

A special thank you, too, to Dr. Dwenda K. Gjerdingen, whose help and direction have been invaluable.

Contents

Foreword

It is sad but true that we are often the least prepared for life's most challenging responsibilities. One such responsibility is that of becoming a parent. Although health care professionals make an effort to teach us the basics of caring for a newborn—how to bathe, feed, and clothe it, for example—we, as parents, still have few opportunities to learn beforehand how to cope with the changes that parenthood thrusts on us, especially on our marriages.

I have seen this lack of preparation on both a professional and personal level. I had just completed my formal training as a family physician when I gave birth to my first child. Medical school and residency had prepared me well for the physical changes that accompany pregnancy and childbirth. The childbirth education classes my husband and I attended taught us more than we ever needed to know about breathing patterns for labor. After the birth of our son, the labor and delivery nurses carefully taught the procedures for breast-feeding, bathing and diapering a baby, and taking its temperature. Then we were on our own. No one had prepared us for the weeks, months, and years that followed after we drove away from the hospital. Our drive home was blurred by tears of joy and fear, all mixed together. And rightfully so, for life was never again the same. My husband and I were two different people with new physical and emotional needs, a dependent infant, a new lifestyle, and a sense of total unpreparedness. It was this intense personal experience, together with the relative lack of clinical information about the postpartum period, that prompted my own research studies on women's postpartum health.

During the time I was conducting and publishing my research, Rhonda

Kruse Nordin came to me for advice and direction on this book. I had realized for some time that, even though I was personally gaining a richer understanding of the postpartum period, there still seemed to be limited educational opportunities on this topic available to the general public. Childbirth education classes continued to focus primarily on labor and delivery, with little time left over to discuss the personal and marital changes that couples might anticipate after their baby's birth. So I eagerly welcomed this book as a much needed resource for new and expectant parents. I feel privileged to have been involved with this project from the beginning.

In *After the Baby,* Rhonda Kruse Nordin clearly lays out for new parents the developments they can expect, good and not so good, in themselves and in their marriage after a baby is born. Her candid, direct style, sprinkled with anecdotes from new parents, makes this topic very approachable and even entertaining. Yet her work is cast in clinically sound principles derived from a large array of medical and psychological research studies. This book provides the educational experience that new parents need and want in order to understand and manage their marriage as it moves into parenthood. It may be one of the most stressful experiences they face as a couple.

If this book served only to enhance our knowledge of marriage and parenthood, it would be enough, but its purpose goes beyond this. It encourages us to become working partners in raising our children, to share lovingly in the labor, stress, and joy of raising a family and running a household. The overarching goal of the book is to strengthen marriages and families, and each chapter and paragraph strives toward that goal, through a skillful interplay of facts, stories, and practical advice.

The premise of the book is that the strength of our society rests on the health of each individual family, and the health of the family is, in turn, dependent upon the strength of its leaders—the parents—and the love and caring that spring forth from that relationship. Therefore, we need to be concerned with bolstering this most vital and basic alliance, and the rest of society will follow.

I have learned a great deal from Rhonda about the needs of today's new parents. This book has heightened my awareness of the changes and conflicts men and women face as they cross into the wildly uncharted waters of parenthood. I learned why many marriages break up in what seems to be inordinate proportions during this time. My medical practice delivers nearly three hundred babies each year. We observe their mothers and fathers and the marriages of these parents. Yet when working on this project, I learned things I did not know. I am sure my colleagues in the health profession will also gain from reading this book.

Those who will gain the most, though, are the many couples who are having a baby or contemplating starting a family. They will be most grateful for *After the Baby.* They will learn a great deal about their marriage and even more about themselves. The information in this book has been largely unavailable to the millions of men and women who become parents together each year. I am well aware of the facts. I work with this information each day, and much of it is available to me as a medical professional. I find it in related journals and periodicals, usually on library shelves and at resource centers I use for my work. Mostly, though, I see evidence of its reality in the lives and faces of those who are my patients. Rhonda brings this information to the men and women who so desperately need to see and understand it. I highly recommend this book. Its information is invaluable and will undoubtedly help many couples at the first critical crossroads in their marriage, after childbirth.

Dwenda K. Gjerdingen, M.D., Family Practice

∾

Introduction

I have met many jubilant new parents. Rosy-cheeked, fresh-faced, just-home-from-the-hospital-green mothers and fathers waded into our interviews purposefully, proudly showcasing their newborn. Eager to take me into their homes, these new parents gushed with enthusiasm. The stories I heard were heartwarming, peppered with good-natured ribbing and an abundance of contagious energy. Within months, though, many of these same couples reappeared, bedraggled, haggard looking, snapping at each other, the tiny bundle strategically wedged between them, creating a physical and psychological chasm. Our second interview lacked the warmth and pleasure I had observed during our first encounter. Their eagerness was replaced with hints of anger, resentment, competitiveness, and a bevy of what I define as unproductive emotions. For many, what may have begun as an easy transition to parenthood had turned into an arduous task-by-task struggle for marital survival.

Jeannie and Tom were in their late thirties when I first met with them. Only months before they had been overjoyed at the birth of their first child. I'd just been seated in their family room with Tom and the newborn when Jeannie entered. Tom was cradling their new son, whose wails were postponing the onset of our visit.

"Give him to me!" Jeannie demanded from across the room. She marched toward her husband, grabbed their screaming baby from his arms, reeled around sharply, then headed down the hall to the baby's bedroom. The child quieted immediately. Sitting in a rocker in that darkened room, clutching her baby to her breast, Jeannie sobbed louder and harder than the child.

Tom sat before me, unmoved, his arms locked at his chest, his eyes cold and hard. "Our marriage is over," he determined flatly. "Divorce is inevitable. We never fought before the baby was born. Now that's all we do. Jeannie criticizes me for how I take care of the baby. I criticize her for the same. We fight over *everything*—who's going to work, who isn't. The house is always a mess. We even fight over sex. I am so tired." He shook his head. "Where did the love go? The trust? The mutual respect? Somehow our communication system—*and* our marriage—fell apart. Honestly, I just don't know what has happened to our marriage," he added sadly. "It's just not the same since the baby was born."

This scene is not uncommon in the homes of many new parents today. Having a baby, cast as such a happy event, does not necessarily set the stage for marital bliss—even when both partners love each other very much. I found this to be true in my own home as well. I had just given birth to the first of our two sons. It was a joyous time for my husband Bruce and me, though we did not yet know the depth or range of emotion, or the intensity of life that lay ahead of us. I felt a tinge of sadness, too, at that time, for I found myself mourning the career I'd put on hold to take advantage of a generous leave of absence that was offered at my work. At my husband's urging, I began to write my first book. It was a simple collection of labor and delivery stories designed not only to help new parents have a more positive and realistic childbirth experience, but to preserve my shifting marriage as well. "You need a project," Bruce had said. "Something more than the baby." I proceeded to interview hundreds of new mothers and fathers who willingly shared firsthand accounts of their baby's birth.

Several months into my research an unsettling pattern emerged. These parents spent more time lamenting the *changes* that had taken place after the birth of their baby than the actual labor and delivery process itself. There appeared to be a need, as well as a desire, to broaden our discussions to include the *changes* and *conflicts* that had challenged them during their transition to parenthood.

Many of the mothers, like myself, had postponed childbirth, for whatever reason—in pursuit of a career, education, conception, or even the right man. Some had spent thousands of dollars to overcome infertility. Pregnancy hadn't always come easily, nor had childbirth. Now ashamed and somewhat reluctantly, many of these parents confessed (most of them for the first time) that perhaps being a parent wasn't all it was cracked up to be.

These parents told me they had been unaware of and unprepared for the changes that would occur in their lives after the birth of their baby. Prenatal classes focused on the mechanics of breathing and relaxation. They sifted through what seemed to be a thousand and one baby names before making their selection. They meticulously created birth announcements, bought the baby's crib, and decorated its room. But they spent little time, if any at all, concerning themselves with the fundamental life changes that would come after their baby's birth, and most importantly, how these changes would affect their marriage. They were wrestling with physical and emotional recoveries from childbirth, questioning their new roles and identities, and reeling in the vast lifestyle changes that proved, they said, to be much greater than expected.

Most alarming was the imbalance the baby had created *in their marriage.* I heard vivid accounts of flaring disagreements over child-care, housework, career, and lifestyle decisions—to have sex, or no sex at all. Emotional and physical exhaustion served to escalate the negative emotions that had accumulated between them since their baby's birth and had created an emotional estrangement that caused many couples, for the first time, to question their marital commitment.

"Being parents is not easy," they confided. "Being parents *together* is even harder."

I listened intently. I knew the characters well. The scenes were familiar. Bruce and I had had our own share of ups and downs after the birth of our first son. It was a relief to learn that we weren't the only couple fighting more after our baby was born, and that yes, there were days when being parents together wasn't exactly what we had hoped for or expected. The similarities led me to question whether or not our experiences were merely a natural and predictable part of becoming parents—inevitable conflicts that come in the quagmire of any transition. I didn't need to look far for an answer. What I found became the basis for this book.

Having a baby, indeed, sets off a chain of discoveries for new parents that greatly influences the state of their marriage. Although couples generally love their new baby profoundly and unconditionally, the changes it brings cause many marriages to become vulnerable and oftentimes to end in divorce. In fact, statistics on divorce following the birth of a child are downright alarming. According to the United States Department of Health and Human Services, National Center for Health Statistics, 42 percent of divorces involving parents take place before their first child leaves kindergarten, and almost 15 percent of these parents end their marriage before their children reach even eighteen months of age.

Sociologists maintain that many parents of young children divorce because they are *unprepared* for and *fail to cope* with the changes that come after a baby's birth. They believe that the *changes* after childbirth, coupled with the parents' expectations that things *won't* change, lead to the high rate of divorce among parents of young children.

After the Baby is the first book written to help couples understand the natural progression of the marital relationship as it expands to include children. In essence, this book helps men and women make sense of their marriage as new parents. Never before compiled in one source, the information presented in this volume clearly depicts how and why common changes after a baby's birth challenge the marital relationship of new parents. *After the Baby* covers each topic in a practical and direct manner, outlines the timetable in which changes and conflicts occur, and helps couples cope by providing marriage-saving solutions.

This book will help couples establish realistic expectations for marriage after childbirth. Most importantly, this book helps couples talk. *After the Baby* provides a framework for discussing sensitive issues which often affect couples for the first time in their marriage.

You will find several philosophies at work throughout *After the Baby*. The first, and the book's central theme, is that changes and conflicts are a natural and predictable part of becoming parents and inevitably affect the marital relationship. It is my goal to help couples understand this so they will not be caught off guard and tempted to throw in the towel at the first sign of marital discord. The second principle is based on current philosophies and research that suggest many parents could avoid divorce if their expectations were more in line with reality. Lastly, the underlying theme that prevails throughout my book is that we, as parents, have a shared responsibility to sustain our marriage for the sake of the family—and even for society.

☙

When I first learned from new parents about the challenges they faced during their transition to parenthood, I set out for the downtown public library, my ten-month-old son, Addison, in tow. With Addison planted firmly in his stroller, bottle and pacifier at hand and a bag of items ready to occupy and distract him, I began my research. I found shelf upon shelf of documentation and scholastic text written, I believe, with professionals in mind, but little information about marriage after childbirth compiled in a reader-friendly, easy to understand volume that brought workable solutions to ordinary parents like me.

Within a few more months, I found myself packing a double stroller and a larger bag of diversions, for by September 1990 our second son, Ian, had been born and I was in the throes of my research. En masse we continued to claim the southeast corner of the sociology section of the library: I spread a large quilt that my grandmother had pieced together years before on the floor beneath the windows, and by some miraculous feat, my two young sons played quietly and long enough so that I could pore over and record the facts I found. I persevered in my search long after my sons had left the stroller and were well entrenched in their own educational endeavors. Now, nearly a decade later, I have finished compiling the findings for this book. They are too startling to ignore.

Forty years ago, sociologist E. E. LeMasters determined that childbirth brings overwhelming tumult into the relationship of new parents. "The arrival of a baby," he stated, "particularly the first baby in a home, usually necessitates considerable change and reorganization for the parents, and some believe this transition is so disruptive that it produces a state of crisis."

An article in the *New York Times' Good Health Magazine*, dated October 8, 1989, referenced the "astonishingly stressful and social consequences of being parents," and more current experts agree: *nothing* makes a marriage more vulnerable than having a child. Ample documentation supports these claims.

ى Seventy percent of new parents said they hadn't thoroughly understood the immense responsibility of parenthood or the impact it would have on their time and relationships—*especially their marriage.*

ى At least nine out of ten couples experienced more conflict after their baby was born and said that adjusting to parenthood was more difficult *as a couple* than as an individual mother or father.

➷ Half of all new parents felt their marital happiness dropped. They argued more, showed and received less affection from each other, doubted their feelings for one another more often, felt ambivalent about their marriage, and lost interest in sex.

➷ Seven out of ten couples reported a decrease in the level of communication after they became parents, which for half became permanent.

➷ Almost *all* new mothers complained that their husband neither helped them enough with the baby or housework, nor supported them emotionally after their baby was born.

➷ Overall, Glenn and McLanahan reported in 1982 that the negative effects of having a child proved to be quite pervasive and, for many, outweighed the positive effects for spouses of both sexes and all races, major religious preferences, educational levels, and employment status.

The bottom line is that, for many couples, childbirth brings the crisis E. E. LeMasters wrote about more than four decades ago. It appears that for all the joys and anticipation of having a baby, its arrival often spurs a long drop in marital satisfaction for new parents that doesn't hit its low point until that child reaches his or her teen years! What happens to these parents? Some of them weather the avalanche of parental stress. With an overwhelming love and a diehard commitment to each other and their marriage, they stay together after the baby. Many, of course, do not. These startling numbers disclosed the overwhelming upset a new baby creates in the lives of new parents and convinced me of the far-reaching need for this book. *After the Baby* is the first book to explore the stunning phenomenon of just how susceptible a marriage is to distress after the birth of a baby.

Not every marriage is challenged after childbirth. Many good relationships are enhanced and strengthened by the presence of a baby. Bruce and I found this to be true, as did many of the couples who related their stories to me. All marriages, though, are changed in some fashion. Perhaps the first step toward staying together after the baby is realizing just what about becoming parents can be expected. What is natural? What is predictable? Should we be fighting about this? What is it about becoming parents together that somehow contributes to marital breakdown? Can it be stopped? How do we stay together when the baby is pulling us apart?

Many chapters end with a Points to Consider section that presents ideas to enhance parents' understanding of the contents and help them apply the information to their own particular situation. They are suggestions, of course, not mandates.

I believe you will find this book logical, inclusive, and easy to follow. I have written it from a parent's perspective. It is not meant so much to be a "how-to" book as a "this is what is happening and why" book. It provides a nuts and bolts description of how having a baby challenges the marital relationship of new parents.

During my ten years of research for this book, I interviewed more than two hundred sets of new parents—many more than once. Their litany of voices was from all walks of life. Some described their own experiences or those of friends and family members. Few were without anecdote to substantiate the claims of science I first thought implausible. Additionally, I cataloged more than one hundred anecdotes from interviews conducted casually at the park, at the market, at churches and schools—wherever there happened to be gathered an intimate circle of new parents. I am especially grateful to the mothers and fathers who willingly exposed the intimate workings of their marriage and their innermost feelings so that I, in turn, might share them with you.

Some one hundred professionals lent me their ear and their expertise. One stands out above the rest. Dwenda K. Gjerdingen, M.D., Family Practice, has served as medical advisor for this book. I first contacted Dr. Gjerdingen following her guest appearance on *NBC Nightly News.* For nearly two decades, her primary focus has been women's prenatal and postpartum physical and mental health. She designed, conducted, and led a team of doctors in compiling the findings that are now a chief part of *After the Baby.* Dr. Gjerdingen and I have been working partners in applying her findings and clinical analysis (along with other supportive documentation) to real-life situations with practical, workable solutions.

I consulted other doctors, psychologists, family and marriage therapists, family educators, and members of the clergy. Their experiences confirmed that the stories I heard firsthand were, indeed, representative of large populations of new parents. My real-life anecdotes are supported with theories and research by leading scholars from a wide range of disciplines concerned with the transition to parenthood, marital well-being, and status of the family. I have dissected my own marriage, and sometimes unwittingly the marriages of my family and friends. Most names have been changed to protect those I love and care about. I am confident I have written an accurate portrayal of how having a baby challenges the marital relationship and offered constructive ideas to help new and expectant parents.

In framing these marriage-saving ideas, I drew on time-honored principles used in the fields of psychology and medicine, marriage and family counseling, and the clergy. I used personal experiences, convictions, and beliefs that stemmed from the turnaround in my own marriage. From other new parents I learned which strategies worked and which ones didn't. All sources contributed uniquely to frame the chapters of this book.

ᗣ

The conflicts we encounter as new parents are linked together in complex ways. There are no simple solutions. It is my hope that this book, written with all my caring and passion, will guide mothers and fathers through the transition to parenthood, that it will help them understand divisive challenges, recover from them, stay close and committed, and rein in thoughts of separation or divorce.

The responsibility of being a parent, you see, extends beyond caring for the baby. Parenthood also means that men and women care for their marriage and plan for the role each plays, not just as a father or mother, but for the very important role of "spouse of a new parent." It is a role few of us consider, yet playing this role well will largely determine the course a marriage will take after a baby is born.

When I speak with mothers and fathers whose marriages did *not* survive, many reflect on the turn their marriage took after the birth of their children and acknowledge sadly that, yes indeed, it was *after* they became parents together that their marriage faltered and they grew apart. My goal is to stop that from happening, to catch men and women before the stressful consequences of being parents pull them apart, and of course, to bind them together while there remains yet a thread of love between them.

As new parents, you won't find yourself in every situation I outline in this book. Nor will you face conflict with every common change known by new parents. Perhaps you are among the fortunate whose marriages re-main unscathed after the birth of a baby. Maybe you have experienced the improvements in your marriage that various parents describe in this book, or with unabashed enthusiasm can proclaim, "*Nothing* has changed be-tween us." Tell others! New parents need to hear encouraging words.

If in reading this book you gain a new perspective that enhances your understanding or communication or encourages cooperation in your mar-riage, or if you glean one suggestion that somehow helps you stay together when the baby may be pulling you apart, then I have accomplished what I set out to do.

I

∼

Marriage After
Childbirth

∾

The challenge couples face after having a baby is adapting to the all-intensive caregiving role of being parents while preserving their marital relationship and maintaining some semblance of self-identity. Will their marriage stay the same? *Can* it stay the same? Why are some couples more susceptible to marital disharmony than others? Can it be stopped? Section I offers a broad perspective of the transformation that occurs at the very core of a couple's union as men and women become moms and dads *together,* and the baby becomes the prism through which they see their world.

1

∾

One Big Happy Family

Carol had been employed in our offices for nearly a decade. She was a tireless worker, focused on her responsibilities, and displayed a great deal of passion for life. Single when she first came to us, we nursed Carol through several failed romances and rejoiced with her when she finally found "Mr. Right." Married to Ted, Carol went through the profound transformations of being newly married, newly pregnant, and newly a mother. One morning Carol arrived at our offices lacking her usual bubble and enthusiasm. She seemed preoccupied, irritable. She snapped at a coworker, then pouted in frustration. I immediately suspected her source of despair. Her baby was not yet one year old—Carol must not have gotten a good night's rest.

"Rest!" she retorted, fighting back tears. "It goes much deeper than sleep. I am so mad at Ted. He wouldn't help me at all last night. The baby was up whimpering, and Ted said that if I wanted to 'baby' the baby I could, but he thought I should just let it cry. So I was up most of the night. Ted said he wasn't going to be a martyr for the baby. "

She sighed. "We seem to fight all the time now. Ted rolls his eyes at me. He seems so distant and disgusted, like he's angry at me. Honestly, I just don't know what has happened to our marriage. I don't feel *close* to Ted. I don't think he even *likes* me anymore. We're always at odds about something!" Carol slumped lower in her chair; her sad eyes searched mine for encouragement.

A few days later, in his law office across town, I spoke with Ted. He had just arrived at his desk. It was not yet nine o'clock and his tie was pulled loose at the collar. He cocked his head from side to side and rubbed the back of his neck, attempting to ease the tenseness that had accumulated there since his child's birth.

A colleague grinned knowingly at Ted and slapped him on the back. "New baby got you down?" he asked.

"Nah, the baby's great," Ted replied. "It's Carol. She's turned into a royal pain since the baby was born. She's on me about everything."

"Welcome to fatherhood!" Ted's friend laughed, moving on. Ted leaned back in retreat. "Is this what it's all about?" he questioned. It wasn't the lack of sleep that was getting him down, he explained; it was arguing with Carol. Everything had become an issue since the baby. Nothing he did seemed to please her. They were out of synch. She drove him crazy. He felt distant. He was filled with anger, resentment, guilt, frustration, and even dislike.

Yeah, he admitted, he actually *disliked* her now—his own wife! He almost felt justified. He didn't want to help her anymore; he didn't even want to be around her. Pretty scary thoughts, but they seemed to fit perfectly. Too bad, with a baby and all, that their marriage was falling apart. He shrugged, though not without concern. He knew they could weather it. *Carol* just needed to change.

What Happened to Our Marriage?

Many of us, like Carol and Ted, remain in the dark about the consequences of becoming parents together until, thrust into the fray of parenthood ourselves, we experience a series of disruptions to our normal routines and behaviors that often result in a gradual, yet definable change in the love we feel for each other and how happy we are in our marriage. Riddling the transition to parenthood are frequent disagreements, an emotional distance, and a stalemate to cooperation.

Although the glow of "having a baby" does not dim, something about becoming parents together often illuminates differences between partners for the first time. In some instances, new parents sink into an uneasy despair that doesn't lift for many months or even years after a child's birth—and that sometimes lasts forever. Few of us respond lightly to these nebulous feelings that "something has changed in our marriage." What we eventually come to realize is that, for better or for worse, having a baby forever alters the course of our union.

When does this happen? It is generally understood that new parents experience a honeymoon period immediately following the birth of a baby that lasts about ninety days. Even this period of increased marital satisfaction is questioned by some researchers. In many cases, it has taken less than ninety days for new parents to experience the threatening conditions that create vulnerability in their marriage. I interviewed several couples who are convinced their marriage changed before they returned home from the hospital; some felt it changed even during pregnancy. Generally, though, the marital unrest that may come after childbirth tends to occur sometime within the first six months after a baby is born.

In this discovery zone, new parents uncover things about each other—each day—that arise out of the very new and serious responsibility of raising a child together. Whatever the discoveries, the bulk of critical ones are usually identified before a baby's first birthday, and whether they represent good or bad changes for a marriage, they often continue for the first one to three years following the birth. Any changes that are still apparent by a child's third birthday can be considered relatively permanent fixtures of a marriage.

Perhaps we have made the transition to parenthood when we no longer experience the change as overwhelming or as a crisis, or when the need for reorganization in our lives seems greatly reduced. An even greater period of instability, however, could be triggered by a second pregnancy.

This period of discovery makes a lasting impact on most couples. It can be an exciting time when a strong marriage flourishes and grows even stronger, or—as is too often the case—a period filled with crisis and conflict as a marriage, weak or strong, is battered and tested to its limits or beyond.

Most of us move into parenthood thinking that our marriage is fine. Then we encounter the stresses that come after our baby's birth, and for the first time in our relationship with each other, we discover that we don't have enough coping skills to survive without a lot of conflict. If we knew what to expect, that our experiences were not uncommon for new parents, and that there were ways to cope, many of us would survive without the devastating loss of intimacy and caring.

Is It the Baby?

When I was growing up, my mother kept one book carefully tucked within her sweater collection in a cardboard box, pushed deeply beneath a tall bureau which stood at the far end of my parents' bedroom. It was a book about marriage and childbirth, and I suspect my mother hid it largely because it contained a photo of a woman whose breasts were exposed. Regardless of how cautiously my mother sought to conceal this book, my sister and I found it and read it on many clandestine occasions, for it contained not only that one photo of a nude woman, but many facts about marriage and childbirth that seemed interesting to us even at that early age.

The book was written in about 1932 by Dr. Maxwell Extner, now long deceased. The title escapes me, and although it was published nearly seventy years ago, most of its content remains applicable to new parents today. At that time, I recall feeling somewhat unsettled by a message in the book's prologue: "Children," Dr. Extner wrote, "are not always a blessing or reward. Just as frequently they become a disruptive influence in a marriage." This frightened me then, and saddens me today, for I have discovered just how close to the mark Dr. Extner may have hit.

My obstetrician, Dr. Maxwell Barr, whose practice of medicine spans nearly four decades, noted that he has delivered hundreds, if not thousands of babies to what appeared to be happily married couples, only to learn that within two or three years of childbirth a significant number of these parents were no longer together. Whether or not their divorces had anything to do with the children is hard to track, he said, but it would almost seem so. After all, childbirth brings about sudden and profound changes to the marital relationship.

Most couples don't want to blame the baby, but when they try to make sense of what they are experiencing, they often attribute the stresses in their marriage to when they first became parents. Obviously, it is not just the baby who influences the state of a marriage. Instead, a matrix of factors set into play after a baby's birth touches both parents—together and individually. Commonsense requirements to compromise, negotiate, sacrifice, and work together challenge them as never before.

Human nature too often casts a pall over what is basically believed to be a high point in the lives of most couples. As parents, we are called upon to deal with the unexpected stresses that come after our baby's birth, and much to our surprise, we are generally unequipped to do so. Many of us just can't get over the hurdle of going from a couple to a threesome, which requires integrating our time and relationships around the needs of a newborn. What we are made of, the substance of who we really are, can't help but come out. We quickly find that leaving our mark on civilization, leaving our legacy—this powerful connection to the future—doesn't come as easily as expected.

Are Marriages Too Weak?

I believe that many of the problems we experience as new parents stem from the fact that our marriages are simply too weak, our characters too feeble, our human natures too freely at play. Many marriages are built without the tough fibers that withstand even minor stresses, let alone major crises. Childbirth brings both to a marriage.

Anne and Neil are in their late thirties. They were married about three years before their first son was born. Each has a lucrative career, and they enjoyed the fruits of their labors—a large home on estate-sized grounds and a full-time, live-in nanny who tended to child-care details and their domestic needs. This arrangement left both of them free to develop personal and professional interests. Nevertheless, with a baby in the family, they were called upon to make adjustments. When they had more children, the stress increased.

Anne sat before me stern-faced, her dark eyes coldly set, defining the distance she placed between us. It was our first meeting. I hadn't asked to pry into her marriage. She offered her story to me because she thought it was an honest portrayal of what led to the demise of her own marriage, and she suspected that the stresses on her marriage were similar to those that dogged the marriages of other new parents, drawing marital harmony to a grinding halt.

"What happened to us is easy to explain," Anne stated curtly. "Our life together was divided by responsibilities to our children and our work. This daily grind of sorting out who did what and when and for how long got tedious." Then she paused and after a quiet moment added, "But it wasn't the responsibilities. We just didn't love each other enough, nor did we ever love each other enough. We weren't committed to each other or to our family. Having to work around the children, the compromise and give and take and sacrifice—all the stuff it takes when one has a family—well, we couldn't do it, because quite frankly, we just didn't love each other enough. Having children brought that out."

Within two to four years of getting married, the majority of couples start their family. At this stage, most marriages are untested by conflict. Having a baby moves a couple into a more mature relationship, and sometimes men and women just aren't ready—or equipped—to move to that next level.

Whatever irritants surface after a baby is born are usually present before its birth, but because childless couples have so much more freedom to bolster their relationship with friends, family, and meaningful outside activities, these differences remain hidden until after childbirth. Husbands and wives are then forced to focus on each other again. This shift, often for the first time, illuminates differences couples have, or a shortage of genuine love and commitment.

"Few couples come to me *because* of the children," agreed Dr. Daniel Nordby, a counselor in marriage and family therapy for more than twenty-five years when we first met. "Usually their problems could have been pinpointed as potential hazards prior to marriage, and certainly before they had children. The problems I see new parents having are not dependent on their children specifically, but relate to issues they have within themselves, their relationship with each other, or with their own parents that didn't come to light until after they became parents themselves."

Children, I'm convinced, only become a bone of contention for new parents when the essential qualities of a marriage have *already* failed. Anne probably had a lack of real love for Neil long before their baby was born. "Oh, things weren't perfect between us before the baby," she added readily, "but we didn't admit it until the children were born. I thought having a baby would help our marriage; instead, our children became a channel for us to express all our conflict."

Do All Marriages Have Conflict After Childbirth?

When my sister-in-law called with the breathtaking news that she and my brother were expecting their first baby, I let out a whoop of joy. Paul and Teresa, in their late thirties, wanted a family very badly, and in my opinion, no two people were more fitted for parenthood or would be better parents together. Then I noted the trepidation in Teresa's voice. "Oh," she responded meekly, "I guess I'm a little nervous about the whole thing. Your brother and I have such a great relationship now—and well, you know, I think about your book and I'm afraid that we'll have this baby and then our marriage will fall apart."

My heart dropped. I swallowed hard. I knew only too well the numbers that had provided fodder for *After the Baby*. I was well aware that the facts I'd collected could be fairly discouraging to couples planning for childbirth. This was certainly not what I intended, nor did I want to cast a dark cloud over my sister-in-law and brother during what I knew firsthand could be one of the most joyous occasions in their marriage. My conversation with Teresa led me to see the need for a disclaimer.

Does becoming parents change all marriages? Do all couples experience conflict after childbirth? Do conflicts new parents experience last forever? Does marriage ever return to the way it was before childbirth? Does marriage actually improve for some partners after they become parents?

It is not my intent to discourage you with the numbers I cite throughout *After the Baby*. Having a baby does not bring conflict to all marriages, nor does it cause all new parents to feel less love for each other or to become less satisfied with their marriage. For many couples, giving birth, becoming parents together, and sharing marriage after childbirth are largely positive experiences. Genevie and Margolies estimate in *The Motherhood Report* that, over the long term, two out of five marriages really do not change that much following the birth of a baby, and one in five marriages actually improves!

I told my sister-in-law about Don and Mary. Don and Mary had been married for twenty-five years when Bruce and I first met them at a backyard barbecue. Youthful-looking and attractive, they were giggling and energetic and fun to be around. Over dinner they told us they would soon be empty nesters and that they were looking forward to this new stage of their marriage.

Several months later the telephone in my study rang. It was Don. "My wife asked me to call you," he began. "We received the overview of your book, and we decided that we have nothing to contribute." He stopped awkwardly. Thinking that I was disappointed, he went on apologetically. "Mary and I talked about it last night," he said, referring to the letter I'd sent asking them for their ideas and anecdotes. "We'd really like to help, but I'm afraid we didn't experience any of what you describe. We asked ourselves if maybe we just didn't remember the conflicts we'd had as new parents since it has been so long ago, but no, we determined after a great deal of discussion that the years after our children were born were some of the best years of our marriage. Those first years were wonderful for my wife and me, and they continued to get better as our children grew."

Without prodding, Don elaborated on the many ways their two children had enriched their twenty-five-year union. He talked at length about their involvement with the children's activities, the years they'd coached their sports teams, the many hours they had labored with their children over homework and school projects, the evenings—rain or shine or even snow—when they'd huddled together on the bleachers as spectators, and of course, the many occasions they'd chaperoned school and church events and gatherings in their own home. These had been fun times, close times full of warmth and laughter.

Woven throughout Don's narrative were pertinent factors that I believe made a dramatic and positive difference in their marriage. "When I vacuumed . . . ," Don started one story. "I did the laundry when Mary was tired," he stated. He also declared proudly, "We have great sex."

Our conversation revealed the side of marriage with children I want my readers to know and live—the teamwork, the support, the give and take of being a family, of being parents together. He closed with, "I love my wife. She's a great person, my best friend."

Don and Mary are proof that all marriages do not become weary after partners become parents. Some couples manage to avoid the destructive chain of events that places a stranglehold on other new parents. Few of us, however, escape the transition to parenthood without some ill-fated impact on our marital relationship, daily living arrangements, or lifestyle—if at least for a short period of time.

Crisis After Childbirth

To most of us "crisis" implies stress—bad stress. But not all stress is bad or disabling to a marriage. Instead, the crisis period experienced by some couples after they become parents marks the start of necessary change, a time when men and women must alter the way they act together, or as individuals, because the way they acted before the baby no longer works. Most new parents simply cannot go on with their lives as they did before their baby was born because they have the needs of the baby to consider.

The responsibility of having a child—of being a family—certainly produces large amounts of stress in the lives of new parents and requires a great deal of adjustment for a couple. Behaviors change, lifestyles change, relationships change. Sometimes these encompass a complete life transformation—socially, physically, and emotionally. But the prevailing view today is that only one in five couples experiences what might be termed a "true crisis" after childbirth, and for the majority of new parents, having a baby is a wonderfully joyous event. For many couples having a baby brings positive changes and provides opportunities for growth and a deepening of the marital commitment. Marriages undergo significant adjustment after each child is born; however, many emerge stronger, happier, and more secure.

I have not written this book to reflect my own individual thoughts and feelings about a life-changing event that didn't live up to my expectations. Quite the contrary. While Bruce and I experienced many similarities to the patterns of conflict and behavioral changes described in the following pages, becoming parents for us has largely been a positive experience that has enhanced our marriage, broadened our perspectives, and increased our circle of love and support. No doubt about it, being parents hasn't always been easy, and being parents together has sometimes been even harder. The disruptions—good and bad—that many couples experience after the birth of a child often result in a decline in marital love and satisfaction. This doesn't have to mean *forever*. By the time most children enter school, *committed* couples have sifted through most small, though not insignificant details and have weathered the first stages of marital imbalance.

As we examine the marriages of a cross-section of new parents described in the chapters that follow, we will find their behavior patterns match those of countless other new parents who, undergoing sweeping changes after childbirth, devote the majority of their time and energy toward the new baby and put the maintenance of their marital relationship on automatic pilot. What happens in the process? For many, the daily mechanics of caring for the baby eventually poison an already stress-filled environment with unhealthy emotions and inconsistent behaviors, leaving two adults—unaware of each other's needs—fearful of a marriage vulnerable to collapse. It becomes evident very quickly that couples who fail to nurture each other as well as the baby eventually let the stressful consequences of being parents pull them apart.

POINTS TO CONSIDER

- Recognize that change of any kind, good *or* bad, is stressful. A baby will take time and attention away from the most important relationship you have—your marriage. This means you must work harder on your marriage at a time when there's the least amount of time to do so.

- Adjust expectations. Do know that having a good marriage after the baby is possible, yet recognize that the good marriage *after* the baby might be different from the good marriage *before* the baby.

- Consider how each of you has reacted to change in the past. Some individuals adjust better to change than others. Think about times when you faced change in your relationship and what steps you took to adjust. Evaluate what good and bad effects came out of the changed situation.

- Don't rush to blame your spouse for all the changes. Most new parents refuse to blame the baby, so their spouse is generally the easiest to fault for adverse conditions in a home or marriage.

- Assess your coping skills. Are you one to roll with the punches, or do you frequently get uptight when things don't go as planned?

৩ Put a positive spin on stress. Think of stress as "good stress." Consider ways to handle it without adding tension to your marriage or your spouse. What parent education or parent support groups might you attend which will help you understand this period of transition?

৩ Look at change as an opportunity. Try to see all the positive aspects of the changes that are occurring. Concentrate on the ways a baby enhances your marriage. Consider, too, the good aspects of your marriage and how these can be further improved through parenthood.

৩ Keep in mind that marriage for many new parents is still a very immature relationship and that you are just starting to learn about each other. Don't allow the baby to interfere with that process. Set aside time to learn about and nurture your spouse as well as the baby.

৩ Find some activities to do together, such as a walk after dinner, pushing the baby's stroller. Maybe your lives are chaotic, but try to set aside time to concentrate on your marriage, doing the simple things that keep you connected.

৩ Keep talking and listening to each other. Strive to be open and honest, and avoid the tendency to turn away from each other or to others when you first discover "bad emotions." This is often the beginning of the separation couples experience as new parents.

৩ Consider that you may have to increase your efforts to communicate with each other almost immediately after the birth of your baby to stay abreast of what each of you thinks or feels and how it is affecting your marriage and your feelings for each other. Talk about the changes you're experiencing and how you feel about them.

৩ Know that you will face marital challenges as new parents. Invite your spouse to work with you on ways to improve conflict-handling skills. Recognize that being able to talk about your concerns and address them together strengthens a marital relationship and is part of the bonding process of parenthood.

৩ Don't fall into the habit of "wishful thinking"—that all concerns will resolve on their own. Determine not to leave your marriage rudderless at its most critical period of evolution. Put a realistic plan in place to protect and nurture your marriage.

৩ Acknowledge that being parents is what you both want and that there will be growing pains along the way. Remind each other that conflict does *not* mean your marriage is weak or that you don't love each other enough. It means, instead, that you need to find a way to cope with the changes so that you don't hurt or alienate one another.

ಬ Try to remain positive in light of conflicts or concerns. Don't fall into the out-of-control despair that creates silence in a marriage and leads to longer and more serious bouts of marital distress.

ಬ Let your spouse know that you are trying and that being a parent is new to you, too!

2

᠗

The Bubble Bursts

I don't recall that Bruce and I had any thoughts about being parents other than that parenthood was going to be wonderful. We had dated without discord, briefly touched on the topic of having a family, married without debate, and made a concerted and successful effort shortly thereafter to have a baby. We hadn't been around many children, but by the time I became pregnant, Bruce and I had nearly a dozen nieces and nephews, and many of our friends had become parents before us. For the most part, however, we didn't know much about babies and had no inkling what being parents entailed. Our exposure to babies was limited to brief periods, after which these boys and girls were gathered up by their parents, gingerly maneuvered to the back seat of a van or station wagon, and driven away until our next encounter, when they were a little older, perhaps a little cuter, a lot more active, and a lot more obviously present.

Having a baby was what we wanted more than anything. We loved each other very much—we were ready! As far as expectations, we had none. We jumped from the comforts of childlessness to the overnight demands of parenthood with no forethought about the impact a baby would have on our time and responsibilities, and certainly not on the relationship we shared with each other. If the lines between what is expected and what happens in the real world have always been fuzzy, rarely have they been more so than when men and women consider what life will be like as parents *together* after the birth of a baby.

Genevie and Margolies revealed in their benchmark study of nearly one thousand new parents that three-fourths had highly positive expectations about parenthood that these couples later believed were unrealistic. They said they had underestimated the immense responsibility of being parents and the impact it would have on their time and relationships, most notably on their marriage.

I found this to be true with many couples I spoke with as well when Dr. Gjerdingen and I participated in childbirth education classes with expectant parents entering their final stages of pregnancy. Those bold enough to explore life on the other side of childbirth came with us to a separate room where we engaged in discussions about their lives and marriages as new parents. These couples were giddy with excitement. There were a few, however, who approached parenthood with what I believe to be realistic trepidation. Our observations coincided with the research Genevie and Margolies had documented several years before. Couples indeed have grand expectations for themselves as mothers and fathers and for their marriage after the birth of a baby.

What Do Couples Expect?

The majority of new parents believe their marriage will return to normal after a short period of adjustment. They give little thought to recovering from childbirth although most have just discussed it in class. They believe giving birth will be a "meaningful, marital-transforming life event" shared intimately between husband and wife. They expect having a baby will bind them together forever. They have no expectations about actually taking care of the baby. Most couples hold onto romantic illusions about marriage and being parents together, and for the most part, couples scoff at the marital stress they've been warned about. They believe that, while marital distress *could* be a possibility, it will most likely strike "some other couple, but not us."

Despite what most have heard from friends and relatives or read about in books, the couples I speak with believe, with all their hearts, that having a baby will be good for their marriage, and that as a couple they will adapt to parenthood without conflict. Those who realistically acknowledge that their marriage *could* change expect the changes to be largely positive, bringing about new, improved models of mother and father. The greatest gap in expectation versus reality seems to be the failure for men and women to foresee the *cumulative* effects a baby will have on their marital relationship—the good *and* the bad effects of going from two, to three, to four or more.

This chapter examines the common expectations of new parents and the startling impact each has on the marital relationship. These expectations play a decisive role in how successfully new parents navigate their marriages through the first turbulent months—and sometimes years—after the birth of a child. Couples who are realistic in their assessment of the impact a baby will have on their marriage tend to be nearly twice as satisfied as those who savor bloated expectations. If reality veers too far from a couple's dreams, or if real-life experiences are actually worse than expected, disappointment can be profound. Disappointment, even to a mild degree, proves intensely debilitating to an individual or a marriage, especially after childbirth.

New Parents Need New Expectations

Lisa and Rick's son Benjamin was nearly walking on his own when they came to my office for our first meeting. Benjamin crawled across the room, groped the edges of my desk, hoisted himself up, then turned to Lisa and Rick and grinned broadly, clearly proud of his accomplishment. "Oh," Lisa, a gregarious and bright young woman, beamed. "He is so ahead of babies his age. He's been such a good baby and so much fun for us. Well, most of the time he's fun," she added with a laugh. "We've had our share of ups and downs, too, this year.

"Our friends hinted at the changes we might expect after Benjamin was born but no one really came right out and described what life would be like as new parents. We love Benjamin so much! *That* was a surprise, too! No one told us how much we could possibly love another human being. However, Rick and I were totally thrown off balance by the massive changes we experienced as a married couple. We hadn't been married much longer than a year when Benjamin was born, yet I thought I knew Rick as well as could be. Neither of us got the parental instincts I thought would just 'kick in.' We took out our inadequacies and frustrations on each other. Once knee-deep in daily living, we realized just how little we knew about taking care of a baby and discovered we knew even *less* about taking care of each other as parents. I expected everything to go smoothly—most things in my life *have* gone smoothly. Rick and I are really capable, upbeat individuals. Who'd have thought having a baby would knock our equilibrium? We didn't listen to all those well-wishing friends and family members who gathered around to support us. We chose to be unprepared for the changes because we didn't want to believe our marriage could be challenged, too, after the birth of our baby."

⌀

When I first learned that the *act* of giving birth plays a role in how we adapt as new parents, I flat-out didn't believe it. However, research supports that in nearly eight out of ten cases the birth event itself proved critical in the relationship between husband and wife following the birth of their baby.

Giving birth, you see, is not only a biological process but a cultural event. It is an important and powerful "life experience," the account of which is reconstructed, retold, and relived time and again by mother and father. It is no wonder, then, that *how* a woman feels about her performance at the birth of her baby significantly influences the feelings she has about herself, her identity as a wife and new mother, and her ability to physically and emotionally recover from childbirth. Furthermore, how she feels about her husband's involvement at the birth—his support and reaction to it—plays an equal, if not greater role.

Most of us fantasize about giving birth. We create expectations that are often hard to meet. We are led to believe the following: "It was a beautiful time, overflowing with emotions. My husband held me tightly and cried more than I did at the birth of our baby. He was so proud and happy—I thought he was going to burst. You'd have thought he'd given birth himself! I let him have the glory. We'll cherish these memories forever."

Unfortunately, about half of all couples fail to capture the highly positive psychological elements of giving birth together. They simply do not connect during this emotionally charged life event. This inability often creates the first ill feelings between partners as parents.

"I thought my husband and I would cry together passionately in each other's arms and be bound together forever after the birth of our baby," offered one new mother. "I expected him to proclaim, 'I love you! Thank you for giving me this child!' Instead, I felt removed from the baby, distant from my husband, and really frightened because I didn't have the intense feelings of love and emotion I'd been led to believe I would have. I was angry at my husband, too. I blamed him that we hadn't experienced the closest, most emotionally shared time at our baby's birth. I thought our marriage was doomed. I felt disappointed, confused, and empty."

"Our birth experience said much about our marriage," said another new mother. "My husband stood three feet from the delivery bed, detached, uninvolved, and void of emotion. Even the labor nurse remarked later that she thought his behavior was unusual. It certainly hadn't been what *I'd* expected. Maybe his reaction to the whole thing was all he could muster, but it hurt me deeply. I withdrew emotionally after that. Why hadn't my husband shown me more love or support? I took out my anger, frustration, and fears about our marriage on him for months. He just didn't know how his distance had hurt me."

So much emphasis is placed on this one individual act that the disappointment is often profound when the real-life experience deviates too far from the fantasy created before a baby's birth. When actual childbirth experiences vary emotionally, physically, or psychologically from what *may have been expected*, women especially take their feelings home to the marital relationship.

Getting Back to "Normal"

Within six weeks of birth most newborns are growing and sleeping longer through the night. The initial adjustment to caring for the baby has been made, and physical healing for most women is either in full swing or confirmed at the postpartum checkup when the obstetrician gives the go-ahead to exercise, have sex, and "get back to normal." I wonder how many doctors smile after saying that word, *normal*. For most couples, life will have changed dramatically by this time, encompassing radical alterations—socially, physically, and emotionally.

During this period, when new parents are enmeshed in the daily responsibilities of parenthood and grappling with the practical aspects of being parents together, many couples succumb to the nagging suspicion that things may have changed between them, perhaps for good. This stage is critical. It is the discovery zone described in Chapter 1. Sociologists believe it is during this period that the *changes* following childbirth first coincide with the expectations new parents had. We expect our lives to return to the way they were before our baby's birth. When this doesn't happen, inevitable conflict results.

According to *The American Way of Birth,* edited by Pamela S. Eakins, 70 percent of couples plan for the birth of their baby; nearly half overcome some type of infertility impairment; one out of ten mothers suffers through confinement during pregnancy; and as a group, we cumulatively spend over $1 billion annually in the quest for parenthood. Despite these difficulties, few of us admit to realistic expectations for day-to-day life after the baby comes. For many couples, being parents is *better than expected.* (Chapter 21 sums up—in the words of parents themselves—exactly why men and women choose parenthood, in some instances, again and again and again.) When considering what parenthood is *really* like, however, the majority say "parenthood isn't all it's cracked up to be."

"I don't know what we were thinking," said one new mother. "Did we think the baby was a toy that we could place back on the shelf when the novelty wore off? The baby was work—real live, hard-core, physically exhausting work."

Much of the conflict couples experience after the birth of a baby centers around their unrealistic expectations about child care. The immense responsibility of caring for an infant surprises most new parents—yet it shouldn't. Being a parent entails at least two decades of sustained attention. It is a lifetime commitment, staggering to most couples who have never put their heads together over such a massive project.

Nine out of ten couples find themselves arguing more after they become parents—usually about taking care of the baby. This aspect alone can be terribly exhausting to any relationship, not only to new parents getting plenty of rest, but to the sleep deprived as well! Relentless in nature, caring for a baby is a daily, minute-by-minute, intense, and necessary part of being a parent.

Couples who fail to sort through the stress related to child care eventually feel its impact on their marriage. As we'll see in future chapters, they suffer an emotional estrangement which often leads to loss of intimacy and caring. Conflicts caused by child care and housework are so prevalent and pivotal to marital well-being that these topics are covered in great detail in Chapters 8 and 9.

The Romance of Parenthood

Most of us move into parenthood with the romantic assumption that having a baby will be good for our marriage. However, when we examine independent studies, we find that the quality of the marital relationship tends to decline between husband and wife after birth and with each successive birth, throughout the active parenting years, and it doesn't improve until a child has grown up and left home.

For the majority of couples, becoming parents brings conflict and causes differences in their relationship to surface, usually early in their baby's life. Twice as many couples said their marriage changed for the worse after they had a baby than said their marriage changed for the better. In *Parenthood as Crisis*, E. E. LeMasters further contradicts the romantic assumption that childbirth is good for a marriage. "The initial responsibilities of caring for an infant," he states, "destroy whatever romantic notions about parenthood a couple may have had." Instead, he points out, new parents feel exhausted, inadequate, and confined.

In only one out of twenty studies do researchers report an increase in marital satisfaction after the birth of a baby. The overwhelming majority expose significant declines in the amount of marital love and satisfaction between new parents.

Census Bureau statistics indicate that although couples with children are less apt to divorce, each year over one million mothers and fathers experience marriage dissolution. Today, one out of two children born to two parents can expect to live in a single-parent home by the time they reach eighteen. Furthermore, an increasing number of children are growing up with no memories of—and no lasting ties to—one or the other biological parent. (Divorce is addressed as a separate topic in Section V.)

I believe our disillusion about being parents relates not so much to "being a parent" or to the baby as it does to our unrealistic expectations about the institution of marriage. I'm idealistic. Most of us are. We believe that marriage should be interesting, challenging, stimulating, and satisfying all the time. But this is not reality. Marriage partners experience peaks and valleys at every stage of the family life cycle, not just after the birth of a baby. For most of us romantics, the highs and lows go against all we hope for or desire in a marriage. The apostle Paul wrote in First Corinthians of "the problems married people will have," and Socrates, with all his wisdom, found marriage challenging at best. Too many marriages crumble under the stress that is simply part of being married, children or no children.

Despite history, despite what others may have told us, most of us believe we will adapt to parenthood without conflict. While most expectations prove to be unrealistic assessments about the impact a baby will have on a marriage, these wildly positive expectations are also a sign of encouragement. They provide a glimpse of the faith and optimism couples must have in each other and themselves as they reach one of the most challenging crossroads in their marriage.

POINTS TO CONSIDER

~ Ask yourself how you expect your marriage to change after childbirth. In what ways do you expect it to stay the same? Are your expectations realistic or are you expecting too much?

~ Can you share your hopes and dreams as well as your disappointments with your spouse? If not, what is keeping you from expressing your true feelings?

~ Keep in mind that while you and your spouse may have attended childbirth education classes and diligently practiced breathing and relaxation, few couples say they are adequately prepared for the pain and exhaustion of childbirth—and certainly not for the psychological whammy it delivers to mothers and fathers.

~ Talk about the birth event. Remember a new mother risks postpartum depression if she isn't able to work through her birthing experience. A woman also needs it acknowledged—and to some degree demonstrated—that she has gone through a profound life event.

~ Remember that a significant number of men and women experience feelings of loss, sadness, disappointment, anger, and other negative emotions following their baby's birth. It is also as normal *not* to bond with a new baby as it is to bond. Not all parents feel an immediate connection with their newborn.

- Visualize your future together as parents. Say goodbye to "normal" as you knew it. Embrace the changes that come after your baby's birth and welcome them as opportunities to grow together and learn about each other as parents in a new stage of your marriage.
- Consider past experiences you've had with other parents. Seek good role models to learn from and others you might lean on for help and support.
- Start early to discuss child-care options and concerns. It's best to do this before a baby is born; however, few couples do. Step through "what if" scenarios to figure out how you'll handle responsibilities and deal with conflicts before they actually occur.
- Name your concerns. Step up to issues and look for solutions before they are needed. Doing so will make you less likely to succumb to stress or to feel overwhelmed as changes come along.
- Be mindful that a new perspective is just as important for your parenting journey as learning new skills.

3

〜

A New Playing Field

Among our circle of friends, word spread about this book, and one evening during its preparation, my husband and I attended a social gathering where I found myself pursued by a gentleman whose wife I had interviewed several weeks before. Dr. Arnold strode across the room, determined to tell me his side of the story. I was well aware of the marital problems that had pervaded the Arnolds' home since the birth of their two children. The difficulties seemed fairly common to me, but I was not unconcerned. Soon we were locked in conversation, much too intense for the gaiety surrounding us.

A surgeon by trade, with a somewhat gallant demeanor, Dr. Arnold was accustomed to being in control of most situations. He expected to control what happened in his marriage as well. "It had been a good marriage," he stated. But much to his astonishment, he hadn't been able to curtail the destructive changes that were sweeping through his household after childbirth—and he wasn't happy about it.

"I don't understand why our marriage had to change," he said, peering accusingly across the dance floor at his wife. "Look at her." A stunning woman, she was laughing and chatting amicably with friends. "We had a great relationship before the kids were born; now I hardly know her. I thought things would straighten around, but it's only gotten worse—and *much* worse since the second baby. Where did all the fun go? The romance? The connection we had? I want my marriage to work, but I don't know," he trailed off before resuming his thoughts. "What happened? Who *is* this woman I married? She tells me I expect too much—that we're normal, but I don't want to be *normal.* I just want my marriage to be the way it was before the kids."

Then he paused, glanced furtively around us to ensure no ears were on our conversation, and turned with the frightened eyes of a child, absent the defiance I'd detected earlier. "Is it ever going to get better? Will our marriage *ever* be the same again?"

I hesitated that evening, measuring Dr. Arnold's need for encouragement, for I couldn't at that juncture elaborate on the many ways I knew his marriage could change following the birth of their children. "The same? No, not the same," I replied cautiously. "Having a baby alters a marriage at its very core. Sometimes the changes are only temporary, but they are almost always predictable and necessary. Your marriage can be better," I added brightly. "It can be enriched in ways you never thought possible."

He looked hopeful, and as we parted I noted his determination to work through their differences. He wanted to understand the changes and their natural contribution to his marriage that now included children. Most important, *he wanted to make his marriage work!*

What I couldn't explain to Dr. Arnold in that short amount of time is outlined in this chapter. *Will* marriage stay the same after childbirth? *Can* marriage stay the same? "Certainly not!" Dr. Daniel Nordby states flatly. "Having a baby changes the whole job description of being married."

I became familiar with Dr. Nordby in the earliest stages of writing this book. I'd never been to a marriage counselor or therapist before, and I was a bit nervous as I found my way to his offices on the second floor of an ivy-clad building in downtown Minneapolis. Dr. Nordby had counseled several of our friends, who occasionally repeated the word-for-word exchanges of these meetings. I also knew the outcome: all of these friends were still married. Dr. Nordby's advice made sense to me, so I sought his contribution to this book.

"Dr. Dan," as I came to know him, too, looked much as I had expected a therapist to look. His lanky frame was topped with long, bushy, graying hair that needed a bit of attention; his eyes were warm and blue and intense. He swept into the room with bountiful energy and with a similar zest, talked at length about what he'd come to know best over his twenty-five-year career—relationships. I was intrigued by what I learned at our first meeting, for at that point I had spent little time in research and was still unfamiliar with accepted theories associated with marriage and the transition to parenthood.

"A couple begins a new phase of their life together after they have a baby. Their relationship will never be quite the same as it was before they became parents." Dr. Dan said this boldly, pausing to let his words sink in. Bruce and I had already discovered this, and I knew that to couples looking ahead to parenthood, this revelation could be fairly incomprehensible and un-settling.

Dr. Dan continued: "Having a baby upsets the applecart. Roles change. New identities emerge, and the inherent needs each parent has as a man or a woman are *forever* rearranged." The word "forever" hit me hard at that time, as I'm sure it has more than one set of home-from-the-hospital-green parents.

We then talked at length about this book and what I hoped to accomplish, and Dr. Dan became a valuable resource. Much of what he told me I eventually discovered firsthand, and I collected countless anecdotes from mothers and fathers which support that psychological research and theory do indeed apply to the real lives of parents today.

All Eyes on the Baby

Jack and Denise had been married for five years when their first child, Charles, was born. They had shared a close and intimate relationship that grew even stronger during the years they'd wrestled with infertility. Both had reluctantly surrendered their dreams of parenthood and poured the majority of their time and energy into their marriage and building Jack's business. Denise had ample time to respond to Jack's every need, and she admitted that, in a way, he became the baby each thought they would never have. This arrangement worked well, until Charles came along.

"After Charles was born, my husband was demoted from being number one recipient of my attention, affection, and maintenance to number two. It was hard for Jack to accept this. He expected me to put him first, like I did before the baby. This enraged me. I thought he was being childish and unrealistic. I directed all my efforts toward the baby; caring for it was intense and necessary. I saw no reason to give excuses for this preoccupation, and I had little tolerance when Jack fussed or pouted. The baby was help-less. My husband was not."

"We'd barely gotten home from the hospital, though, when things changed," Jack countered. "Denise forgot about me. She was always with Charles. I knew I shouldn't be mad—we'd tried so hard to have our baby, and we were both extremely happy about its birth. I loved the baby, too, but I was angry that my wife neglected me. I hadn't caught up with her dedication as a parent, and deep inside, I guess what I was *really* afraid of was that my wife had somehow changed and that we were growing apart already."

ᔍ

Of one thing we can be certain: a baby becomes the prism through which most new parents see the world. This is pretty obvious very quickly. The baby, which upsets the applecart, becomes the apple of its parents' eyes as well. What time and energy most parents once devoted to strengthening their marital bond is now redirected toward the new baby. This is a natural process. It is also a necessary one. The first year of a baby's life is crucial to its development. It is a time for bonding with the baby, caring for it, and responding promptly to *all* its needs. During this time a baby's conscience is formed, and its roots of self-esteem, confidence, and safety are first planted. Babies who do not receive adequate love and attention from their parents during these early months are robbed of the jump start needed for their healthy growth and development.

Letting a baby become the focal point of the family also upsets some unspoken marital rules. We expect our spouse to nurture us, to encourage us, to give and take, and to make us feel loved, wanted, needed, and secure. We expect to offer the same in return. Most couples take this daily exchange for granted, and it is usually doled out in fairly hefty portions during pregnancy. Having a baby changes that. When Denise put the baby first, Jack moved lower on the totem pole. He was forced to wait his turn. He no longer felt loved, needed, wanted, or secure. He wasn't ready for this change, and he wasn't happy about it.

"Women typically take all nine months to get ready for a new baby," explained Dr. Dan. "During this time they make room for it in their hearts and lives. They make plans to care for it. The process is quiet and gradual, yet it makes a tremendous impact on a woman and consequently on her marriage. A father usually needs some time after the baby is born to catch up. Most women aren't ready to refocus on their husband until they are willing to let go of the baby. This could be when a woman goes back to work or feels comfortable with a baby-sitter—or it may not be until that child enters school! This change in focus or behavior can be mystifying to a husband and terribly upsetting to his marriage."

This Isn't the Person I Married

A man brings a different woman home from the hospital after a baby is born. A woman finds a new man at home.

"I thought I'd been duped," admitted Peter, referring to his wife, Monica. They'd been home from the hospital about three days when Peter first noticed the subtle, yet alarming changes in his wife. "I gave her a lot of leeway those first few months. I tried to be patient and understanding, but Monica, in my opinion, was never really her old self again after she became a mother. She'd always been so independent, but she became as dependent as the baby. She used to make good decisions on her own, but after the baby was born, she sought my advice for everything—everything, that is, but how to take care of the baby. *That* she knew all about! And could she boss me around! I saw a side of my wife that I'd never known. She just wasn't herself. I started to wonder if I'd been tricked. You know, we hadn't been married much longer than two years; still, I felt I knew my wife. Not after the baby was born. It was *some* adjustment!"

Monica wriggled uncomfortably in the chair next to him. "Well, you weren't exactly yourself in those days either," she retorted. "I had so much I wanted to say to you, so much was happening in our lives, but I couldn't talk to you. You were preoccupied with something! What did *you* have to worry about? I was the one taking care of the baby all the time." Then she turned to me. "Peter could be very warm and loving one minute; other times he was cold and distant—and he was always so serious. He'd never been like that before the baby. I didn't know how to react to my 'new' husband. It was a very lonely time."

∾

In many ways, having a baby brings about a "rebirth" of a couple, with new roles, responsibilities, and needs for each spouse. It's not so much that *individuals* change; it's more that the differences each has as a man or woman come to light. Generally, if we recognize and understand the differences, we can also manage them.

A new mother needs to know that her husband is sensitive toward her feelings. "Does he hear me? Does he understand what I'm going through?" Most important, "Does he care?" A wave of insecurity causes many new mothers to yearn for assurance at every turn. "Am I doing a good job taking care of the baby? Am I a good wife? Do you still love me? Am I still attractive? Am I attractive as a *mother*?"

This need for a husband's approval is evolutionary. If a husband doesn't affirm his wife when she needs it the most, it lays the groundwork for the disappointment referenced by many new mothers in the early months of their baby's life, which often contributes to early feelings of marital unrest.

New fathers, on the other hand, become absorbed in the role of "provider." Maybe they hadn't thought much about putting money in the bank, or buying a house, or earning more than enough to cover the bills. Now they have a baby to feed and clothe and diaper—a child who eventually needs an education. Seventy percent of women leave the workforce during the first year of motherhood. Some never return. On average, newly formed families experience a drop in income, sometimes by as much as 40 percent. These facts are frighteningly real to most new fathers and cause them to think more about their performance as the breadwinner than about their role as a husband or new father.

Men also express a need, as never before, to feel respected and appreciated for their contribution to the family. Maybe they never needed a pat on the back or a few good words of praise for going out to "slay the dragon" each day. As a father, they do. If a woman fails to meet this need in her husband, he, too, is disappointed. Disappointment can be debilitating to both spouses as well as to their marriage.

Few men and women respond appropriately to the changes in their partner's needs. We shouldn't be surprised. Most of us struggle to figure out what we need individually or from our spouse as we make the transition to being parents together.

Changes in behavior and personality leave many new parents dumbfounded. Who is this person I married? I've never seen my spouse act like this before! What has having a baby done to my wife? To my husband? The impact might occur gradually, or seemingly overnight, as it did for Peter and Monica. Few can predict the exact transformation. Most often, though, it pivots on the care of the new baby and how a new mother and father were raised.

But That's the Way My Mother Did It

My husband and I share common backgrounds and a long list of similarities in how we were raised, but after we became parents several blinding differences emerged which challenged our mission to care for our baby without conflict. While we were in concert on the larger issues, the devil was in the details! We disagreed whether the baby should wear socks or a hat, if he had too many blankets on or not enough, if it was too warm or cold in the house, whether or not the sitter was qualified, and how long to let the baby cry. We bickered all the time, yet before the baby was born, we'd seldom disagreed on anything. It didn't take long to discover that however many similarities we shared, parenting together brought our differences to the forefront.

Who we become as adults—who we become as *parents*—is largely dependent on our individual backgrounds, the homes we were raised in, the values we possess, as well as our individual biology, method of socialization, and personal and family histories. Any variations in how we were raised or in the attitudes we developed in our homes growing up become increasingly problematic after we become parents. Couples who have the fewest problems adjusting to parenthood together usually share similar values or accept each other's ways of orchestrating them when different. Few of us were raised exactly alike, so problems involving parenting decisions—however minor—are bound to set in, and they only get bigger, as do the children and their issues.

More often than not, though, as new parents we're guilty of exerting our own agendas. These are based on a lifetime of experiences—separate and different from our partner's. We believe we're right because we're following what our parents did. It's seldom that one new parent is right and the other wrong; our ideas are just different. While many of us are willing and able to compromise *before* a baby is born, after its birth we're not.

A baby increases the risk for differences to surface because there are just so many details to work out. What many parents discover is that they do not have a good enough communication system to survive without conflict and less intimacy in their marriage.

"Bill and I cared for our baby in different ways," explained Linda, a retail salesperson. "We both thought we were right because 'that's the way my mother did it.' This led to huge disagreements, and sometimes we had yelling fights over something as small as when to change a diaper. I usually gave in when we disagreed, just for the sake of not arguing."

As differences come out, power shifts between spouses. Somebody has to compromise. Routine tasks, perhaps casual backdrop before the baby's birth, require delicate negotiating skills afterwards. Daily living often becomes taxing.

"I held so much inside," said Linda, sighing deeply. "I didn't realize our disagreements over such small things could affect our marriage in such a big way. I grew to resent Bill for always getting his way, and I was mad at myself for always giving in."

How to survive? Reach beyond the differences. New parents need to say, "Let's put our heads together over this one." Come to the table with mutual respect, trust, communication, and cooperation—despite the differences in how you were raised or the attitudes you developed while growing up. This sounds simple in theory yet is difficult in practice. The more differences two people have, usually the more work they have to do. Sometimes the help of a professional is needed.

"We both mellowed over time," concluded Linda, "but not without the benefit of a therapist who helped us understand what was getting in our way of working together. She helped us find solutions that were agreeable .to both of us. Having an action plan that was not *his* plan or *my* plan but *our* plan enabled us to act without the blame and resentment that was hurting our marriage."

A Working Relationship

The key word here is *working*. Parenthood transforms a marital relationship into a true working relationship because one thing that a child brings to any marriage is *work*. The conversion takes place almost immediately.

Workloads shift and increase. Stressful situations develop that are unique to being new parents together and are almost always based on who takes care of the baby or who doesn't. The importance of values and backgrounds becomes even more crucial to solving the problems we encounter as parents when men and women move away from the roles they knew and tackle the duties of caring for their family together.

"I can't remember what it was like to love my wife *before* the baby," reflected Peter thoughtfully. "Monica and I are so different today. I want to feel the way I did before we became parents, but I'm afraid those feelings are lost forever."

Most marriages grow out of a romantic relationship. When we become a family, we often move away from each other as lovers and are reintroduced to each other as parents. Much to our surprise, loving and respecting each other under the arrangement of "family" doesn't always happen overnight. Many parents are inclined to look at each other as partners after their child's birth. Their marital relationship decreases as a romantic relationship—and sometimes as a friendship during the process.

As parents, we're in the trenches together. It's in the trenches that love either grows or dies. It doesn't take long for parenthood to test romantic love. That's when romantic love needs to be replaced by *real* love, the type that one stays in, rather than falls into or out of. It's the commitment type of love discussed more fully in Section IV, for once romance fades, a marital relationship is built on what is left.

No doubt about it, becoming parents creates a new playing field for both spouses. Marriages are changed at the very core. As parents, we are asked to let go of the relationship we shared *before* our baby's birth and embrace a new relationship that is built on a different foundation, around new sets of rules and roles for each. Too often, though, we're guilty of putting our marriage on automatic pilot, sacrificing our adult relationship for the sake of "being a good parent." Narrowly focused on the baby or on individual survival, couples lose sight of each other's perspectives; they also lose momentum in their marriage. As couples devote less time to each other—however unintentional it may be—it is not uncommon for misunderstandings and ill feelings to widen gaps in communication and decrease intimacy—sexually, emotionally, and intellectually. Are some couples more susceptible to this than others? The next chapter helps us determine just that.

POINTS TO CONSIDER

ᴄᴏ Discuss with your partner the changes that often take place at the very heart of a marriage after a baby is born. New mothers shouldn't be afraid to say, "I'm probably going to get caught up with the baby. It doesn't mean I love you less. Please be patient with me." New fathers shouldn't hesitate to say, "Having a baby is a big responsibility. I might become preoccupied with my work. It doesn't mean that I'm not thinking about you or the baby. Please be patient with me."

ᴄᴏ Keep in mind that couples who acknowledge changes are usually successful at managing them.

ᴄᴏ Take into account the different ways men and women respond to becoming a parent. Anticipate that a new father will thrive on praise and appreciation for the work he does (or the efforts he makes) on behalf of his family. Appreciate, too, the special needs a woman has to be reassured she is doing a good job and is loved, valued, and attractive as a mother.

ᴄᴏ Think about the traits you consider necessary to be a "good parent." Do you possess these traits? Does your spouse? This isn't the time to point out shortcomings, but a time to consider where extra attention might be needed. Knowing that one of you lacks patience, for example, or doesn't respond well to a disorganized household may spur you both to make changes in these areas before they become issues in your marriage.

ᴄᴏ Recall personal histories, family backgrounds, and relationships you had with others growing up that were important to you. Sort out what you would like to see continued in your own home and what you'd rather "throw out."

ᴄᴏ Keep in mind that your spouse was raised in a different home and possibly with a very different reference point than your own. There are no absolutes for parenting styles. It might take time to work out "whose way is the most appropriate way" to parent together. If one way doesn't work, agree to try another. Remain flexible and patient. You are both learning!

ᴄᴏ Praise your partner's strengths. If your husband does a good job quieting the baby, *tell him* so. If your wife demonstrates selflessness and patience as she cares for the baby, let her know you admire or appreciate those qualities.

ᴄᴏ Set limits with intrusive or judgmental family members and friends. Thank them for helpful ideas or suggestions and tell them you'll consider them. Let them know that you and your spouse will make the ultimate decisions. If your family or friends drop in uninvited and you find this disruptive, convey that however happy you are to see them, you'd prefer that they call ahead of time so you can be rested and ready to visit.

ى Be mindful that however helpless a new baby is, the most important relationship is the "couple relationship." The health of the entire family pivots on the health of a marriage.

ى Think about times when you and your spouse compromised in the past. What was helpful? Did you listen respectfully to each other? Did you both give a little, or did one of you make the decision and the other wallow in anger or self-pity?

ى Think about changing roles you and your spouse have experienced before, such as those related to job changes or positions. How did you react? What was helpful?

ى Fine-tune compromising and negotiating skills by attending classes on conflict resolution. These are available through many churches, schools, and community education centers. Doing so early in parenthood helps couples build skills they can use throughout their marriage.

ى Guard against a new father feeling left out by giving him opportunities to participate in the care of the baby. Let him do his child-care tasks his way, or agree on methods so you are both comfortable that the baby's needs are being met. Fathers should care for the baby *on their own* periodically so they, too, become adept at child care. Many men don't feel an immediate bond with the baby, and engaging them in its care increases the likelihood of making the connection that much sooner.

ى Run through "what if" scenarios before the baby is born to get a feel for how you might react to child-care issues, housework matters, and other parenting concerns. What if the baby gets sick and both of you are working? Who will provide backup child care? Who will do the laundry, buy groceries, arrange for sitters? Who will get up with the baby during the night?

ى Lighten up if your spouse seems overly dedicated to the new baby. Researchers believe it is impossible to give a baby "too much love," just as a baby won't be spoiled if you respond promptly to its needs. Trust that you'll eventually find a balance between focusing on the baby and your marriage.

ᗌ Start *before* a baby's birth to locate trustworthy, responsible, and mature baby-sitters. Your baby's development will not be hindered if left in the care of a reliable sitter or family member for a short period of time; however, your marriage *will* be helped if you devote time to each other, as adults, and keep in touch as marriage partners.

ᗌ Consider the qualities that make your marriage special and commit to doing things which make your spouse feel loved, needed, secure, and appreciated.

ᗌ Try to be patient when you detect changes in your spouse that may confuse, alarm, or annoy you. Accusing your spouse of changing can be a painful charge, as well as harmful to your marriage. Allow leeway as you and your spouse strive to adjust.

ᗌ Refrain from feeling hurt, disappointed, or angry if your spouse does not respond to your needs the way you would like. Recognize that you both are struggling to incorporate being a parent into the world you knew before.

ᗌ Anticipate that the love you felt for each other *before* the baby can return— and grow.

4

∾

Candidates for Chaos

Amy was wildly enthusiastic about the baby, much more so than Rod, who hadn't been all that gung-ho about having a baby in the first place. In fact, Amy admitted, he hadn't been too excited about getting married either. She told me she had to coax him down the aisle and then trick him into fatherhood. She giggled then, out of embarrassment I suspect, and I also detected a bit of alarm in her voice.

Rod had had numerous girlfriends before they married, and while he hadn't been reluctant to give them up, he *had* alluded to the "finality of being married." If not for Amy's ultimatum, Rod would have preferred to continue living with Amy as they had happily for the previous two years. Amy and Rod had good jobs with hefty incomes. They traveled a great deal and lived an enviable lifestyle. "Why change?" thought Rod. In fact, Rod had just earned a promotion that was to take him to both coasts frequently, and he was excited at the prospect of seeing new ports of call and the challenges presented by his new business opportunity.

Within a year of their marriage, Amy became pregnant. Rod wasn't angry, necessarily, but he hesitated to embrace parenthood, for he knew it would mean a great deal of change. How could this have happened? Wasn't Amy on birth control?

Unbeknownst to Rod, Amy had wanted a baby so badly that she went off the pill without telling him. She wasn't really trying to have a baby, she said, nor to trick Rod into parenthood. They'd just never discussed having a family. If they had, Rod might have revealed the reasons he did not want to become a father and that he was still haunted by his own father's abandonment years before and his mother's aggressive, depressive behavior after his father left them. Amy, in turn, might have told him that she was tired of her job and felt that having a baby would rid her of the insecurities she'd carried around and give her the chance to be the mother her own mother had never been to her.

In the early stages of pregnancy, Rod was supportive. He encouraged Amy to eat right and helped her a great deal during the first trimester when she was sick. As the impending birth drew near, he became quiet and withdrawn, sometimes angry and frustrated. Twice he didn't show up for the childbirth education classes he'd committed to attending with Amy, and by the time Amy gave birth, Rod, though present at delivery, had plotted his own quick exit. Within months, Rod moved out of their home.

∽

Could we have predicted Rod and Amy's problems? Was their marriage more susceptible than others to marital disharmony after the birth of their baby? Can we predict which couples will experience marital distress after they become parents together?

After ten years of motherhood and spending nearly the same amount of time researching and writing this book, I watch new and expectant parents, fully anticipating the patterns of behavior that will color their transition to parenthood. Based on what I see and hear, I predict the pitfalls—or the lack of them. I've become fairly accurate. Eventually, you will too.

I wouldn't have been able to foretell the problems that besieged my own marriage after Bruce and I became parents together, but I know more today than I did. I know now that some couples are simply more prone to marital distress than others after they have a baby, and that some preexisting conditions set the stage for marital disharmony. Some men and women are simply more susceptible than others are to marital distress. They possess the classic symptoms that make them, as parents *together,* candidates for chaos.

Who Wanted This Baby?

Key to making sense of some of the marital conflicts which arise after a couple gives birth is understanding whose decision it was to have the baby. If having a baby is a mutual decision and both parents are happy about the birth (planned or unplanned), couples are more cooperative in the care of the child and experience fewer marital difficulties adapting to parenthood than do couples in marriages where the decision to have a baby leaned more heavily toward one or the other parent. Rod never came around to accepting his child's birth and was put off by his wife's deceit.

Sometimes the decision to have a child is not clear-cut for both spouses, and reaching consensus marks a turning point in a marriage. Like Rod and Amy, husbands and wives may have very specific reasons for whether or not they want to become a parent—or to become parents *together*. These might be very different reasons. They should be discussed prior to childbirth, prior to conception. If they're not, they inevitably come back to haunt a couple after their baby's birth. Not a pretty picture. The greatest risk to marital stability after childbirth is to have a baby when the husband did not feel ready or did not want to become a parent. Dr. Carolyn Pape Cowan and Dr. Philip A. Cowan of the University of California, Berkeley, found that all couples facing this dilemma divorced before their first child entered kindergarten.

How Do We Feel?

Couples who not only share the excitement and anticipation of having a baby but also feel good about themselves and each other usually experience fewer conflicts after their baby is born than the parents who prematurely fret about becoming a family. Anxieties about child care, career decisions, and changes in responsibilities often threaten an otherwise well-tuned household. Having a child may also conjure up painful memories of experiences that men and women had with their own mothers and fathers growing up, making them leery of just what lies ahead.

One of the preexisting conditions that affected Amy and Rod was Amy's low self-esteem. She expected that having a baby would change the way she felt about herself and that motherhood would somehow fill the emptiness that had existed within her since she was a young girl.

Few of us are fortunate to feel good about ourselves all the time. Approximately one third of parents suffer from low self-esteem and depression, and an even larger fraction experiences these and other negative feelings about themselves during the first year postpartum. We expect pregnancy to be a fulfilling life event. We hope pregnancy will generate positive feelings that last into parenthood. This isn't always the case. However, it is important. Parents who feel good about themselves, each other, *and* the baby tend to experience less parenting stress and less conflict as a couple and to raise children who are happier and better adjusted.

When I was young, I thought that men and women chose to have a family because they loved each other and because they both wanted a family very much. Not a bad assumption to take into adulthood. As I grew older, however, I learned that couples have babies for a variety of reasons, and sometimes it isn't as an expression of love for one another. Goldberg, Michaels, and Lamb documented that the quality of the marital relationship remains the most critical factor in a couple's adjustment after childbirth. Men and women who cross the threshold to parenthood with good feelings about each other and their marriage typically have a better chance of surviving the transition without conflict than those couples who are already striving to find traction in their marriage. It should be of no surprise, then, that the couples who report the greatest marital problems after they become parents are the same ones who had the most strain in their relationship prior to giving birth.

Caring for the baby and taking care of oneself and a marriage are big tasks, made even more difficult when we face distracting personal and career goals or relationship problems. Judy arrived at our lunch, groggy from a sleepless night. She was tense and weary of the day ahead. As she spoke, she tried to hide her bitterness, but soon angry words revealed the dismal chain of events that had transformed her household into a single-parent home almost overnight. Shortly after the birth, her husband took a new job. It required long hours at the office, involved considerable travel, and propelled his self-image to lofty heights.

"My husband was more excited about his new job than he was about being a father," she explained. "He was upbeat. I was worn out. His career was moving ahead. I had just resigned. He showed the baby little attention and even less attention to me. He didn't help with the house or the baby. He just wasn't there for me. I resented my husband and let him know it. I was angry all the time. He thought I was trying to hold him back in his career—he thought I was jealous. We never understood how each other felt and he eventually moved out."

Mark, another new father, explained that his mother-in-law had died just months before his wife delivered their first daughter. "My wife was angry at me because I was so excited about our new baby. I don't think she had had enough time to grieve the loss of her mother before having to enter into another close relationship as demanding as motherhood."

Then there are Jeff and Becky. Just weeks before childbirth, Becky, a product manager, was granted a massive assignment at her office that afforded her the exposure she'd sought throughout her career. Becky felt unprecedented pressure to succeed. Should she take a leave of absence after childbirth or return to the office to finish the project? Her situation detracted from the excitement they felt about the new baby. Becky returned to work full-time. "Full-time! It was more like time and a half!" Jeff bellowed. "She made the decision, putting her career ahead of our family. She became very driven and spent more and more time away from the baby. We fought a lot about it. I saw a new side of my wife that I didn't like. I think she was afraid she'd fail as a mother, and being away didn't give her the chance to see."

It is surprising that statistics don't reflect even higher stress levels between new parents since most become mothers and fathers between the ages of twenty-five and forty-four, long before they have settled into their careers or altered efforts to get ahead. Those who start their families when they are older or who are enjoying more established careers generally stand a better chance of moving into parenthood unscathed. These couples have worked through the so-called formative career years and tend to experience fewer life crises related to personal and work goals or relationships. On the other hand, as couples become parents at increasingly later ages, they may get caught in the sandwich generation and find themselves caring for an aging parent or mourning the death of one while rejoicing over a child's birth.

The Sex of the Baby

I don't wish to set any insecurity into motion with this factor, however farfetched it may sound, but studies indicate that the sex of a baby predisposes some couples to marital conflict. Cowan and Cowan found that couples were less likely to separate or divorce if their firstborn child was a boy. There could be several reasons for this. Their findings suggest that men are more apt to push for a second child sooner if their firstborn is a girl. When a second birth follows soon after the first birth, couples are subject to additional stresses. They are generally still recovering physically and emotionally from the first transition to parenthood. Another birth forces them to go through a second transition soon after the first and make even more choices, sacrifices, and trade-offs as family dynamics go from three to four or more.

Men tend to describe themselves more favorably if they have fathered a son. "Our second baby was a boy," offered one new mother. "'John got his boy!'" Another exclaimed, "My husband was a new man, boasting about his son—not at all the way he reacted to our daughter's birth. He had a cigar for *everyone!*"

Cowan and Cowan also found that men tend to be more careful and protective of the relationship they have with a son than the relationship they have with a daughter. Research indicates that boys are more vulnerable to parental divorce. Furthermore, both mothers and fathers believe that boys are more difficult to raise alone and that boys need the influence of a father. With courts granting custody most often to mothers after divorce, many fathers make greater efforts to stay married, choosing to avoid the painful loss of contact with their sons or lose influence in rearing them.

Lastly, Cowan and Cowan found that a man whose firstborn is a girl and who has a troubled relationship with his wife often experiences an equally troubled relationship with his firstborn daughter. A father tends to spend less time nurturing his relationship with that child and makes fewer attempts to overcome differences between them. These men are also more apt to relieve themselves of what they *perceive* to be an overwhelmingly difficult relationship by separating or divorcing.

Clearly, there are a number of pressure points in each marriage that hint at potential marital distress after a baby's birth. These are more apparent for some couples than others. The key is to recognize them *before* becoming parents and to get help ahead of time, hopefully bypassing some of the ill will that unfortunately accumulates between marriage partners.

POINTS TO CONSIDER

∾ Determine the pressure points in your marriage. What areas might be stumbling blocks to marital satisfaction following the birth of your baby?

∾ Try to reach a mutual decision about whether to have a child. If you need help making this decision, attend a workshop or other educational program that addresses the pros and cons of having a family. Couples report that such classes helped them clarify their feelings about becoming parents and enhanced their communication and problem-solving skills. They also felt better informed about parenthood and able to make more personally satisfying choices about the decision to become parents.

∾ Address negative emotions tactfully without worsening the situation. At a quiet, convenient time, when you are both rested and not distracted or under stress, ask how your spouse feels about the impending birth. Acknowledge that negative thoughts and concerns are normal when facing this magnitude of change.

∾ Discuss the reasons you want to become a parent as well as the reasons you hesitate. Take into account short-term and long-term considerations for choosing or postponing childbirth. There is no perfect time to have a baby and no perfect transition to parenthood.

∾ Attend childbirth education classes or a prebirth intervention group if you suspect your marriage will be at risk. These programs help couples learn to resolve conflict, work on communication skills, and face the realities of early parenthood. Couples who participate in this type of education and planning tend to experience fewer marital difficulties after their child's birth and are more optimistic about being parents *together.*

∾ Decide what changes you must make to accommodate your baby's birth. Are you willing to make these changes, or are you stubbornly adhering to old ways of doing things, making pregnancy and childbirth more stressful than they need be for you and your spouse? What obstacles prevent you from welcoming your baby's birth?

∾ Realize that if having the baby is your idea and your idea only, your spouse may balk at becoming a parent. Be prepared to carry the bulk of child-care and household responsibilities alone *without* complaining. Be patient while your spouse warms up to the idea of being a parent and the responsibilities it entails.

ɷ Talk about your concerns with each other. Share them with friends or family members who have made the transition successfully. Participate in child-birth education classes where you'll find an opportunity to ask questions, voice concerns, and gain a richer understanding of pregnancy, delivery, and the parenting transition from other parents and healthcare professionals.

ɷ Think about what dark memories from your background might cause you to be leery of parenthood. How did your own parents respond to being parents? Your spouse's parents? How have other family members or friends adapted to becoming parents? What helped them? Establish friendships with other couples who are experiencing similar changes and who can offer a support-ive ear and an understanding voice.

ɷ Try to do those things that make you feel good about yourself. Begin by tak-ing good physical care of yourself, getting plenty of fresh air and light exer-cise. Emotional healing often follows. Remember, those who suffer low self-esteem *before* a baby's birth are more susceptible to emotional problems and postpartum depression afterward.

ɷ Assess the status of your marriage. Do you openly share love and warmth? What might be straining your relationship that you need to work on before your baby's birth?

ɷ Try to avoid having a baby when your career is taking a toll on time and en-ergy, or when you're facing other personal crises or problems. Put off moving to a new home, changing jobs, or that big remodeling project if you are hav-ing a baby. Say no when people ask for help that taxes your time or energies. Direct your attention to your spouse and new baby and put extra efforts into making a smooth transition to parenthood.

ɷ Be resolved to nurture your marriage as well as your baby, keeping in mind that *both* sexes, boys *and* girls, face gender-specific consequences to parental divorce.

II

∾

Stress for New Parents

~

Why does the "honeymoon" end? What happens to the level of love and support between new parents? Why does a new mother often perceive a decline in her spouse's expressions of caring and concern shortly after the birth of her baby? This section details the common incidents unique to new parents that often bring stress to their marriage. Conflicts encountered at this time cut across all class and ethnic lines and tend to revolve around the needs of the new baby and its parents.

Chapters 5 through 7 explain how the healing process is significant as it affects the overall temperament of the marital relationship and impacts how readily men and women adapt to the day-to-day consequences of being parents. Other practical everyday issues are addressed in Chapters 8 and 9. These relate to increases in child care and housework, the newness of parental roles, and a total re-arrangement of time, energy, and priorities. Even in the best of circumstances, when men and women love each other very much, we find these challenges combine and intersect at a time when new parents are least able to cope. Detracting from the marital relationship, these stressful situations chip away at the foundation of love and support new parents are able to offer each other, and they sometimes send marriages careening wildly off course, causing new parents to abandon their commitment to each other, their marriage, and their family.

5

∽

Recovery After Childbirth

Childbirth marks the end of pregnancy and its related risks. Giving birth, however, marks the onset of other physical and emotional hazards, ones which can be far more disturbing to a new mother and her marriage—and last much longer.

It's a rare woman who does not give birth and a still rarer one who does not live to tell about it. According to the U.S. Department of Health and Human Services, approximately 90 percent of all women in the world give birth—almost 145 million each year—and for the majority of them, childbirth and recovering from it run a relatively uneventful course that lasts about six weeks. Few of these mothers have the luxury of medical care afforded to women in our society, nor the availability of goods and services to cushion their transition to motherhood. Childbirth for many is largely a natural event, taking place without circumstance.

Although childbirth is a natural process, researchers are now taking a serious look at the recovery requirements following the birth of a baby, for they are learning that the period of healing has a widespread and a long-lasting impact on the lives and marriages of new parents. Not only is the time immediately following the birth of a baby believed to be one of the most stressful periods in a couple's marriage, but it is also clearly one of the most stressful times in a woman's life. During this time a new mother undergoes enormous physical and emotional challenges as she recovers from childbirth. The healing process coincides with the baby's first months, which require total caregiving. A new mother may not know how to care for her baby nor have the instincts to do so. She also has needs of her own that often go unmet, and she may be juggling her new role as a mother with responsibilities outside of motherhood—marriage, household, extended families, community, and career—all of which were established when her life did not include children.

Giving birth touches every aspect of a woman's life and every relationship close to her. Even when the birth of a baby is a welcome event, changes of this magnitude frequently create adverse conditions in a new mother's life and place tremendous stress on her marriage.

Hidden Hazards

The prevailing opinion among medical professionals is that the marital metamorphosis referenced throughout this book begins to accelerate during the stage of physical and emotional recovery that immediately follows childbirth. Recovery, while perhaps not debilitating, can be distracting. If prolonged, it often becomes a hotbed for marital tension. Some fathers, when first called upon for practical and emotional support, simply fail to meet the needs or expectations of their wives. This perceived lack of understanding or support is often interpreted as a lack of caring or concern. Against the backdrop of a new mother's needs, this apparent failure sparks some of the first ill will between new parents.

Furthermore, women tend to be the emotional caretakers of the family, maintaining the emotional integrity of the family by paraphrasing, reflecting, talking about feelings, and playing them out. In many families, women are the relationship builders. They nurture, send cards and well-wishes, organize events for family unity, and work hard to ensure that family members are happy and content. Besides being emotional caretakers and chief housekeepers, many women are also the household managers. They keep schedules on track, sort out who's supposed to be where on which day, and figure out what is needed to make sure everything runs smoothly. When a baby comes, there may be so much to keep track of that a woman's whole finely tuned system falls apart. Women typically perform one more task essential to marital satisfaction: they edit their husband's comments to keep conflict from escalating.

After childbirth, when preoccupied with the needs of the baby and their own recovery, many women stop performing these vital tasks. The role of caretaker may fall vacant, leaving the emotional climate of a marriage unprotected and vulnerable. If a husband is unequipped or unwilling to perform caretaking duties, the position remains dangerously empty, with no one at the helm, sifting, sorting, cushioning egos, or tempering marital satisfaction.

An alert father (the *wise* father) steps into this role. However, decades of research indicate that most men have a difficult time grasping exactly what to do. When a new father fails to respond, or his efforts to support his wife physically or emotionally fall short of her needs or expectations, it seldom goes unnoticed. A man's inability to carry out these duties *at a time when they are needed the most* has profoundly negative consequences to his marriage. He also misses an enormously rich opportunity for personal growth.

Who's the Star?

While moms may be in the spotlight during pregnancy and childbirth, dads have the chance to star afterward. If a man pays close attention to his wife's needs and responds appropriately, he may well turn out to be a hero. Simply "being there," not only at the birth, but during recovery at home, to help with the baby and the housework, to lend a hand or a shoulder to cry on, to listen, is a very important part of fatherhood. We see many beautiful examples of men who support their wives during pregnancy and really connect with them at their baby's birth, but then, when they go home from the hospital, all efforts stop. Yet that is when women need nurturing and help the most.

A man's level of love and support before, during, and after childbirth does more to influence his wife's physical and emotional recovery and well-being than any one single factor. *It also sets the course for his marriage.*

The following chapters describe the physical and emotional healing process after a woman gives birth. It is a journey for both parents. Once we match the needs of *both* types of recovery against the backdrop of practical needs—in a world that has been *totally* rearranged—we start to see more clearly the patterns that lead to a shift in marital love and satisfaction after the birth of a baby.

6

∾

Physical Healing

A friend told me this story nearly twenty years ago. While living abroad in a relatively poor, undeveloped country during the early 1960s, a family employed a young woman as a servant. It was Christmas Day and the young woman was "with child." She prepared the holiday meal and served the main course, then quietly disappeared to the cellar to give birth, returning within minutes to serve the dessert. She hadn't missed a beat. Thank goodness this is not what we expect of mothers today in our society. A deeper look into the needs of this young mother might have revealed a number of healing requirements, but due to her duties and status as a servant, they were perhaps largely ignored.

What is a natural recovery from childbirth? What is to be expected by the many new mothers and fathers who become parents together each year? What is it about the recovery process that often accelerates changes in a marriage, causing many couples to stingily withhold affection, attention, and common courtesy, and temporarily—or forever—sever the ties that bind them together as family?

∾

Patty's baby was just four weeks old when we first met. Before I reached the front entry of the large, gray, cedar-shake colonial she shared with her husband Jon and their new baby, its double doors burst apart and Patty beckoned me inside. "Oh, I'm so happy you're here!" she exclaimed breathlessly. "Please come in." I'd never met Patty. The doctor who had presided at the birth of our first son several months before encouraged me to visit with Patty about what he believed represented a very "normal" recovery from childbirth.

Patty motioned me into the kitchen. She removed some old newspapers and a few towels from a sofa so I might sit down, then shoved her newborn into my empty arms while she poured hot coffee into two cups. Patty had tons of energy. She bustled about the kitchen and playfully interacted with her son, then proceeded to enthusiastically detail the highlights of his birth and her recovery, which she felt was moving along as it should. She really didn't know *what* to expect, she said, since this was her first baby, but she felt good, and that was what was important to her at that time.

Patty had had a quick, easy delivery. She was thirty-five years of age, had exercised regularly throughout her adult life and during pregnancy, and appeared to be in excellent physical condition. Within a year, though, we met again, and Patty revealed that her recovery was less than complete.

"About the time I expected to be healed from childbirth and participating in 'real life' again, I developed mysterious aches and pains. I just didn't feel right. My hips were sore, my pelvic bone hurt, and whenever I moved the *least* bit vigorously, I felt like my insides were going to tumble right out of me. I stopped exercising—and making love, too! I suspected that giving birth had left a gaping hole down there." Patty related that her breasts were tender and sore even though she wasn't breast-feeding.

Her symptoms were not only painful, but distracting and irritating. "I was always aware of these unusual sensations in my body," Patty told me. "I'd never thought too much about my health before, but after giving birth, I became preoccupied with my physical well-being. Mentally, I felt great. I told my husband what was going on, and quite frankly, he thought I was imagining things or just looking for attention. Well, that was far from the truth. My aches and pains were *real*. Even with what should have been adequate rest, I was exhausted all the time. I needed help with the baby and taking care of the house. Anyway, Jon found all this very annoying. He accused me of using my health as an excuse when I didn't want to do something, or when I wanted *him* to do it, or when I didn't want to make love. I made conscious efforts not to talk about my physical condition because I knew it irritated Jon."

Sometime after that first year, Patty felt more like herself again. "I really think that time healed me. No one had told me that recovering from childbirth could be such a lengthy process, or that it could affect my marriage in any significant way," Patty said. "I felt very lonely during that time because

I couldn't confide in my husband. I saw the limits of his care and concern, how much he was willing to help me or to even *try* to understand what I was going through. I felt distance between us, a deep disappointment in how Jon responded, and a great resolve to care for the baby without his help. I also resented Jon for his lack of support. I was overwhelmed but I didn't know where to turn."

The Puerperium and Beyond

Patty and Jon had traveled through the *puerperium*—and beyond. The puerperium is the period of recovery following childbirth. It is commonly believed to last about six weeks and begins when the placenta is expelled. It is a time of physiological and psychological changes for a new mother when both she and her new baby need extra care.

The changes that occur within a woman's body during the puerperium are called *involution*. During involution the body's reproductive organs return to their nonpregnant state. At this time, new parents establish the foundation of their relationship with their baby. The mother recovers from the actual stresses of pregnancy and childbirth; she starts to care competently for her newborn and reenters society in a whole new role. All within six weeks! Few new parents move through this time without minor, if not major, disturbances to their health and marital well-being.

The puerperium is generally punctuated by one quick and routine postpartum trip to the doctor's office about six weeks after the birth. Few new mothers contact their doctor after that. Most continue to recover without additional medical assistance, coping alone with any small, yet irritating conditions.

Smack dab in the middle of childbirth's honeymoon stage, most new mothers and fathers overlook minor irritations and moderate discomforts. "I ignored whatever pain I had during the first months after our son was born because I had my baby to care for," explained Rachel, a new mom in her early thirties. "I didn't feel well. I was exhausted, but I didn't complain. I had my baby, which was all I cared about. He was healthy and we were happy. I could put up with a lot of pain and discomfort just as long as I had a healthy baby."

Doctors believe Rachel's reason also explains why so few new mothers seek medical attention postpartum. Caught in the afterglow of giving birth, women put their thoughts and energies into caring for their new baby, sometimes at a cost to their own physical and emotional well-being.

This doesn't mean that women don't need additional medical treatment. Patty could well have benefited from it. Perhaps she would have had a faster recovery and experienced less pain. A doctor might also have unearthed the disappointment and sadness she felt due to Jon's lack of support and directed them to seek help. In turn, Jon and Patty might have bypassed some of the marital distress they experienced as new parents.

Dr. Gjerdingen and her team of researchers at the University of Minnesota spent considerable time tracking the recovery needs of new mothers. Their work reveals that although physical and emotional needs vary by individual, most women require much longer time to heal than the six weeks normally allotted. Even after six *months* postpartum, more than half of the new mothers they studied had not fully recovered from giving birth. While fewer than 6 percent of these women sought medical treatment for themselves during this time, the majority suffered from minor to moderate discomforts, and some faced more serious problems that limited daily functioning.

Many of their recovery concerns were caused by the actual process of giving birth. This is expected. However, more often listed as obstacles to full recovery were fatigue, lack of sleep, weight loss, the increased responsibilities of caring for the baby or taking care of the house—while juggling a job *outside* the home, too—and the overall emotional upheaval brought on by the balancing act.

Furthermore, new mothers seldom recovered drug-free. On average, they received more than three different medications to combat one or more symptoms. Fewer than one in a hundred received *no* drug treatment whatsoever after they returned home from the hospital.

Clearly women have unique characteristics for recovery from childbirth that impact daily functioning as a mother *and their role as a wife*. "I suppose Jon was disappointed in me," Patty noted, "but he never said that. What he *implied* hurt the most. He didn't seem to care how I was feeling or about what I was going through at the time." Because he didn't seem to care enough to help her at this difficult time, Patty grew to resent Jon. His behavior marked a turning point in their marriage that had an impact for several years.

Researchers have found that what is viewed as a natural, expected, and welcome period of recovery often marks the first of many intermittent cycles of emotional poverty experienced throughout a couple's marriage. The period of recovery may in fact be an irritating, alarming time of marital transformation, as it was for Patty and Jon. Far from a time of recovery, these months may be laced with disappointment, frustration, alienation, and increased marital conflict.

What to Expect

Travel back in time to seventh-grade biology class. We were all wildly curious about the human reproductive system. To conceive and give birth calls upon every bodily function we studied at that time. A constellation of symptoms results from the gynecological, respiratory, endocrine, gastrointestinal, and musculoskeletal systems. Few visible signs, however, reveal a woman's true healing requirements after she gives birth or hint at their potential and sometimes widespread influence on her marriage.

At the top of the worry list for most women is how they will look after they have a baby. It's not far down on the worry list of most new father's either. General guidelines indicate that a weight gain of 25–30 pounds during pregnancy is not uncommon for most women and is considered healthy. Most of us want to lose that extra weight immediately. We're concerned, though, if we'll be able to do it.

When researchers from the University of Alabama at Birmingham School of Medicine studied a group of women over five years, they found that those who had had one child gained only about four pounds more, on average, than women who had never given birth. Furthermore, the gain appeared to be a one-time-only deal; second or third pregnancies didn't add extra weight.

Prenatal education classes, however, make it clear that leaving the hospital with a flat stomach rarely, if ever, happens. I know women, though, who boast of wearing their stiff, unforgiving blue jeans home from the hospital. A good share of new mothers—and new fathers—continue to be disappointed when this doesn't happen. There are good reasons it doesn't.

The shrinking of the uterus is gradual. The greatest reduction in uterine size is visible the first ten days after delivery. Oxytocins (hormones produced while breast-feeding) aid in contracting the uterus and shrinking its size. The uterus, however, seldom retreats to its original size until at least six weeks have passed.

"My stomach was soft and mushy," said one new mother. "I could pull out folds of skin and drape it over the waist of my pants. I didn't want my husband to see this. I doubted that I would ever get my waistline back."

Mothers tend to change shape a bit after giving birth. Their waistlines become larger in proportion to their hips, compared to women who have not given birth. Stomach muscles, however, can return to washboard tautness—with time and effort. Exercise is key.

Of course, what *is* "normal"? It is certainly easier to get back into shape if one was in shape before pregnancy and childbirth. Yet even stomach-crunch fanatics don't believe their abdomens are as flat after pregnancy as they were before. On the other hand, I know women who gained 50 or even 60 pounds during pregnancy and are smaller today than they were before their babies were born. Much of our resilience is due to luck, according to Dr. Felicia Stewart, coauthor of *Understanding Your Body*. The size of one's pelvis, the size of the baby, and one's genetic makeup have a lot to do with how quickly and effortlessly a new mother gets back into shape.

Stretch marks might also leave their stamp. These most often occur in women who gain a great deal of weight during pregnancy, but they're not an impossibility for mothers who gain only 10 pounds either. Stretch marks tend to show up on the breasts and belly as little scars. Ask your mother about stretch marks; they also can be genetic.

A side effect during the shrinking of the uterus might be uterine cramping. It's seldom severe in intensity or duration, but nonetheless, it can be distracting. These "afterbirth pains," as they are often called, are little contractions that occur two or three days after birth. They are more pronounced in women who have given birth before, as the uterus must work harder to recover from a second and each subsequent birth.

A new mother might quickly retreat to her prepregnancy weight and size, yet suffer common symptoms of healing we just can't see. Many women complain of the following characteristics in higher incidence at one month postpartum. For the majority of new mothers, these and other symptoms continue to plague them throughout the first year after birth and sometimes into a second year. When these symptoms continue for longer than expected, they often become sources of irritation to both parents, as they were for Patty and Jon.

Vaginal Healing
The vagina becomes soft and enlarged during pregnancy. After childbirth, it never returns to its exact original condition. Although the changes to the vagina are usually so small that they fail to affect sexual functioning and enjoyment, women who give birth vaginally are more prone to vaginal discomfort, pain during intercourse, and difficulty reaching orgasm. (The effects of these symptoms on the sexual relationship of new parents are discussed in Section III.)

No doubt you've been encouraged to do Kegal exercises after the baby is born to strengthen the pubococcygeal muscles that form the pelvic floor between your legs. Toning these muscles, which contract during orgasm, helps many women climax more easily. To do Kegals, tighten your muscles as if to stop urine flow; hold for three seconds. Relax for three seconds, then repeat, building up your repetitions to thirty. Do the exercise with your legs slightly apart, pulling up with your pelvis. Try to isolate only the pubococcygeal muscles. If you find the exercise tiring, it may be that you're also tensing your buttocks and abdomen. In due time, and with faithful dedication to the Kegal exercises, most women can restore much of the vaginal muscle tone that is lost when giving birth.

Episiotomy
Nearly 95 percent of women have an episiotomy during childbirth. This procedure enlarges the birth passage and reduces the incidence of tissue damage from tearing. About half of new mothers complain of discomfort from the stitches that reconnect the tissue. This might affect them daily, often during sexual intercourse, and perhaps throughout the entire first year postpartum.

Lochia
During the first weeks after childbirth, a bloody discharge flows from the vagina. This is called *lochia*. It comes from the uterus and is often accompanied by an unpleasant or unfamiliar odor. Two out of five women cite this as more of an irritation than an impediment to daily living. The amount and intensity of the discharge vary by individual. It is usually reddish in color for the first three or four days, pink after five to nine days, and whitish by the end of three weeks. While physical movement and light exercise increase lochia drainage and urine flow, they also help restore a woman's strength and make her feel better physically and emotionally. An offensive odor along with the discharge could indicate the presence of an infection. This should be medically treated.

Hemorrhoids
Just under half of all new mothers suffer from hemorrhoids (swollen rectal tissue). For what seemed to be weeks on end following the birth of our first son, I sat in a tub of warm water on the donut-shaped cushion provided by my gynecologist. While hemorrhoids do eventually disappear or shrink in size, they can be painful—and painfully embarrassing. Hemorrhoids are caused by the stress of pushing during the process of childbirth, or by the pressure of the baby as it moves against the vaginal walls and pelvic area.

To reduce discomfort from hemorrhoids, women should eat a healthy diet of roughage, drink plenty of liquids, and take sitz baths. Pain and itching can be treated with the use of a commercial ointment, available without prescription. More severe hemorrhoids, however, may require surgical removal. Mine did.

Constipation
Over half of all new mothers become constipated. This further complicates hemorrhoid healing. Cases of constipation tend to increase at the first month postpartum and some may last well into the ninth month. Constipation is caused when the gastrointestinal tract (pushed aside by the enlarged uterus) attempts to regain its original position within the body. Over-the-counter stool softeners help relieve the symptoms of constipation, as do increasing the intake of dietary fibers and liquids, and exercise.

Breast Concerns

Problems associated with breasts are most likely to occur in the first days after delivery and are more common and aggressive in women who breast-feed. Breast concerns are *not* confined to women who breast-feed, however. Nearly a third of new mothers who do not breast-feed complain about general breast discomfort, infection, and nipple irritation. More than 50 percent of all new mothers complain of breast concerns at their sixth-week postpartum checkup. Symptoms usually disappear between the ninth and twelfth months postpartum and are largely due to the hormonal changes that occur during the first year after a baby's birth.

Sagging is an issue, too, for breasts after they've been touched by pregnancy, childbirth, or nursing. Once the glandular tissues primed for lactation are no longer needed, breasts shrink back to their normal size. Many women think they just keep shrinking, getting smaller than they were before the baby! Yet just as prevalent are women who believe their breasts became larger after becoming a mother. Differences could relate to the weight gain or loss a woman experiences after she gives birth. Aside from wearing a good bra, try exercise and weight conditioning to keep the chest and upper arm muscles toned and as supportive of the breasts as possible.

Hair Loss

Hair loss shouldn't be too alarming, but it is distracting to many new mothers who, for the first time, find large clumps of hair gathering in their hairbrush, in the drain, or trailing them around the house. One in five women experiences temporary hair loss after childbirth. The stresses of pregnancy and childbirth cause hair follicles to enter a resting stage prematurely. This interrupts the regular cycle of hair replacement. When normal hormone patterns kick in, all the hairs start to fall out at once, resulting in excessive shedding. This peaks at about the sixth month but can occur up to one year postpartum. "The big fall-out," explains Dr. Gjerdingen, "might clarify why everyone seems to know someone whose hair texture 'totally changed' after having a baby."

Other Common Recovery Concerns

Poor appetite, anemia, increased sweating, acne, hand numbness or tingling, dizziness, hot flashes, and increased days of illness accompany many of the typical recovery symptoms and almost always persist beyond the first month postpartum. These are often joined by "later recovery symptoms" such as respiratory ailments, sexual difficulties, and hair loss.

As women move through the first year of motherhood, many experience an increase in flu, bronchitis, tonsillitis, laryngitis, sore throats, coughs, colds, earaches, and sinus infections. These strike one in every three new mothers and affect more than half of those who work outside the home. This could be due, in part, to the increased exposure these women have in work and day-care environments, the additional stress in their lives when they work outside the home as a new parent, and the decrease in protective antibodies after pregnancy.

More Serious Concerns

Reported by less than one tenth of new mothers, serious concerns include thyroiditis, urinary incontinence, and late hemorrhaging. All should be medically treated. Incidents of carpal tunnel syndrome—on the rise in the general population—affect less than 3 percent of women giving birth. New mothers often complain of tingling or numbness in their hands. Most cases heal naturally without treatment within forty-eight hours of delivery, yet some cases don't begin until the third month postpartum and may persist for another fifteen months. Treatment includes resting hands, splinting hands at night, or taking steroid injections. Surgery may eventually be needed if symptoms become incapacitating and other treatments haven't worked.

I'm Just So Tired!

The obstacle to recovery most often overlooked or treated trivially by health care professionals and new parents alike is fatigue. Yet fatigue can be extremely damaging to the marital relationship after a baby is born. We expect to be tired. Most new parents are. However the impact of fatigue on an individual as a mother or father, and on a marriage, is nothing to be treated lightly.

We all need rest. Without it we become short-tempered, ill-humored, and incapable of viewing our world with rose-hued optimism. Interrupted sleep patterns for infant care or sleep disturbances due to physical and emotional distractions contribute to a lower quality of life for weeks and even months after a child is born—for new mothers *and* new fathers.

Four out of five women report fatigue after childbirth. Actual occurrences may be higher but go unreported. Incidents of fatigue are even more serious when they go hand in hand with sexual dysfunction, marital difficulties, or postpartum depression.

Being tired hits at a bad time. We need all our energy and faculties while learning to care competently for a new baby and for making a smooth transition to parenthood. However, the effects of fatigue, more often than not, result in negative consequences for many couples. Fatigue proves to be one of the leading causes of postpartum depression, and postpartum depression (discussed in the following chapter) continues to be one of the leading causes of marital dissatisfaction. If left unchecked, it often leads to marital dissolution.

Some Heal More Quickly Than Others

While a woman's body recovers remarkably well with little intervention within a relatively short period of time, several factors affect how readily each new mother physically and emotionally heals after childbirth.

General metabolism before birth affects how quickly and easily a new mother returns to her prepregnancy weight and size. Personality and general outlook on life also hint at what her psychological state might be during recuperation. A woman with a gloomy attitude before the baby is born often has the same tendency to dwell on each ache, pain, or obstacle without recognizing its role in the miracle of childbirth.

Infections of any sort, during or after birth, also tend to slow recovery and make a new mother more prone to depression. Furthermore, a new mother's recovery depends on her general health before pregnancy and childbirth, the type of delivery she had, demographic and social variables, if she returned to a demanding position in the workplace, and not surprisingly, whether or not she received adequate help with the baby and the housework after she returned home from the hospital.

The greatest factor by far that sets the parameters for recovery is whether or not a new mother receives—or perceives she receives—the level of support from her husband that she needs or expects.

POINTS TO CONSIDER

- Recognize that recovery from childbirth often calls for marital adjustment and could very well mark a turning point in your marriage if not properly managed.

- Be patient, as a new mother, if your husband does not respond as needed or expected. Nurturing and caregiving are learned behaviors.

- As a new father, consider where you can help *before* being asked. Assist with routine household duties as well as emotional caretaker responsibilities. Plan a family event, write thank-you notes, send out cards and well-wishes—send one to your wife, too! Spend more time with your family during the first year postpartum. Be mindful of the very important role you play in how quickly and successfully your wife heals after childbirth.

- Avoid habits that slow recovery, such as excessive alcohol consumption, overeating, junk foods, or smoking. Eat regularly and nutritiously, exercise lightly, and get plenty of fresh air. Take the baby out, too. A baby's immune system is very efficient in the early months of life. Dressed appropriately, babies have few health risks from being out in the fresh air.

- Attend the sixth-week postpartum checkup *together*. This provides emotional support for a new mother and shows that a new father cares. It also gives him a chance to ask questions about his wife's recovery. The doctor can be a third-party buffer that enables new parents to discuss sensitive issues, chronic health problems, or marital concerns.

- Monitor the progress your wife is making. If she seems preoccupied with her health, or if health problems persist past the sixth-month postpartum checkup, suggest that the *two of you* return to the doctor. It could be that she has thought of going to the doctor herself, but the idea of handling the baby alone is too overwhelming.

- Do not hesitate to tell your practitioner if you feel that healing is not progressing as it should. Problems healing physically often lead to problems healing emotionally. Postpartum depression is treatable.

∽ Attend parent support groups or parenting classes where you can talk with other new parents. Knowing you are not alone, that what you are experiencing is not uncommon or unusual, can be very helpful.

∽ Remember that birth by cesarean section is major surgery. It requires a longer period of recovery, and extra help around the house and with the baby will be needed.

∽ Be open with each other about negative feelings you might be having. It's okay to have them, and expressing them is healthy.

∽ Empathize with your wife but *don't say you know how she feels!* This can be very annoying to a new mother. Emphasize the outcome instead, such as, "I'm so thankful for our new baby. I admire your courage. I am proud of you." Statements such as these offer support and encouragement.

∽ Acknowledge that giving birth and recovering from it can be rough. Be sensitive to the emotional changes your wife experiences which may keep her from responding to you in her customary fashion. She's taking a break from decoding every word you say. Give her some leeway, too, if she seems a bit touchy at this time.

∽ Don't criticize your wife's weight gain. Let your wife know that you love her and that you know healing, dropping pregnancy weight, and getting back into shape don't happen overnight, nor do you expect her to do everything she was doing before the baby was born.

∽ Share your fears and overall feelings you might be having about yourself with your husband. Remind your husband that while you are now a mother, you are above all a woman with needs and wants, goals and dreams of your own.

∽ Try not to compare your healing process to how others might have healed. Each woman recovers at her own rate.

∽ Know that returning to the size and weight you were before the baby was born probably requires attention to diet and exercise. Design an exercise routine that fits into your schedule. Walking is a great stress reliever, and you can take the baby with you, too.

∽ If sexual intercourse is painful or you find lovemaking unpleasant or uncomfortable after childbirth, assure your husband that it isn't *him*, but feelings you have about your body that keep you from being an enthusiastic sex partner.

◊ Take a nap when feeling overwhelmed. Sleep calms our nerves and rejuvenates our bodies and minds so we can cope better. Sleep when the baby sleeps. Go to bed early. Reduce work hours during the early months of a baby's life, if possible, so you do not get overworked, overstressed, and overtired. Acknowledge that fatigue might be tied to the emotional tension, sexual dysfunction, or relationship concerns.

7

∾

Emotional Healing

Caught in pensive reflection, Connie, a film production specialist, spoke of the psychological shifts that surprised her after the birth of her first baby and plunged her and her marriage into an alarming tailspin. "It was the last thing my husband Brad and I expected. We couldn't have been happier with my pregnancy and delivery, and the new baby. Everything was about perfect—even our marriage. I thought giving birth and recovering from it would be the last dramas we'd face before reclaiming the life we'd known before the baby. Was I wrong! Shortly after I returned home from the hospital, my emotional rearrangement came without warning. It was swift and decisive. Whatever happiness I felt about the new baby melted into an uneasy darkness that failed to lift. I was content, yet irritable. Motivated, yet inert. I felt frustrated, confused, and vulnerable. This just wasn't me."

Connie continued relating her story to me, a confessional of the emotional defeat she suffered after giving birth. She told about the rapid descent into a depression filled with feelings of loneliness, confinement, and entrapment. Enslaved to the baby's needs, Connie mourned the loss of her former self. She'd given birth at age thirty-two and left a demanding position in the workforce to stay at home and care for their newborn. "Brad and I discussed this decision at length. He was very supportive." Nevertheless, Connie stated, "About two months into motherhood, I felt my former self fade into oblivion."

Connie witnessed profound changes in her body, in the way she thought, how she dressed, in the responsibilities she performed as a new mother, and even in the way she interacted with others. Her sexuality vanished, along with her rapidly diminishing freedom. Connie became increasingly dependent on Brad, and less confident. Convinced that he could not love her as she was, she determined that Brad would eventually leave her.

"None of this was good for our marriage," Connie added. "And of course, I blamed it all on Brad. I loved the baby but hated what it was doing to me and my marriage." She was disappointed in herself, too. "I felt so guilty that I reacted this way after our baby was born. I alienated Brad and withdrew from the very people who could have offered me the love and support I needed and longed for." When Connie's dark mood failed to lift within ten months, she sought professional help.

"I don't know why we waited so long. I guess I thought I would recover on my own. I didn't want to admit that I needed treatment! That was for other people. I'd never had an emotional problem before, so I didn't understand its course or how it might affect our marriage. A counselor helped us talk about my feelings, and Brad really listened to me. He helped with the baby and the housework, too. We are fortunate that our love and commitment kept us together. Still, it wasn't a good time in our marriage, and certainly not a good way to begin our life as a family. I am ashamed of what I put us through and afraid to have more children. What if this should happen again?"

ᶜᵃᵒ

The emotional journey a woman takes after giving birth proves to be one of the leading causes of marital distress. If left unchecked, it often leads to long-term emotional estrangement, the loss of intimacy, connection, and caring—and sometimes marital dissolution. Of this, most couples remain painfully unaware.

Depression in the arduous months following childbirth is well documented. Becoming a mother begins a fragile time emotionally for many women. More than eight out of ten new mothers profess a period of tearfulness and anxiety after childbirth that often lasts for days, if not for months. At least a fifth of new mothers experience a clinically diagnosed depression. Many go undiagnosed. Yet a new mother faces her greatest prospect ever of being admitted to a mental health facility in the first year after she gives birth.

These psychological changes bring conflict to many sets of new parents. These conflicts can be complex, divisive, distracting, and potentially destructive to a marriage. Far from mythical, these conflicts are real. They affect the lives and marriages of men and women everywhere and are one of the leading causes of marital breakdown during the early years of parenthood.

A good share of seemingly stable and fundamentally happily married couples are challenged by a bout with one or more of the three known classes of postpartum mental illness—the blues, puerperal psychosis, and later onset postpartum depression—all of which fall under the umbrella of postpartum depression. This chapter describes the characteristics of each condition and the timetable in which they occur. Each strikes with varying intensity and duration and does not fail to leave its mark on individual parents and their marriage. This chapter also outlines a contingency plan for couples at risk and helps new parents determine when to seek treatment and how to find an appropriate doctor.

The Baby Blues

The quiet time of reflection in which new parents revel in the delights of having a new baby fades about the third day when the needs of a mother's recovery and child-care responsibilities converge. These are often accompanied by a collection of confusing and alarming emotions. Known as the maternity blues, the weepies, baby blues, or milk fever, all are an expected sequel to giving birth and are considered temporary, self-limiting, and short-lived.

More than four out of five new mothers report a postpartum period filled with anxiety, nervousness, irritability, insomnia, loss of appetite, sadness, loneliness, or depression. New mothers might cry uncontrollably and for unexplainable reasons. Like Connie, they know they "aren't themselves." They feel vulnerable, fearful, and unpredictably angry (usually with the new father), and they have a very strong yearning to feel safe or belong. Many new mothers question their ability to care for the baby and become overwhelmed by the dramatic changes they now understand are a very real result of giving birth.

For the majority of new mothers, these feelings disappear within a week to ten days and seldom last beyond eight to ten weeks postpartum. However, some women suffer these symptoms throughout the first year of their baby's life, and others experience them at recurring intervals until their last child enters school.

The blues are not considered serious. Seldom do they interfere with child-care responsibilities, and few new mothers and fathers view them as much more than a minor inconvenience. Some cases of the blues, however, indicate tendencies toward later episodes with postpartum depression. Roughly 12 percent of blues cases become serious enough to cause greater emotional disturbances that persist past the sixth week postpartum and often last up to a year. This is considered later onset postpartum depression.

Puerperal Psychosis

During the first days after a woman gives birth she may suffer from a very serious category of emotional illness, clinically described as *puerperal psychosis*. Puerperal psychosis affects only a handful of new mothers, about one in one thousand. Although it most likely occurs after a first birth, it can strike after any pregnancy. Seven out of ten cases result within the first month of delivery, and if a mother experiences psychosis once, she stands a one in three chance of developing it again after subsequent pregnancies.

As with the blues, symptoms of psychosis generally appear within the first few days to first six weeks of delivery. Symptoms, however, are much more severe and the duration longer. They prove *extremely* debilitating to a new mother and her family.

Hallucinations, delusions, periods of great agitation, and marked deviations in mood define this disease, and they often reflect themes of childbirth. The victim may appear grossly disorganized or display catatonic behavior. Another symptom is severe depression alternating with mania. Fleeting or persistent thoughts of suicide are common, and sometimes a mother wants to physically harm her baby. Cases of infanticide, however, are rare.

Less extreme cases of psychosis could lapse into the elongated state of postpartum depression. It is imperative to seek treatment in the early stages of psychosis.

Later Onset Postpartum Depression

Roughly four million women give birth each year in the United States, and of these, approximately 800,000 suffer from *later onset postpartum depression.* Researchers believe the actual rate of occurrence falls somewhere between 20–40 percent of all women. Many cases go undiagnosed.

For most new mothers, the common blues pass within the first few weeks of parenthood; however, for many, a surprise stage of postpartum depression sets in, accompanied by emotions unrelated to those they may have experienced immediately after birth. Later onset postpartum depression usually begins twenty to forty days after a woman gives birth, but it has been known to occur *anytime* within the first year of motherhood. Some doctors believe a mother is susceptible until her child reaches age six or her youngest child enters school.

Later onset postpartum depression incorporates elongated periods of sadness, fatigue, futility, loss of energy, acute sexual unresponsiveness, and feelings of total inertia. Women have good days and bad days. Some identify this condition as a "smiling depression." It comes at a time we're supposed to be happy—we've just had a baby! There should be no reason for depression, we think. Consequently many new mothers try to hide behind a smile while inside they lack the joy and passion usually associated with such a momentous event as childbirth.

The symptoms of later onset postpartum depression sneak in slowly, infiltrating a mother's being until she sinks into a dismal, paralyzing abyss. "At first I just felt low," said Mary, a sales representative. "I was so sad. Nothing made sense to me. Chronically tired, I had little energy for anything. I wasn't interested in the baby or anyone or anything else—and *certainly* not my husband Steve. My days were filled with empty moods, inconsistent bouts of anger and irritability, futility, and indecision. I felt worthless, frustrated, and guilty. Sometimes I raged at my husband."

Mary couldn't understand these feelings. "I loved my baby. It was what I wanted more than anything," she said. As the symptoms continued, however, Mary lapsed into silence and found solace only in routine, mundane tasks. "Sleep escaped me. My menstrual cycle became a thing of the past. I developed mysterious aches and pains, and sex—without a doubt—repulsed me."

Neither Steve nor Mary knew how to cope with what was happening. "We should have gotten help," Mary acknowledges. "Our marriage might have lasted had we been able to control the symptoms, and education might have enabled us to understand that I hadn't gone totally bonkers. *I had a disease*—the most common form of mental illness, and common to a substantial host of new mothers." Help is available for postpartum depression, but Mary and Steve didn't seek it. "We let my depression break us apart," Mary told me. "Who'd have thought we wouldn't stay married after our baby was born?"

Mary's postpartum depression, of moderate intensity, allowed her some level of control, and she continued to feel great affection for her baby; however, her marriage was unable to survive the damage. She and Steve eventually divorced.

Mary's symptoms were not unlike those experienced in most cases of classic depression. Each symptom presents itself in various levels of intensity—mild, moderate, or extreme. The more severe the symptom, the greater its disruption to a new mother and her family. In more severe cases of postpartum depression, a new mother might not be able to eat or sleep. Out-of-control anxiety could give way to panic attacks, long fits of crying, or intermittent or persistent thoughts of suicide. Depression might also cause her to become so sluggish that getting out of bed and caring for herself and the baby appear unattainable goals. In some cases a new mother might want to hurt herself or the baby, if she can stand touching it at all.

"I'd never experienced anything like it before," Mary reflected later. "I had always been a very happy individual, spunky, with lots of drive. Having postpartum depression was totally out of my character. Who would have thought I'd fall victim to it?"

The Impact on the Family

Postpartum depression affects not only the new mother, but the new father and the baby as well. More than one weary new father has spoken to me about the frustration he experienced as he watched his wife suffer with postpartum depression. "I felt helpless and abandoned—so alone," Steve said openly. "I tried to be supportive of my wife, but she wouldn't let me get close to her. She wouldn't tell me what she was going through or how I *could* help. Mary actually *drove* me away. We argued all the time, I'm sure out of frustration. I also felt guilty, I'll admit, because I thought, 'Hey, what if Mary doesn't snap out of this? Can we ever get our marriage back on track? Could I *live* like this?'"

Being physically and emotionally out of touch is often a result of postpartum depression. Most new mothers don't have the energy—or the inclination—to be intimate. They withdraw from the very people they love and need the most. In the case of postpartum depression, misery does not love company.

Outside of sexual problems, depression is the main reason couples seek marital counseling. Frequent disagreements and misunderstandings are far more common to couples when one or the other partner is depressed. In fact, if depression hangs on for too long, it can be totally devastating to a marriage. A marriage is nine times more likely to end in divorce if one or the other partner is depressed.

Treating postpartum depression promptly is crucial for a new baby. Researchers find that a mother's postpartum depression has a significant effect on her baby's intellectual development. A newborn usually relies on its mother for the stimulation it needs—to be touched, to be soothed, to be talked to, to smell, and to play. Alarmingly, efforts in this vein are often the first to go when a woman is depressed.

Causes of Postpartum Depression

Postpartum depression is an intriguing phenomenon. Not all experts agree on why it occurs or why it affects some mothers and not others. One school of thought is that postpartum depression has nothing to do with childbirth, that mothers who become depressed were depressed *before* their baby was born, just undiagnosed. Other researchers believe that the psychological process tied to the life-changing event of becoming a mother sets the stage for this and other postpartum mental illnesses. Still another cast of experts believes that the chief cause of postpartum depression lies within a woman's biochemical response system, that her hormones "act up" after she gives birth.

The following paragraphs examine the common causes of postpartum depression, outline which mothers are most likely candidates, and explore situations which render a fitting environment for its siege. Special attention is given to the changes a woman's biochemical response system goes through after she gives birth. Here we learn that the answer to "Isn't it just my hormones acting up?" might very well be "Yes, to a certain degree."

Caring for the Baby

As new parents, we must chisel a surprisingly large block of time from our schedules to care for a baby. This reality sets in very quickly. Few of us know how to care for a newborn (it is intense and demanding), and within weeks of childbirth many couples, overwhelmed and discouraged, admit that the responsibility of being parents is much greater than expected. This gap between expectations and the reality of baby care is one of the main reasons postpartum depression strikes a wide swath of men and women in the early days of parenthood.

Caring for a baby is even more stressful if the child is a difficult, demanding infant who cries a lot, is not easily comforted, vomits frequently, and sleeps little. Add to this any unsuccessful attempts at bonding or breast-feeding (common to about 40 percent of new parents) or the divisive pull to care for other children in the family. It's easy to see why roughly half of all new mothers and fathers are discouraged within weeks of becoming parents together. Difficult child-care situations often evoke stress between husbands and wives, and their baby responds by becoming more demanding. Eventually, the stresses of baby care can bring about symptoms reflecting postpartum depression.

Sleepless Nights and Broken Sleep Cycles

We all need sleep. It is essential for normal bodily functioning. We need sleep to process information, relax our nerves, and rejuvenate our bodies for the challenges of the next day. Getting adequate amounts of sleep also improves the prospects for a speedy recovery after childbirth, both physically and mentally. Not getting enough sleep can lead to irritability, paranoid thinking, emotional rages, and hallucinations. Without adequate rest, we also lack the ability to process good *and* bad emotions—which, of course, are mixed turbulently together during the first days, weeks, and even months of parenthood. Few couples understand the devastating loss of sleep before it makes its unwelcome claim on their lives and marriages.

A Bad Birthing Experience

For some new mothers, childbirth entails more than the usual discomforts. They may experience a complicated delivery, an unfortunate reaction to medication, poor treatment from the medical staff, or problems with the baby's health, well-being, or sex. For some, the depression they feel could be due to the letdown that comes if the birth experience is anything less than the emotionally charged life event they expected.

Career and Child-Care Choices

Dealing with career and child-care decisions propels more than a few couples into the stranglehold of postpartum depression. Adapting to the consequences of motherhood proves to be no small task for the career mother as well as for the mother with a career. No matter which role you choose, the transition can be an emotionally riddled time, laced with high psychological costs. Both groups of women often question their ability to care for the baby, discover divided loyalties, and experience intense exhaustion and great consternation over the choices they face. Should I work or stay home? Should I give up my career or just reduce my hours? Who will care for my baby? Why do I have to make this decision? Where is my husband in all this? Should we *really* have had this baby?

Leaving an established career to care for a child—if even for a short period of time—can affect a woman's well-being. Career mothers often face increased incidents of loneliness, irritability, and frustration, as well as lower levels of self-esteem and decreased marital satisfaction. Yet new mothers who return to the workplace can succumb to nagging sensations of postpartum depression when they go back to work.

Most new mothers return to the workplace within a very short period of time and continue to participate in the workforce throughout the formative years of their children's lives. More than 53 million working women wrestle with career and child-care decisions annually, weighing the pros and cons and the numerous and sometimes inadequate choices available. Despite mammoth strides in workforce policies and practices that aid new parents and expanded programs of support to help the mother with a career, for many new mothers the level of available support proves inadequate, leaving many women floundering in indecision as well as postpartum depression.

A Shaky Marriage

The mothers most likely to experience postpartum depression are those who have a baby that is not wanted and those who do not feel loved. The level of love is often gauged by the level of support. A new mother's postpartum mental health is greatly dependent on the support she receives from the new father. His support—practical and emotional, real or perceived—does more to influence marital satisfaction and a new mother's mental health than any one single factor.

Other Factors

Other factors influencing postpartum depression include a mother's attitude about caring for and raising children, anxiety and hostility she may have felt during pregnancy, if she has an excessive preoccupation with negative events, or if she feels helplessly out of control over her life. Women who are physically inactive, use alcohol and cigarettes, experience chronic health problems, fatigue, or other medical illnesses, or are in a lower socioeconomic status have a higher incidence of depression in general and face a much greater chance of being depressed after they give birth.

Some women are naturally more prone to postpartum depression because of personal histories and genetic makeup. Women who suffer from irregular menstrual periods or frequent bouts of PMS or who have a history of depression or a genetic predisposition towards it are much more likely to experience negative emotions after they give birth. These negative feelings often lead to postpartum depression.

Many couples don't realize that depression in the father is a possibility and they are totally thrown off balance when it happens, so much so that a marriage is terminated. If new parents only knew that new fathers might need professional help too, perhaps some marriages could be saved.

Hormones

Whenever my mood shifted after we became parents, Bruce would tell me, "It's just your hormones acting up." To a certain degree, he was right. But I wish it were that simple. The changes in a woman's biochemical response system do indeed provide answers for some of the unregulated mood swings and alarming symptoms experienced by many mothers postpartum. These are as uncontrollable yet as predictable as those experienced by young people in their adolescent years.

Our biochemical system influences hormonal output. This in turn affects how we react emotionally to the changes that take place in our body and in the world around us. The biochemical system works overtime during pregnancy and childbirth and throughout the transition to parenthood. Combined with the changes in lifestyle, roles, and responsibilities as parents, the stress of becoming a mother rocks the balance of our hormonal system, rendering us, in many cases, incapable of responding emotionally as we normally would. Many women are able to cope with a great deal of stress before pregnancy and childbirth. After giving birth, however, they may find even the most minor stresses too much to handle. Whereas before childbirth their biochemical system was able to efficiently process their emotions, after childbirth it becomes less effective, competent, and aggressive in processing them—or it may shut down altogether.

During pregnancy a woman's body produces more hormones in order to maintain, protect, and nurture the baby in the uterus. Within twenty-four to thirty-six hours of giving birth, the greatest hormonal changes take place as hormones start their rapid descent to prepregnancy levels. This causes many women to be highly emotional, to cry erratically for seemingly no reason at all, or profess that they just aren't themselves. Progesterone and estrogen levels, which are 50 percent higher during pregnancy, plunge 50 percent within hours of birth. This often brings about feelings of anxiety, agitation, and depression. These same two hormones, used to treat depression, are now linked to the very erratic behavior that coincides with their descent immediately after a woman gives birth.

Thyroid output also falls to prepregnancy levels at this time. This sudden drop often causes new mothers to feel lethargic, sad, nervous, and highly emotional. They may feel mentally sluggish and experience a slight loss of memory, noticeable hair loss, and an acute lack of sexual responsiveness and sex drive. Thyroid imbalance is more often associated with later onset postpartum depression than with the baby blues. One out of every ten new mothers suffers from thyroid imbalance. It is diagnosed by a simple blood test and is very treatable, yet most cases resolve on their own.

Prolactin, which brings about the breast changes necessary for lactation, often induces postpartum depression when it is combined with the use of oral contraceptives. Prolactin is also responsible for lower estrogen levels, resulting in a lack of vaginal lubrication and other problems during sexual intercourse.

Getting the Help You Need

If you or your spouse experiences symptoms that fall under the umbrella of postpartum depression, *do not wait to seek help.* Depression can progressively worsen and become more difficult to treat. If dark moods are apparent at the sixth-week postpartum checkup, by all means tell your practitioner. Women should not feel ashamed to seek help any more than they would feel ashamed to be treated for pneumonia. However, many people are embarrassed by the stigma of depression and isolate themselves from the help or support they need. Steve and Mary did this. The National Institute of Mental Health reports that 18 million Americans suffer from depression. Depression is the most common form of mental illness. (It is the mental health equivalent of the common cold.) Sadly, only one in three victims seeks medical treatment, yet of those who seek treatment, *almost all are helped.*

The baby blues tend to resolve on their own. More severe cases might be helped by talking to a physician or by participating in new parents' support groups. Hormone replacement also relieves symptoms brought on by the rapid descent of hormonal levels after delivery. Later onset postpartum depression usually needs the attention of a skilled medical professional who can rule out other factors which might be confused with postpartum depression, such as incorrect medications, endocrine disorders, or other chronic diseases. Treatment could include psychotherapy, medication, antidepressants, and in severe cases, electroconvulsive therapy. Cases of puerperal psychosis require great scrutiny. These mothers are referred to psychiatrists, prescribed major tranquilizers or antidepressants, and may require hospitalization.

Keep in mind that help is available! Under the watchful eye of a medical professional, treatment can be striking in its speed and thoroughness—almost magically effective. Many obstetricians, however, are guilty of ignoring the symptoms of the battle-weary mothers who drag in for their sixth-week postpartum exam. Many dismiss too quickly the complaints of these women who are often too physically tired or emotionally weak to convey their concerns accurately—or convey them at all. Unsympathetic ears have left many new mothers trying to cope with undiagnosed postpartum depression, until they drag themselves back at a later date, their condition worsened and battle scars already formed between marriage partners. In fact, unless psychotic, many mothers do not receive any treatment at all.

Speak up! Tell your obstetrician how you're feeling and how it is affecting your marriage. Few doctors will pry, so it is up to you to ask for help. If your own doctor does not treat postpartum depression, ask him or her to recommend a professional who does. You can also find a specialist by calling a local teaching university. Seek treatment from a professional who is skilled in the proper treatment, is a sensitive and sympathetic listener, and has training in the careful administration of drugs, for drugs are used widely as effective treatment for moderate to severe cases of postpartum depression.

Ongoing therapy might also be needed. It's a good idea for both new parents to attend these types of sessions together. Recovery tends to occur more quickly when the new father is involved and supportive.

Clearly, a new mother is at risk for a number of postpartum physical and emotional disorders that can coexist and persist for months or even years after she gives birth. These greatly impact her marriage! Couples need to be aware of how prevalent these types of problems are and form a contingency plan to get help whether or not they feel at risk.

THE CONTINGENCY PLAN

ⓐ Assess your situation. Ask yourself the following questions: Can you honestly say that you don't want to have this baby? Do you often feel your husband doesn't love you? Did you feel depressed after your last birth? Do you have marital problems? Are you single or separated? Do you regret that you are pregnant? Have you and your spouse attended childbirth education classes? Do you feel adequately prepared for childbirth? Do you have a demanding job, work long hours, or have little flexibility, allowing only a brief maternity leave? Are you comfortable with the arrangements you've made for child care? Is your spouse supportive of them? Have you secured adequate backup?

ⓐ Tell your spouse if you feel at risk. Discuss this possibility before the baby's birth. Review the factors that make a couple more susceptible and the common causes for postpartum depression. Explain why you feel you are at risk, what you believe might help prevent it, and what could possibly help you cope should postpartum depression set in. Keep in mind that while some women are more inclined toward postpartum depression and even exhibit qualities that predict it, *most victims have never experienced anything like it before.*

ⓐ Consult your doctor *together.* Ask your obstetrician to help you learn as much as you can about postpartum depression, what you might expect, and your individual roles in dealing with it.

ⓐ Confirm that your doctor treats postpartum depression. (Not all doctors do.) Ask your doctor the following: What is postpartum depression? Do you treat it? How would you treat it? What do you advise me to do if I think I have it? What are your expectations for my having postpartum depression based on what you know about my pregnancy and personal health history? Make sure you disclose to your doctor any possible threats to physical and emotional recoveries, concerns about your marital well-being, lack of support, or lifestyle characteristics. Mention any other stress points in your life. The more information you provide, the better your doctor will be able to help you. If your doctor doesn't treat postpartum depression, ask him or her to refer you to someone who does.

ⓐ Acknowledge the negative emotions that each of you may have. Seeing them as a real possibility often helps put them into perspective. Encourage your spouse to talk about thoughts and feelings by saying something like, "Help me understand what you are going through." Then really listen.

ဖ If you identify any of the common symptoms outlined on the previous pages, contact your health-care professional. Have a complete medical evaluation that includes a thyroid screening. This could eliminate physiological causes due to thyroid problems.

ဖ Learn how to talk to your depressed partner in a helpful, empathetic way. Don't say, "Snap out of it!" or "Just try a little harder," or "What you *really* need is . . ." Comments such as these often seem patronizing or judgmental to the depressed person. Draw on every ounce of patience when dealing with depression. Sometimes the best response is silence. Lend an ear or a shoulder—sometimes just "being there" is more important than being heard.

ဖ Consider the extent of practical and emotional support needed by a new mother after she gives birth. Is it available? Who can offer relief in child care and housework? Go out of your way to be helpful, anticipating where efforts might help the most. Plan to spend more time at home than you would normally; perhaps cut out the weekly ball game for a while or work fewer hours.

ဖ Assume a healthy lifestyle. Minimize stressful events until well after the baby's birth. Put off moving to a new home, doing extensive remodeling, or changing jobs.

ဖ Discuss contraception. There *will* be a time when you feel like making love again! Select a method of contraception *before* giving birth. Another pregnancy too soon after the first will add to an already stressful situation.

ဖ Keep in mind that sexual difficulties frequently accompany depression. Don't blame each other for a lack of sexual interest or an inability to arouse. Recognize that antidepressants and other medications used to combat depression often contribute to sexual difficulties, such as a weakened sex drive, a delayed orgasm, or the inability to reach orgasm altogether.

ဖ Arrange for adequate maternity leave from work, and possibly part-time hours for several weeks after returning to work. Talk to your employer about the company's policy and benefit coverage for a longer leave of absence should you not be able to perform career-work or require extended hospitalization, medical treatment, or therapy. What about child care? Are day-care or sick-care programs located close by or onsite? What policies are in place for breast-feeding on the job? Ongoing continuing parenting and family education is also helpful. Keep in mind that more and different support is needed for mothers who return to the workplace and that an absence of these kinds of support may trigger postpartum depression.

ᴗ Choose not to get uptight about new or unfamiliar responsibilities, unexpected interruptions, or the total upheaval of time, tasks, and relationships. Strive for a stress-free home. This is important to the growth and development of your baby, too.

ᴗ Take good care of yourself. Eat regularly and nutritiously. Cut out the extremes of caffeine and alcohol and eliminate junk foods. Get plenty of rest, fresh air, and light exercise.

ᴗ Simplify your routine for daily hygiene. There will be less time for personal care, so plan accordingly. Think clean. Look your best. If you wore makeup before the baby, wear it afterward. Select comfortable clothing that reflects your personal style. Try to feel good about yourself even when you're carrying a few extra pounds from pregnancy or not feeling up to par.

ᴗ Sleep when the baby sleeps. This is the best way to prevent sleep deprivation. It is also helpful to arrange for assistance with child care and housekeeping. Resist the temptation to rush around trying to catch up with personal tasks and housework while the baby sleeps.

ᴗ Stay abreast of current events by listening to the news or reading a daily paper. Read an article of interest you might later discuss with others.

ᴗ Maintain interests or hobbies. Too many couples give these up after they become parents, but having an outlet other than the baby is good for both parents and their marriage.

ᴗ Go out of the house every day, with or without the baby. Some mothers find that a daily walk or running errands fulfills their need for social interaction.

ᴗ If you're caring for the baby all day, anticipate the need to be away from it. Ask your husband to develop a schedule that includes time for you to get away. Let it be a time of adventure, self-renewal, or self-indulgence. You will not be shirking from responsibilities: *every worker needs a break.* Your husband will also benefit from caring for the baby without your help.

ᴗ Structure some aspects of motherhood as you would a job. Maintain as normal a routine as possible. Schedule the baby's meals and naps. "Motherhood on demand" gets to even the most loving and patient mothers. Take a break when the situation gets the best of you, and reward yourself in some way for accomplishments.

ლ Exercise, exercise, exercise! Enough can't be said about the benefits of light exercise. It speeds physical *and* emotional healing. Endorphins, the body's natural opiates, are stimulated by exercise and act on stress immediately. New mothers, however, should limit the intensity of their workout. During pregnancy and childbirth, a woman's body produces the hormone relaxin. It relaxes joints for delivery, and if a woman exercises too strenuously too soon, these joints and ligaments might be damaged permanently.

ლ Tell yourself it is okay to have negative emotions. Most mothers do. Acknowledging them makes a woman less susceptible to despair. A few good cries rid the body of poisonous toxins and do wonders to improve a mother's mental outlook. Keeping a journal might also be helpful.

ლ Find someone to help you keep your emotions in check. All new mothers speak about the need to have someone *outside the home* in whom to confide. Another new mother is often able to lend an empathetic ear. Talking tends to reduce tension, and it is comforting to share similar experiences with other new parents. Be watchful of what you say, though. A professional counselor might be a better target for those deeply personal or assaulting thoughts. If possible, participate in a new parent support group.

ლ Do seek help that is needed. A marriage is only as healthy as its weakest link. Do all you can to restore emotional well-being before it affects marital well-being.

ლ Don't be discouraged. Give yourself credit for the very difficult job you are doing as parents! Caring for a baby is one of the most important jobs on the face of the earth. Too few of us acknowledge this contribution to our families and society. It could be the most important job you'll ever have.

8

∽

Workload Shifts

The novelty of our new baby wore thin very quickly for my husband," one new mother told me. "He stopped sharing nighttime feedings, seldom changed a diaper, and resumed most of his old habits and activities. It suddenly hit me that the baby was 'my thing.' Caring for the baby, making decisions about its well-being, finding child care, doing the housework, *and* my part-time job all fell onto my shoulders."

Eventually this young mother felt totally exhausted. "But I don't think my husband even noticed or cared. I felt hurt, betrayed, angry, and resentful. I took two courses of action; neither worked. Nagging and yelling only worsened the situation." Finally this woman lapsed into a defeated silence about her husband's behavior.

"Caring for a child was an enormous responsibility, the most serious responsibility we'd ever had," she stated. "Why didn't my husband help me? Couldn't he see that I needed his help and support?"

∽

Similar anecdotes for this chapter ran wild as I continued my research for this book. I heard them on the street, in the park, at the market, wherever I encountered new mothers. Few story lines deviated from a central theme: new mothers are exhausted, overwhelmed with responsibility, and want and need more help and support. All too common is the scenario offered by a battery of new mothers. For many it is generally the perception that a new father *fails to help when needed or expected.* This is interpreted by his wife as a lack of caring and concern. His lack of responsiveness at a time when she *needs it the most* sets the stage for physical and emotional estrangement—or their first big fight as new parents.

Fighting over domestic responsibilities may seem trivial to some, but independent studies show us that when spouses differ over child care, housework, housekeeping habits, and expectations, marital frustration inevitably escalates.

ی Nine out of ten couples say they argued more after they became parents, usually about taking care of the baby and the home.

ی Three out of four new mothers feel they do not receive adequate help and support with the children and housework. Moreover, they believe they and their spouses could lead more balanced, less stressful lives and have a better marriage if these responsibilities were shared.

ی The amount of child care and housework increases so dramatically after childbirth that most couples experience a drop in social and recreational activities by as much as 40 percent.

ی Activities *shared* by husband and wife were cut by two-thirds over the first three years as parents, and fewer than one in five couples found time to spend a weekend alone together within the first year of their baby's birth.

ی For many couples, child care and household responsibilities caused them to long for "excitement" in what they said had turned out to be a "particularly dull marriage."

ی On the whole, new mothers perceived diminishing levels of practical and emotional support at a time when the need for this support was greatest. This did more to influence their level of marital happiness and personal well-being than any single factor.

As a statistical composite, these numbers display withering versions of the American household. Let's hope they overstate what is happening at individual addresses.

This chapter does not depict the nuts and bolts of parenting responsibilities. Nor is it designed to point fingers of blame at those who don't pitch in and do their fair share. Rather, it vividly and honestly sheds light on the very *nature* of child care and housework and explains how factors combine to create obstacles to the sustained marital love and satisfaction of new parents.

The Division of Labor

One of the toughest issues to remain unsolved for new parents is the division of labor. Besides finances, choices within the home over child care and housework create more disharmony between mothers and fathers than any other issue. Sociologist Arlie Hochschild argues that sharing work at home is vitally linked to marital harmony. Somehow we think marriages should be made or broken on loftier issues than who takes out the garbage or who changes a diaper. However, it is this daily grind of sorting out who does what and when that steers many couples to divorce court. In fact, "neglect of the children and the home" is listed as a cause for divorce in almost as many cases as mental cruelty.

Caring for the baby becomes the primary mission of new parents; caring for each other and their marriage becomes secondary. The marriage is instantaneously transformed from a romantic relationship to a true working relationship. The immense responsibility of caring for a baby and the intensity of it occur at dizzying speed, confounding the majority of new parents who have never put their heads together over such a massive project. The amount of child work and housework surprise most couples, who admittedly had grand expectations and made elaborate preparations for their baby's arrival but spent little time concerning themselves with the daily mechanics of caring for a baby or how doing so would change the relationship they shared.

Caring for a child is a demanding physical commitment that requires an equally intense emotional commitment. Nothing we do as husband and wife proves more relentlessly demanding, nor calls on a wider range of physical and emotional resources. Most of us become mothers and fathers with little or no training in the basics of feeding a baby, holding it, changing its diapers, or bathing it. Couple the newness of these necessary tasks with the stress of dealing with a variety of constant but unpredictable dilemmas like crying, colic, fever, rashes, or cradle cap. You easily have one stressful environment, involving two individuals struggling urgently to respond to the baby in the best way they know how.

New parents are also called upon to judge their baby's development, sometimes with conflicting ideas about what is best for their child. When parents disagree over child-care practices and philosophies, conflicts inevitably impact their marriage.

Caring for a child changes the landscapes of our homes and relationships and challenges the physical and emotional resources necessary for daily living. If these resources run short between husbands and wives *before* the birth of a baby, they will surely reach deficit levels *after* its birth. It is not uncommon for new parents to experience more distractions, work harder but less productively, and spend less time focusing on each other and their relationship, while conflicts gnaw away at what may have once been a harmonious marriage. Gone is the laughter, gone the warmth and cooperation, the joy and spirit of togetherness. In their place we find overwhelming fatigue, drudgery, disenchantment, and a division of spirit. Homes become worksites for overworked, underappreciated women and men, potential battlegrounds for intense disputes over who does what, or who doesn't.

Fighting over responsibilities is terribly exhausting to any relationship. Every time a couple fights over child care and housework, husbands and wives are a little less happy with each other, a little less happy with their marriage, and a little less satisfied with their lives. New parents fight about who does which tasks of baby care or housework, who gets time alone or for personal activities, who works, who stays home, who sacrifices, who compromises (who doesn't), and which way and whose way is the best way. Conflicts can occur daily, hourly, and minute by minute as couples lurch from one stressful situation to the next, consuming an ever increasing portion of their time together.

What new parents are really fighting about, however, is equity—or rather, *perceived inequity.* They fight about time—his time versus her time. They fight about adult responsibilities that affect the well-being of the baby and the family. For many couples, it is a battle of will over each other. In today's busy households, most parents simply do not have the time, inclination, or resources to do it all—or the time to argue.

It's Not Fair

One of the greatest sources of tension between new parents is the mother's perception that she is the one who "does it all," that she is the one who makes the biggest compromises and that parenthood means change for her only. Half of all new mothers resent the way their husband shares child-care and household responsibilities, and one in five says her husband doesn't help at all. Many women try to live with these resentments, but they often remain a source of irritation long after tempers have cooled. "Pure and simple," states Dr. P. J. Schwartz, sociology professor at the University of Washington, Seattle, "mothers and fathers who do not share tasks evenly or who *perceive* these responsibilities are not shared fairly are more likely to be miserable and divorce."

While researching this book, I heard a spate of stories lambasting spouses who didn't do their fair share. One such narrative came from Jane. With a pensive face, and immersed in uneasy analysis, she took me within the walls of her home, unveiling the sorry state of affairs which later led to her divorce.

"I got the baby ready for day care, dropped her off, and picked her up each day after work. Then I fixed dinner, cleaned up the kitchen, bathed the baby, put her to bed, and with whatever energy I had left, picked up the debris left around the rest of the house. On weekends I ran errands, picked up groceries, *really* cleaned the house, did laundry—and, oh yes, spent 'quality time' with the baby. I lost track of family and friends, dropped all volunteer activities, and gained 10 pounds. Now, how could I have gained weight? I was moving nonstop from morning until night! Bedtime became an opiate. And of course, I didn't feel like making love. I was exhausted," she said.

"Now, let me tell you about Ben's schedule," Jane continued, referring to her husband. "He'd pretty much describe it the same way. Ben's day began with a hearty breakfast and a thorough perusing of the daily paper. He exercised regularly, squeezed in breakfast or lunch with friends or colleagues, arranged for cocktails after work some evenings, and even managed a weekly game of golf or tennis. He amazed me. Seldom tired, he was always ready to play. Somehow Ben's life stayed intact after the baby was born while mine became consumed by child care and housework. I tried to get him to help me, and in his defense, I think he made some effort at first, but he just didn't get it. Lying in front of the television with the baby on his stomach did help in a way, I suppose, but it didn't make me feel better. He seldom *offered* to help me or commented on the work I did. He never thanked me or showed any kind of appreciation. I came to the conclusion that he wasn't just inconsiderate, lazy, and stubborn; he didn't respect me either. I'm not sure he even cared about me. There was no affection between us. I resented him and even grew to dislike him. I had enough to worry about with the baby and my job to worry about our marriage, too."

∾

Jane and Ben stayed married for only a short while after our interview. Jane, who worked for a computer software company, took the baby and left Ben, a financier, opted not to seek counseling, and without looking back, threw in the towel on a seven-year marriage she determined was void of love and respect. I am convinced their marriage might have been saved had they taken the time to understand the issues that divided them. I'm not sure Ben ever saw his wife's red-faced anger, or that Jane understood the pain and bewilderment Ben felt when she left. Perhaps it would have helped them had they understood that similar situations are found in countless homes across America, and that there are remedies for these missteps that have become a way of life for many new parents.

With or without children, women carry most of the responsibility for housework, period. It's not just a matter of perception. According to Dr. Gjerdingen and her team of researchers at the University of Minnesota, women spend an average of two to five times as many hours performing household chores as do their husbands. These differences become even greater after the birth of a baby when mothers usually assume primary responsibility for both child care and housework. There is evidence that men are inclined to help with the baby in the early months of a child's life, but even that involvement tends to fall off markedly over the course of the first year postpartum. During this same period of time, Dr. Gjerdingen found, many mothers perceive diminishing levels of practical and emotional support and fewer expressions of caring and concern. This results in hurtful, angry emotions, increased feelings of distrust and alienation, and lower levels of love and marital satisfaction.

While most parents *believe* child care and housework should be shared equally, in reality barely one in ten couples splits domestic responsibilities evenly. Dr. Jay Belsky, of the University of Pennsylvania, provided conclusive evidence of this. His research revealed that women consistently performed 275 percent more of the feeding, diapering, and bathing of a child, while fathers did 100 percent more of reading the paper and watching TV. Arlie Hochschild in her book *The Second Shift* similarly detailed the division of labor between husbands and wives. "Women," she stated, "typically do 250 percent more of the baby chores and 15 percent more of the household chores. This equals about 15 more hours each week of domestic tasks— about two and a half more hours each day."

Another example comes from sociologist Patricia Ulbrich, who analyzed more than 1,200 couples and found that the average wife performed 32.3 hours of housework each week compared to the 8.7 hours her husband did—and this doesn't include time spent in child-care. These differences in workload, which become more extreme after childbirth, stand out as targets for disagreement after partners become parents.

To some, these numbers may not seem plausible, but I found them to be consistent from one source to the next. Moreover, when asked separately about individually named tasks, men and women generally agreed about who did what around the house and who didn't. Regardless of today's purported attitudes on equality, it appears that most women do most of the housework and remain the primary caretakers of their children.

Time Wars

Domestic battles aren't always waged over actual chores or the inequity of handling them. For many couples, the battle is over time. Most parents simply do not have the time to do it all. The breathtaking loss of personal time and space and freedom is a common theme in the lives of new mothers. This loss, paired with the perception that the new father has been spared this devastating impact on his life, leaves many women angry and bitter. Two-thirds of new mothers said being a mother was more stressful than they'd expected, largely because they felt tied down, with no relief from the time-consuming, all-consuming responsibility of taking care of the baby.

Several factors are a certainty when partners become parents. They will have less free time and less control over their time; they will be less productive with the time they have; they will be less independent and more accountable for their time; and they will need to be more selective with how their time is spent.

Few of us have the financial resources to employ people who will completely relieve us of child care and housework. Therefore, it is essential that new parents divide up the tasks in ways that seem fair to both parents. Choices may be based on whichever parent is most available or best qualified to do the work.

An unequal division of labor tends to emerge if a woman takes time off from employment or from other responsibilities to stay home and care for her newborn. Nearly half of today's new mothers leave full-time employment after childbirth, sometimes for as long as one year. During this time, the mother usually becomes the more competent of the two parents in caring for the baby and frequently takes on the majority of this caregiving role. The traditional pattern of "mother knows best" often parallels "mothers do most."

A mother who breast-feeds further stakes her claim as the primary caregiver. While nursing, the baby gets to know the mother as a source of nourishment, develops a close relationship with her, and usually prefers the mother over the father for quieting and comfort. Men tend to be less involved with the care of the baby and generally have fewer opportunities to do so unless arrangements are made to supplement breast-feeding with bottle-feeding, or to share in baby care in some other way. Consequently many new fathers do not develop the same level of emotional attachment to the baby as their wife does in the early months of the child's life.

Some new fathers don't help because they just don't know what to do. For other new parents, tradition from one generation to the next dictates that the woman is the primary caregiver for the baby and the home while the man is the provider. More often than not, women end up performing the requisite tasks for the family and the household, driven by the creed "My children will not suffer."

In the majority of homes today, more than one parent brings home the bacon. Nearly half of all working mothers contribute 50 percent or more of their household's income, and many women see themselves as breadwinners as well as caretakers for their family. While most women applaud their opportunities in the workplace, they are scandalized by the inequities at home. What real life confirms is that even when a woman works outside her home, the majority of domestic responsibilities fall on her shoulders. This leads many women to feel they carry two full-time jobs, one at the office and one at home—what Arlie Hochschild calls "the double shift."

Women who "do it all" eventually feel used or exploited. They are more likely to suffer from depression, low self-esteem, and chronic exhaustion, and to eventually direct their anger and resentment at what they perceive to be the "nonparticipating father." It's no secret, too, that the arrival of a baby to a dual-career couple is a tragic, yet common cause for divorce.

Tag-team parenting is one solution for two-wage-earner families. However, this arrangement is no panacea. About one third of two-income households with children under age five have parents who work a back-to-back shift. One parent works from seven in the morning until three in the afternoon, then races home so the other parent can make it to the next shift. Children seem to be happy, confident, and secure when continually in the presence of one or the other parent, which the back-to-back shift allows. However, the arrangement is not so good for the parents involved. Mothers and fathers are, in essence, working around the clock, with little time for themselves and certainly no time left over for each other or to enjoy what might be considered "quality time" with the entire family. This set-up boasts a substantially higher rate of divorce than other work and child care arrangements. It can work, though, and tends to be most successful when employers are tuned into the benefits for the children and honor each parent's obligation to arrive home on time to relieve the other parent. Also, the hurdles tag-team parenting presents are surmountable when couples have a strong partnership and a shared belief that this arrangement is ideal for their children.

The arrangement that prevails in most homes today, however, remains beating the clock, fighting the traffic, making it to day care to pick up the baby or home to relieve the sitter. Moms star, of course, in the balancing act; fathers are cast in the supporting role.

Why Don't Mothers Demand More Help?

I heard a variety of answers when I posed the question, "Why don't mothers demand more help?" One person I asked was Ellen, a thirty-eight-year-old stockbroker and the mother of two preschool daughters. Her husband Will is equally ambitious, and they share a comfortable lifestyle.

Ellen's nerves were thin, her voice thick with irritation on the morning we spoke. "I *have* asked for help," she assured me. "I used to ask all the time. More than once I *implored* Will, 'Won't you *please* help me?' You can only ask so many times before you give up and figure out another way to get the job done—*if* you don't want to nag all the time and *if* you want to save your marriage."

Ellen went on to explain that after a while she did, indeed, stop asking Will for his help and she did, indeed, stop harping at him when she didn't get it. Did it improve her marriage? "Well, I'm not sure," she replied thoughtfully. "We had fewer arguments, but I remained just as disgusted with Will. I reduced my hours at the office. I lowered my standards. The house isn't as clean and tidy as it could be, our meals are less elaborate, and I don't pressure myself to look perfect and be the perfect mother anymore. I gave up being the perfect wife a long time ago," she laughed. "The hard part has been spending less time with our daughters. I still feel that I'm doing it all. I cut corners everywhere. I guess I just learned to accept things the way they were and to somehow love Will for who he was, rather than for what he did around the house or for me and our children."

Other mothers replied with similar themes. More than a third said they had asked their husband to assist them with housework or child care, and while some got the help they needed, others received minimal help, and some thought their husband provided a kind of "substitute" assistance.

Ellen explained, "I asked Will to take care of the children while I prepared dinner. This seemed fair enough, but rather than occupy the girls' time, he went outside to work on the lawn. Obviously, it was easier for him to mow the lawn than to care for a fussy two-year-old and a baby. He thought he was helping because our lawn *did* need attention. However, he wasn't helping me with what I needed him to do. Consequently, I didn't feel he helped me at all."

Some women don't ask for help because, pure and simple, they are fearful of divorce. Janet is an office administrator for a large insurance company. When five o'clock rolls around, she scurries home to relieve their baby-sitter and prepare dinner for her husband Matt and their two preschoolers. Matt is the major breadwinner, works long hours, and travels periodically. "Help me?" she exclaimed. "Matt never helps with the housework or the kids. 'It's not my job,' he maintains. He has a full agenda of his own and is seldom around for me or the children."

In our discussions, I learned that Janet thinks Matt takes advantage of her. She knows things are not quite "fair" at their house, and overall, she feels Matt neglects her and the children. Would she like him to help? Her response was filled with resignation. "Oh yes, I'd love my husband to help me, or at least to be around more, but when I say something about it to Matt, he tells me to stop nagging. He says that I don't appreciate what he *does* do. So to keep peace, I don't say anything. I'm afraid to express my anger and resentment because I am afraid he'll leave me. I'm afraid we'll have a major blowout, and I can't risk having things escalate to the point of conflict. I mean, what would I do? I can't support the children and myself on my measly salary. I have no education or any real job skills. So I work hard at home, hard at the office, and harder still 'to earn my keep.' I work like a dog. Oh, I know my husband notices. He just doesn't seem to care."

Some partners do not accept the idea of an equitable division of labor. Perhaps they have grown up in a home where their mother took care of the children and the house, and the father worked to support the family. Whether or not a woman works outside the home becomes irrelevant for many a husband after his wife gives birth; based on how he was raised, he believes that any domestic responsibilities rest on her shoulders. Consequently, many new mothers give up or reduce their expectations for getting their spouse to share the labor. They might have to decide what is most important. Is it their marriage or their idea that household responsibilities and child care should be shared? Perhaps they talked to their partner in all the right ways, and maybe they've seen some change, but not as much as they'd hoped. They choose to let go of their expectations. It's a less than ideal solution, but a common one at that.

"Jay and I started our family later in life," remarked Anita. "My husband had already determined his role and his habits during the seven years of our marriage before we had children. Almost immediately after our first son was born, I sensed that my husband wasn't going to change. I wasn't going to change my husband, and he certainly showed no signs of changing himself, so I decided to take control of my own satisfaction. Someone needed to care for the baby. This was evident very quickly, and without discussion I knew it was going to be me. I gave up a very rewarding career to care for our family. Luckily, Jay was supportive of my role and ambitions as a mother. I was every bit as fulfilled in this capacity as I had been while working outside the home.

"Perhaps to keep harmony in the home," concluded Anita, "more women need to understand that their husband is not going to change, then make the necessary adjustments to accommodate parenthood without overwhelming consequences to their marriage."

Of course, some mothers "do it all" because they want to. Monte Vanton wrote about this in his 1977 book, *Grounds for Divorce*. Vanton believes, as I do, that even when women work outside the home, deep inside they also aspire to care for their children competently and to make their homes havens of happiness, health, and comfort. *They just want help making it happen.*

What Do Fathers Want?

My husband Bruce helps a great deal around the house and with our two sons. He loves spending time with the family, he likes to be home, and he doesn't find housework distasteful. Even before we were married, Bruce vacuumed the carpets and pitched in around the house. His father is much the same way. I know, though, that I don't always credit Bruce as he deserves, and more than once, in the forum of good friends, I have joined in the complaints about husbands who don't pitch in and do their fair share.

Fathers, I have learned, are tired of catching the blame, tired of being the scapegoat for marital tension, and tired of hearing they don't do enough. While some fathers I spoke with admitted that their actions appear to drip with disrespect, many explained in manly prose that their actions aren't necessarily a clue to how they really feel.

Most new fathers want to help. Most believe that they do. In fact, the men I interviewed believe they do much more than "just help": they believe they are not only good fathers, dedicated to the healthy growth and well-being of their children and family, but that they are good husbands, good helpers around the house, and that yes, their wives are "lucky" to be married to them. These men took a great deal of pride in their contribution to the household and family and resented accusations their wives had made and the statistics that supported them.

Unfortunately, there is a gap between reality and perception. Fathers *do* help—just not as much as they think they help nor as much as their wives wish they did. Years of detective work by psychologists, marriage therapists, and family research workers reveal exactly what mothers and fathers want. I heard from parents firsthand. When men sat before me, their number one complaint was, "Don't nag me!" Husbands simply do not want to be harangued. Constant carping alienates a man and brings about his resistance to cooperation. Nagging builds walls, closes minds, and hardens hearts.

We're all guilty of nagging at one time or another. Wives seem especially prone to telling husbands what to do, when to do it, and how to do it. Never is this truer than in the child-care arena. "I really don't have a say in the matter," Edward lamented, referring to how he takes care of their newborn son. "My wife dictates how I should care for the baby and what I need to do around the house. Every detail of child care is spelled out, and you know, I could do it my own way and our baby would probably be just fine. My wife, though, throws a fit if I fail to place a dirty diaper in the garbage pail rather than throw it in the refuse pile, tightly bound as she instructs. She has rules and regulations for everything, where before the baby was born, we did our own thing as far as housework went and we got along fine. So, yeah, I'm mad at my wife as much as she's mad at me. Do I like having her tell me what to do all the time? Not really. I work longer hours than I used to, and when I am home, I try to appease my wife by following her orders—but I am seething inside. She makes me feel incompetent. Heavens, I know how to change a diaper. I can use Windex, too. I'd just like to do it my own way."

Men cannot read minds. They admit they don't always see what *needs* to be done, and that they don't always care about what needs to be done, either, or necessarily how *well* it is done. The men I spoke with, however, do want their wives to ask for help when it's needed, and they want help doing the job correctly. They don't want to hear their wives complain later about *how* the job was done or see them brooding about the help they failed to get when they hadn't asked for it in the first place. Men were specific about this.

Closing the Gap

Women long for physical and emotional support from their spouse. They do *not* want to have to ask for it. They need tangible help with the baby and the housework, but most importantly, they need the emotional assurance that they are loved, needed, appreciated, and understood. Regardless of how much *real* help a new father provides with the housework and the baby, his expressions of caring and concern affect his wife's level of marital satisfaction more than any other factor, real or perceived, practical or intangible. The new father's *efforts* to help are also important when his wife faces the energy-intensive responsibilities of taking care of the children and the home.

"Sure, caring for the baby is hard work and the house is always a mess," said Anita, the former telecommunications specialist. "But I know my husband appreciates what I do. Jay tells me every day. He tells me that he loves me and that what I do is important. He makes *me* feel important, and I know that he respects the work I do and loves me for creating a happy environment for our family. He even helps me some days! Taking care of the house and the baby is something we do in our 'together time.' We get away to rekindle the romance often enough to have a very satisfying marriage."

Most women want more than a balanced budget or a stuffed pocketbook: they want the benefits of appreciation, respect, unconditional love, compassion, and yes, help around the house with the baby! The responsibility of caring for the children and the home causes the stress that wracks many marriages. Under this pressure, new parents may grow increasingly distant or resentful. Most couples, however, wait for something to happen that somehow ends their impasse, and more often than not, nothing happens until one or the other parent makes a concerted effort.

Of all the conflicts we face together as new parents, those over domestic responsibilities seem to me to be the most fixable. They are easy to grasp. There's housework to do, a baby to care for, and tasks that can be listed and divided. There is action that can be taken in the home, straightforward steps that bring about results immediately, daily, hourly, and with the impact of changing the course of a downhill marriage. The following chapter examines how mothers and fathers can master the complexities of child care and housework together in ways that strengthen and enhance their marriage.

9

⌀∾

Fixing the Problem of
Work, Work, Work

The intensity of child care and domestic responsibilities and the number of chores are not likely to diminish for a good number of years after a child is born, but what can change are how the chores are done, how we feel about them, and most importantly, how we act and feel toward each other. Throughout this chapter you will find strategies to help you cope with the tasks necessary to being new parents together.

Working Toward Change

- First of all, do a relationship checkup. Is the way you are handling child-care and household responsibilities affecting your feelings for each other? Do patterns of behavior contribute toward feelings of less love, greater resentment, frustration, and anger, lower self-esteem and marital satisfaction, or negative feelings toward the baby?

- If you are dissatisfied with your partnership in these areas and feel that disagreements over them are hurting your marriage, resolve to do something about it. Little improvement takes place without a concerted effort by at least one partner in the marriage.

- Ask yourself: "Have I done all I could to make my home run more smoothly? Am I carrying my fair share of the work? What is *my* role in the dissatisfaction?" Your answers may lead you to make changes that improve living conditions in your home.

- When is a good time to address your concerns? Steer clear of bringing them up right after a heated dispute. Wait until both of you are calm, then with volatile issues aside, explain tactfully and specifically what you believe is at the root of discord and what you believe needs to change. Be kind, yet direct. It would be nice to inject some humor into the discussion, but by the time most couples get around to talking about their concerns, it's usually far from funny.

ဖ Reach consensus that change is needed. This might be the most difficult step. One or the other parent may find it hard to shake the conviction that the way child-care and household responsibilities are being handled works just fine. Often, though, we find that if one partner feels dissatisfied, the other feels the same way. Some couples can't agree on *when* things need to change, or on how to change. Ask your partner what changes or improvements he or she would like to see. Communicate your feelings before disparities on this issue divide you on *all* issues in your marriage.

ဖ Acknowledge what each of you does that is helpful and elaborate on how it helps you and benefits the family. Praise the things your spouse does well and refrain from criticizing.

ဖ Concentrate on how you *feel* rather than on what you think your spouse is doing wrong. Use a variation of the "feeling" technique that proves effective when communicating conflict. For example: "I feel overwhelmed and anxious because there is so much to do after I get home from work each day. I feel tired and cranky when I don't get to rest, and I'm afraid I take it out on you and the baby. Can we sit down and plan together what each of us might do to make our home run more smoothly? I feel we could handle our chores in ways that would make us both happier and give us more time together as a family."

"Our kitchen became a certified disaster area after our daughters were born," Marci offered apologetically. "Dirty dishes piled up, newspapers and mail were stacked unread in corners, and groceries were unpacked and waiting by the pantry. Baby paraphernalia closed in on us—the high chair, jumping swing, baby bottles, and old Gerber jars to be used for school projects mixed in with toys strewn carelessly about the floor. The refrigerator and stove needed cleaning. In fact, there wasn't much that didn't need attention. I knew the disarray upset Joe as well—but goodness, I was working as fast and furiously as I could. There was never enough time to get caught up before the next wave of activity. And I was tired after a full day at the office and with the children. It was starting to hurt our marriage, though. Sarcastic remarks about my housekeeping habits had turned into angry barbs more than once. I knew I needed to do better, but there really wasn't time to do it all—work and care for the kids—and I was exhausted just thinking about it! More exhausting though was thinking about the hours my husband spent doing just about anything but helping me!"

Sensing open warfare at hand, Marci led Joe away from the mess and into the family room. "I'm not happy about the state of our kitchen, and I know you aren't either," she told him. "I want to do better, and I believe if we both pitch in we can eliminate the problem. I work all day, too, and when I see you watch TV and rest while I fix the meal and clean the house and care for the girls, well, I feel angry and resentful. I feel tired with no energy left for anything—*including you!*"

Marci offered a solution. "I need help," she said pointedly, cushioning her words with a smile. "I'll clean up after each meal, and perhaps you can go through the mail and take out the garbage. If we keep up with little things daily, on weekends we'll have time to tackle the big jobs and more time to spend with each other. I think we'll both be happier." Joe agreed.

 formula Sell your partner on the benefits of change. A Roper Organization poll revealed that seven out of ten women felt they could lead more balanced lives if *everyone* helped around the house. Both parents felt they'd have more time to spend together and as a family. Each felt that the mother would be happier and more fulfilled because she had time to do things other than just take care of the kids and the home. Mothers and fathers thought the respect they showed each other when sharing domestic responsibilities would lead to a better sex life. They expected to spend more time with each other and, as a result, have a better marriage. Children, too, learn about sharing when they see their parents working together.

formula Define what "help" means to you. Without being bossy or demanding, come up with specific ways your spouse might contribute. If having your husband make a trip to the supermarket would help, by all means tell him so and prepare a list of items he should pick up. If he comes home with margarine instead of butter, keep still. If you truly want him to fold the laundry, ask him to do it. Be sure to show appreciation for the help you receive.

ဟ Make a master list of responsibilities. Getting out pen and paper is a sure sign that you mean business. Ask your spouse to make a list, too. Compare the lists. Discuss their differences. You might find that half of what you believe is essential doesn't even make your partner's list. It could be your partner will come up with good ideas you hadn't considered before. Determine together how often these tasks need to be done and outline the standards for doing them.

ဟ Divide the tasks. Each spouse should pick those they are most comfortable doing. Some tasks will be more appealing than others, so make the split according to each partner's strengths, abilities, interests, and time.

ဟ Negotiate an equitable split. What's important is that the split feels equitable. If partners perceive a plan is fair, it is probably going to work.

ဟ Gain agreement that the plan seems workable. If your partner is skeptical, change the plan immediately or agree to try it for a period of time. Remain flexible, and if the plan doesn't work, agree to revise it so it does.

ဟ Delegate tasks to others outside the home. There will be some duties that no one wants to do or that seem impossible to do because of time constraints. Be willing to delegate those to others if you can afford to—*or if it will save your marriage.* Perhaps you'll have to give up something for this to happen. A therapist became frustrated after counseling one couple over their domestic work disputes when none of their attempts at solving their problems seemed to work. Finally the therapist suggested that they hire a housekeeper. The couple took the money they spent on the therapist and put it toward a housekeeper.

ဟ Help your partner learn to do new jobs. Be specific with directions. Eliminate the guesswork. However, if you sense your partner is resentful of your instructions, let your partner do it his or her way. There are many means to the same end.

"I usually arranged for our baby-sitters," began Sarah, a twenty-eight-year-old sales representative and the mother of two small children. This could be challenging when school and teen activities were in full swing. Her husband had several evening commitments, and when Sarah had overnight travel every few weeks, arranging child care was a nightmare.

"One day it dawned on me that my husband was just as capable as I was of getting a baby-sitter. He assumed this responsibility reluctantly, but I encouraged him by telling him how much easier it would be for him to make his plans if he didn't have to depend on me as the middleman each time he needed a sitter. I gave him a list of sitters. This was a big step. He then had the necessary tools to do the job. It relieved me of the tremendous burden of coordinating his schedule with a sitter's schedule, and it gave him the flexibility to make his own plans. Most important, he gained an understanding of just how difficult and time-consuming arranging child care can be."

ဟ When changing responsibilities, change expectations, too. Many husbands and wives hold each other to standards far too rigid to meet. Not everyone performs tasks in the same manner or using a like set of standards. Tidiness and cleanliness habits differ, just as fashions vary in the care and feeding of a child. Be flexible and allow room for your partner's creativity. Resist the temptation to be critical or to redo your partner's efforts.

ဟ Remember that our capabilities as parents often improve with experience and training. Parenting is a lifelong process, and each of us will be better at it at different stages in the family cycle.

ဟ Learn to deal diplomatically with the precious commodity of time. Establish ground rules within your home and with friends and family members. Determine what interests, activities, and friendships are most important to you and be prepared to give up or cut back on others. Trade-offs will probably be necessary. Double up on activities that fulfill two needs at once. For instance, if you want to keep up your tennis game, stay in contact with your friend Mary, and check out a new restaurant, why not play tennis with Mary, then go to the new establishment afterward for lunch?

ဟ Allocate a weekly "off-duty" night for each parent. Having an evening to maintain interests and friendships without feeling guilty is good for each partner and a marriage.

ဟ Be punctual when you have a time commitment. Be up front about this when making plans to meet someone. "I'll only have an hour for lunch. I need to relieve the sitter at two o'clock, so please be punctual so we can spend as much time together as possible." Or "We'll arrive at three o'clock, which is after our baby's nap, and we'll need to go home by eight."

ᥫ Angry, bitter, or resentful feelings usually get in the way of cooperation. Being nice to your spouse is often the quickest way to get the job done. Go out of your way to help your spouse. Men especially tend to do work around the house if they are treated kindly and know their efforts are appreciated.

ᥫ Be aware of the potential for deadlock. At the mere suggestion of change, you may encounter an empty stare or experience a walkout altogether. If your concerns are strong enough, press on in an even tone of voice. Tell your spouse, "Our marriage is much too important to me to ignore this issue. I don't think we're as close as we could be because of our differences over child care and housework. Can we talk about this?"

ᥫ Remind yourself that clashing openly sometimes clears the air. One good argument might open up the channels of communication so you both can move ahead and make improvements in your home.

ᥫ Tell your partner you expect things to change and that you expect your partner to give your ideas some thought and consideration. Thank your partner for listening. Listen to your partner in turn. You'll probably both feel better having said tactfully and honestly what was on your mind.

ᥫ Pick your battles. Small children create massive amounts of details, and most are too insignificant to fight about. Isn't it easier to care for your children when you are working in partnership, trusting that your spouse is doing the best job for the family, in the best way he or she knows how?

The good news, of course, is that not all new parents war over domestic labor disputes. For some couples, it is just these undying responsibilities that bind them together for life. I spoke with plenty of couples who were mostly satisfied with how they shared child care and housework. These parents had mature attitudes about the responsibility of being parents and about their obligations to each other, their marriage, and their family.

"I think being parents is part of life—part of growing up," said Patrick, a forty-something manager of a large computer software and services company. He and Gina had three preschoolers at the time and a house full of animals—a house full of love. "I thought parenthood would be like this," he said enthusiastically. "I anticipated the responsibilities and I was ready for them. I even expected the conflicts. They seem natural to me, and a vital part of being a parent. In fact, they are, in a way, what make being a parent worthwhile. Handling the responsibilities and the stresses of parenthood makes me feel good about myself and my marriage. Gina and I don't always agree on everything or make the right decisions, but we do the best we can. I'm sure my parents faced similar challenges. My wife and I work as a team. We have cooperative spirits; we respect and understand each other's role and acknowledge that we are both important for the good of our family. We love each other and support each other. I think this is important."

Other mothers and fathers cited "the big picture." They said they were willing to make sacrifices in time and efforts for the sake of their family. They didn't let the enormity of caring for their children tear their marriage apart. They set aside quality time to concentrate on each other, and whether they stated it or not, their marriage remained a top priority after the children were born. It became clear to me that couples who experienced the least strife in their marriage over child care and housework were those who were committed to each other and their families, valued the institutions of marriage and the family, desired a strong sense of family, and made sacrifices to preserve them.

The Smoke Screen

Squabbles about child care and housework might be smoke screens for suppressed tension caused by some underlying conflicts within a marriage. More than one set of puzzled new parents, while reflecting on the state of their union, discovered that the issue of who took care of the baby or who took out the garbage was lighter than air compared to the deeper issues weighing more heavily on their marriage. One mother confessed that the conflicts she and her husband experienced didn't revolve so much around specific chores as they did around the fact that she felt her actions were never appreciated. Another couple's nagging suspicion that something was missing from their marriage was indeed confirmed.

New parents must ask: Is something lacking between us or from our lives? Are we missing the intimate connection that builds a healthy marriage? Do we spend enough time alone? Do we spend enough time together? Have we eliminated fulfilling activities outside our home? Has life become all work and no play?

Robert traveled a great deal for his work, and Debra left a demanding post in the headquarters of a Fortune 500 company to care for their three small children full-time. "I was tired of wrestling with the beast of child care," she so aptly put it. Then she turned to me with sad, tired eyes and said, "I know what our problem is. We don't laugh anymore. All we do is work. We take care of the kids and our home. Robert goes to his office. I do family things. We love each other," she added hesitantly, "but the spark is gone. We're worn out and we're not even forty years old!"

The notion that all conflicts over domestic responsibilities will be resolved quickly, quietly, and forever is foolish. There will probably be no letup for years ahead. But of course, most parents, though bruised and frustrated, will continue to care for our children and our homes, taking stab after stab at ending our vexing sessions over household and child-care responsibilities—*and most of us will succeed.* The goal is to do so before workload disagreements affect how you feel about each other. Prolonged brooding, resentments, and arguments over domestic imbalances eventually gnaw away at two good things: sex and intimacy. Skirmishes such as these erode affection and communication and destroy attraction, which are vital components to a good marriage—vital, too, to a good sex life. These aspects of a marriage, so often altered after the birth of a baby, are addressed in Sections III and IV.

III

∾

Sex, Intimacy, and Communication

In this section, you will discover how changes in sexual behavior and patterns of communication combine and intersect with the issues outlined in previous chapters of this book to bring about a deterioration of both physical and emotional intimacy and sometimes pose serious marital problems.

10

∾

We're Not "Doing It" Anymore

We had just been seated for dinner when my friend Susan asked what I had done earlier in the day. "Oh," I smiled, with a gleam in my eyes, "I started to write the chapter about how sex changes after a couple has a baby."

She leaned closer, her eyes darting around to ensure that no one else was listening. "You mean you are finding parents to interview who actually *have* sex anymore?" Susan and Michael were proud parents of a child not yet one year old. Susan had told me several months earlier that their sex life abruptly deteriorated after their baby was born, and that she missed the closeness and reassurance that making love with her husband provided.

"It's stressful being a parent," she admitted. They were juggling two careers, changing child-care providers frequently, and trying to maintain a myriad of interests and family responsibilities. "It isn't easy," Susan sighed. She and Michael were feeling stressed, conversation between them had become stilted and dissatisfying, and she felt physically and emotionally disconnected from her husband. Susan's story did not surprise me. In my preparation of this book, I came across countless anecdotes from couples who told about the changes they experienced in their own intimate relationship and the distance that had developed between them since becoming parents.

"I felt so far away from my husband during that first year," explained another new mother. "Not only had our conversations ceased, but lovemaking had too. I didn't feel sexual, but I craved intimacy. I was so tired, making love sounded like work. By the time I took care of the baby and the house, all I wanted to do was sleep when I got to bed."

A young father lamented: "Where did all the romance go? We used to give each other cards and flowers and make love three or four times a week. Now we are both exhausted, distracted, or uninterested in sex. I don't initiate it and neither does my wife. We give the baby more attention than we do each other."

ᴄᴏ

Changes in sexual behavior and communication patterns intersect with the issues outlined in previous chapters to bring about a deterioration of physical and emotional intimacy. Childbirth, cast as such a happy event, does not necessarily strengthen the intimate relationship of new parents even when they love each other very much. What mothers and fathers told me firsthand, researchers have readily confirmed. Having a first baby has the greatest negative effect on a couple's intimate relationship, sexually and emotionally.

ᴄᴏ Sex experts Masters and Johnson document that sexual and marital satisfaction decline from the birth of a first child until the last child leaves home.

ᴄᴏ Two out of five new mothers—and an even greater fraction of new fathers—said their sex life deteriorated sharply after they became parents.

ᴄᴏ A University of Michigan study documented that the incidence of sexual intercourse for new parents dropped by more than 40 percent the first year after childbirth.

ᴄᴏ In 1990 researchers at the Kinsey Institute found that more than half of all couples had not resumed their normal sex lives within a year after their first baby was born.

ᴄᴏ When Masters and Johnson studied the sexual relationship of new parents, they discovered a loss of sex drive, great psychological distress that altered their erotic relationship and self-images, difficulties reaching orgasm, and lower levels of overall sexuality and sexual activity.

Only two things were blamed more than parenting for rapidly diminishing the intimate relationship of marriage partners. These were the death or the loss of a spouse.

Having a baby does not destroy the intimate relationship of *all* new parents. I spoke with plenty of mothers and fathers who were satisfied with their sex life and who continued to feel emotionally connected. Other new parents experienced only minor blips in their sexual routines and behaviors, while still other couples suffered major challenges that rocked the very foundation of their union. For many, what started as a sexual problem turned into a marital problem, too. The goal is to keep that from happening.

Couples ask: Is it natural to stop making love after a baby is born? Why does making love change after partners become parents? Does the frequency of lovemaking return to prepregnancy levels? What do men and women *really* think about sex after childbirth?

What couples want to know is: Are we normal? Should we be fighting about this?

Like so many things in the rapidly changing world of new parents, the intimate relationship of a couple undergoes a new interpretation of what is acceptable and what is not. Some changes in intimacy mar the happy event of childbirth and alter the overall temperament of a marriage.

Sexual and Emotional Intimacy

Philip sat confidently before me, his broad forearms stretched across the table, his fingers loosely interlocked. Jennifer sat quietly beside him, in the shadow of his huge arms. Looking boldly into my eyes and without hesitation, Philip opened the book on the intimate relationship they shared. He and Jennifer had been married about three years when their first son was born, and their second child was six months old when we first met.

"One thing that changed after the baby was born," Philip said, "was that we were always tired and seldom had the energy to make love. I was patient and understanding when my wife told me she was tired. I knew the exhaustion wasn't going to last forever. If I'd thought it was going to be a permanent problem, I would have suggested we seek professional help, but we talked and remained close. We don't make love as often as we did before the kids were born, but we hug and kiss a lot. We talk about the fact that we are too tired for sex. We actually laugh about it, and I think talking about it—this communication we have—helps us ward off any misunderstandings we could have because we're not sexually active."

Although Philip served as their spokesperson, Jennifer nodded silently in agreement. It was evident that they loved each other and their family very much. They seemed to be well-adjusted parents who were actively engaged in parenting and with each other. They also shared a mutually satisfying sexual relationship. "Less active now, mind you," Philip laughed, "but nonetheless satisfying."

We chatted amicably for the next hour, during which time I learned a great deal more about their marriage and what made it work. Among other things, Philip and Jennifer had the good fortune to differentiate between *sexual intimacy* and *emotional intimacy.* They understood that their relationship was not threatened when they failed to make love, *because they remained emotionally connected.*

"Intimacy" Means Different Things

Physical and emotional intimacies are important when building a longlasting union. Effective intimacy breeds good will and is essential to adult happiness. Many of us, however, struggle to understand the *separateness* of physical and emotional intimacy, as well as the *connection,* and few of us realize the importance of each until both are threatened after childbirth.

Women want to be physically close *and* emotionally connected. "If my husband doesn't talk to me while we make love, forget it," remarked Ellen. "I want to share my thoughts and feelings with Will *while* we make love! To me, the emotional connection is what's important."

For most women, the emotional connection *is* intimacy and probably means more to them than the physical act of sexual intercourse. For many men, however, *sex* is intimacy. Making love is about as intimate as most men can imagine, and verbally expressing thoughts and feelings may or may not be part of their sexual union.

After a baby is born, a woman's need for lovemaking often takes a backseat to her need to connect emotionally with her husband. Touching, cuddling, or being verbally encouraged sound just as good as making love, to many new mothers. Consequently, when the marital relationship is unbalanced at childbirth, sexual intercourse—a man's usual method of communicating intimately—plummets to the bottom of his wife's priority list. Many men become vulnerable, as do their marriages.

"Just talk to me," many wives say to their husbands. "Talking sends the message that my husband is there with me, that he's concerned about what I'm concerned about," observed Ellen. "Maybe he'll tell me I've done a good job or that he's proud of me. These are the things that are meaningful to me."

Most of us anticipate some level of sexual adjustment throughout the years of our marriage, and especially so after the birth of a baby. On the other hand, we don't expect *emotional* intimacy to change—*unless it deepens.* We expect it to grow, as should the connection, the closeness, the sharing and affection, the give and take we find in healthy marriages.

While sexual and emotional intimacy differ, they intersect at various stages of the family life cycle and remain an integral component to marital happiness. Understanding the difference makes it easier to accept your spouse's comment that "I don't feel like making love tonight, but I still love you."

Seldom do couples stay together because of sizzling sex, and seldom do couples part because their sex life fizzled. Collectively, however, the couples I spoke with agreed that their sexual relationship was a significant aspect of their marital union. Research by Cathy Stein Greenblatt confirms this. Eighty-five percent of couples surveyed rated marital sex as "important" or "very important" to their marriage, and almost as many men and women qualified marital sex as more encompassing than "just sexual intercourse." Sex, to them, included feelings of closeness, tenderness, love, companionship, togetherness, affection, cuddling, friendship, and trust.

11

∾

Sexual Turning Points

It was the night I had been dreading," began Rachel. "I had just returned from my sixth-week postpartum checkup where I had gotten the go-ahead to have sex. Secretly, I hoped my husband Dan had forgotten that I had gone to the doctor that day. We hadn't made love for four months. We'd been afraid of hurting the baby or triggering an early labor during my last trimester of pregnancy, and since our baby was born we just didn't feel like making love. I think we forgot about it. We were both negligent in initiating any type of physical closeness."

In the week leading up to Rachel's checkup, however, as their conversations about making love increased, Dan indicated he was eager to resume their sex life. "Sure enough, that night, the lights went out and within seconds Dan confirmed my visit to the clinic. Like a young boy, he entered me suddenly and without foreplay. I was shocked and alarmed—almost frigid. I wasn't lubricated at all. I wasn't physically or emotionally ready to make love. I was afraid of so many things: that it might hurt, that the size of my vagina might have changed, that my husband wouldn't find me attractive anymore, and even that I had forgotten how to make love. What was most alarming was that I hadn't gotten wet. Surely my dry vagina concerned my husband, too. I seemed unable to become aroused the way I had before I had a baby. We'd always had a good sex life. I couldn't understand what could be happening. I was embarrassed for myself—and for Dan—fearful that this was a problem that would endanger our sex life forever.

"Then I became angry. Why wasn't Dan more sensitive? Surely he knew that it might hurt me if he was that aggressive. I felt hurt and confused. We never talked about our feelings. Instead, I shied away from making love after that. Our sex life never returned to the way it was before the baby, which left me feeling discouraged and distant from my husband."

Another new mother stated, "It took us forever to make love again. I certainly didn't feel sexual when I had a baby hanging at my breasts all day. I don't think my husband was too eager to get back into it either. It bothered me that we didn't make love, but more so that we didn't seem to miss it. When we finally made love, I don't think either of us really wanted to. We just did it because we thought that was what we were supposed to do."

Some new parents experience little change in sexual habits. "I felt great after delivery," offered Mindy, a stay-at-home mom. "My husband and I were so in love with each other and the new baby that we made love within days of childbirth without any concerns of infection or pain. Resuming sex was just what we needed to alleviate the anxiety that was building because of the baby and the extra work it brought and all the visitors who came to see us. So much was happening around us, we needed sex to pull us back together."

When to Resume Lovemaking

One issue that often raises at least a temporary dilemma for new parents is just *when* to start making love again. Many couples, like Rachel and Dan, refrain from sexual relations during the last trimester of pregnancy. For some, making love is awkward or even downright uncomfortable. However, it is during the last months of pregnancy and the first months of parenthood that both partners often benefit from being physically close.

When to resume sexual relations depends on a woman's type of delivery, her ease of recovery, and the interest level of each new parent. Some doctors encourage a couple to wait until two or three weeks have passed after a vaginal delivery, by which time the cervix has closed and opportunities for infection have decreased. Other doctors say it is best to wait until after the sixth-week postpartum checkup. By then, bleeding should have stopped, the episiotomy is healed, and risks of infection have usually passed. Overall, any physical obstacles to sexual intercourse should be gone within three to four weeks of giving birth.

Birth by cesarean section has its own set of circumstances that influence a couple's decision to resume sexual intercourse. Few women are up to making love soon after this major surgery. However, it is usually healthy and safe to resume sexual relations after six weeks postpartum. While women who give birth by cesarean face a longer recovery period and often complain about tenderness at the incision, they tend to experience fewer sexually related problems than women who give birth vaginally.

While there are no clear-cut guidelines for resuming sex after childbirth, new parents *do* have clear-cut expectations. These are formed by generations of societal, legal, and religious traditions that shape what we believe should happen in our homes and in our marriages. If we aren't ready or willing to make love within the medically approved time frame, many of us feel threatened or anxious, concerned that something is amiss with us or in our marriage. Studies, however, reveal that most new parents aren't as sexually aggressive as many of us might think. Research indicates that at least a third of new parents—and perhaps as many as 80 percent—have not resumed lovemaking by their sixth-week postpartum checkup. The Kinsey Institute reports that the majority of the couples they studied had not resumed their "normal" sex lives even a year after the birth of their first baby.

Moreover, when couples resumed making love, many shared concerns about sexual functioning. According to Gjerdingen and others, two out of five new mothers expressed at least one sexual concern at three months postpartum; even when one year had passed, the bulk of new parents continued to be plagued with obstacles to sexual fulfillment: pain and discomfort during intercourse, decreased sexual desire, emotional tension, fatigue and trouble reaching orgasm, as well as general vaginal discomfort and irritating hemorrhoids—problems which remained well beyond the first year postpartum for some, and caused many couples to establish new norms or expectations for sexual functioning.

Actually, I expect the numbers to be much larger, and the mood among medical professionals is that they probably are. Many new parents, however—embarrassed, discouraged, or frightened by the surprising sexual imbalance at home—simply choose to remain silent.

New Patterns in Lovemaking

I became more alert when Karen's sarcasm hit home. "Yeah, you're just happy because you got your quarterly roll in the hay last night," she quipped to her husband Jim. Once again, Bruce and I were lamenting the aftermath of childbirth with another set of new parents. Were they that sexually inactive, too? My goodness, Bruce and I had not made love in several weeks, and this had become fairly routine for us since starting our family several years before. We *talked* about making love, we *felt* like making love, but we were both usually too tired or too busy to do much more about it than talk. Somehow, just acknowledging that we were still interested was enough to satisfy our desires and prevent the misunderstandings that often occur when couples are sexually inactive. We'd heard other parents joke about having a meager sex life. It was comforting to learn that our closest friends didn't have much of one either.

Most couples expect that, after a relatively short period of recovery and an insignificant adjustment to being parents together, the frequency of their lovemaking will pick up. When this doesn't happen—as is often the case—many couples suspect they are no longer making love as often as they *should* be, nor as often as everybody else does. Consequently, they worry that they are falling outside the "norm" for sexual functioning. The marital sex domain, however, has few known cultural norms. Little valid statistical material is available about marital sex.

Researchers of late, however, are attempting to expose what goes on sexually in the homes of married couples today. The survey *Sex in America*, designed by the National Opinion Research Center in Chicago, illuminates Americans' sexual behaviors and attitudes. Its findings coincide with data collected for the most recent *Statistics Handbook on the American Family* (Chadwick and Heaton, editors). Both sources show that most married couples enjoy an active sex life, from which they derive great physical pleasure and emotional satisfaction, despite pauses or infrequencies which occur at various intervals in a marriage.

From the American Medical Association, though, we learn that about 30 percent of men and 43 percent of women experience *sexual dysfunction*—a catch-all medical term that includes lack of interest, impotence, difficulty reaching orgasm or lubrication, and pain during intercourse. One or more of these factors are prevalent after the birth of a baby. The bottom line: not everyone else is having great sex *all* the time, and if you're having problems, *you are not alone.*

Seven out of ten couples begin new patterns in their sexual relationship after the birth of a baby. By the one-year postpartum checkup, Dr. Gjerdin-gen and her team of researchers found that *more than half* of all couples had not returned to prepregnancy levels of sexual intercourse, and the majority reported a persistent reduction in sexual activity that lasted well beyond the first year postpartum. Few couples make love as often as they did before their kids were born. Moreover, sex falls under the use-it or lose-it category. Continuity does count. Once couples stop making love or allow large gaps of time to pass between lovemaking, it gets harder and harder to get the ball rolling again. Great pauses in sexuality can also cause hormonal levels to shift—and many times the mood of a couple shifts, too, as well as their marital wellbeing.

In light of my interviews, I came to the conclusion that most of us take our sex life a tad too seriously. We forget that lower rates of sexual intercourse and declines in sexuality in general are not confined to parents with babies or small children. All couples are affected and at various stages of the family life cycle. There will be hot and cold times of sexual functioning. Job demands, the responsibilities of taking care of a family or the household, physical, emotional, and financial worries are as influential as childbirth in changing our sexual behavior.

Sexual satisfaction should not be about "how much" or "how often," but about "what kind." Unfortunately, for many new parents the quality of lovemaking falls into question, too. Underlying the litany of complaints about *when* to make love, or how *often* to make love are all the reasons couples *don't* make love. The following chapter pinpoints these reasons. It addresses the physical obstacles to an active and satisfying sexual union, as well as the psychological deterrents. Chief among them is sleep deprivation. Let's face it, sleep sounds more exciting than sex to most new parents!

12

What Mothers Say About Sex

Pinpointing the exact cause for sexual change is no easy task. However, if the secret to a good sex life lies half in the body and half in the mind, then understanding the physical and mental challenges we face as new parents could explain why our sexual relationships often go through a tumultuous spin.

Pam sat with me in her back yard, watching her two toddlers squabble over a plastic golf club. She raced up to separate them, then flopped back down in her lawn chair. After a deep sigh, she opened our discussion with a frank admission that making love with her husband hadn't been that great since they'd started their family a few years before.

"For one thing," she said, "it hurt. It was just plain painful to make love after giving birth, and I had no interest in it for a long time. I was always tired, but it was more than fatigue. I was afraid that I wasn't as much fun to make love to anymore. I thought my vagina had stretched. My breasts seemed different, too. They were round and firm before the children were born; now they droop like hanging bags with no elasticity or tone. More than sex, I longed to hear my husband tell me that he thought I was attractive and desirable even though my body had changed after I had our babies."

Recovery from childbirth can be a stressful and lengthy process, altering not only a woman's physical and emotional well-being, but her sexuality as well. Even if a woman has a relatively easy birth with few or no complications and a rapid recovery, her body often reminds her that it was used for something other than physical enjoyment.

If pain or discomfort isn't enough, many of us are also uneasy about the ways our body might have changed. The extra pounds added during pregnancy that failed to come off after birth can be a real distraction for many women and men and take away from sexual arousal or pleasure. Stretch marks or changes that occur to the breasts can be equally troubling or embarrassing.

"I was self-conscious about making love after our son was born," explained Kate. "My body was soft and flabby. I had hemorrhoids—big purple hemorrhoids, the size and color of grapes—and an unusual odor came from my vagina. I didn't think that making love to me would be very pleasant, so more often than not, I said I was too tired when really I was too embarrassed."

In a University of Minnesota study, Dr. Gjerdingen found that two of the top five complaints women made about their transition to parenthood centered on how they felt about their body after giving birth. New mothers were concerned that they had lost their figure, and they expressed unhappiness about their general appearance. This in turn affected their sexual appetite and reduced their level of sexual satisfaction.

The following pages describe the most common fears or complaints that new mothers experience after childbirth.

Is My Vagina Bigger?

New mothers and fathers worry that the vagina will change due to childbirth and that making love will not be as enjoyable. But the vagina is a remarkable organ. It stretches to accommodate the baby during delivery. It can be swollen and bruised in the process, and for several months after childbirth the vaginal opening is larger and its tissues more relaxed. These changes are temporary. In time, and with faithful dedication to the Kegal exercises outlined on page 56, a woman's body can recover fully from giving birth with no marked effect on sexual functioning or enjoyment.

I'm Not Lubricating

A concern shared by many new mothers is vaginal dryness. "I didn't lubricate," Marci said, her voice a whisper. "I just didn't get wet. I couldn't get as excited about making love and sex wasn't as enjoyable because I didn't lubricate. It seemed to scream to my husband that I wasn't sexually aroused. I seldom climaxed after the baby was born, yet before childbirth I always had. We eventually overcame these physical handicaps to our lovemaking, but it took a long time. I never said a word to Joe about it, or to anybody else. I started to think that being dry after childbirth was part of the process, you know, just part of the great mystery of giving birth."

What Marci hadn't realized, and a fact of which many other couples remain unaware, is that the biochemical responses to childbirth temporarily limit a woman's ability to lubricate for sexual intercourse. Estrogen and progesterone levels hit rock-bottom lows and thyroid output decreases. These low levels keep the vagina from stretching and lubricating as well as it did before childbirth. However, hormonal levels usually return to normal sometime within the first year or shortly after the first year postpartum. The vagina eventually regains its ability to lubricate, but prior to that time, the period of sexual dysfunction often triggers some valid concerns about a woman's sexual performance. Whereas a man's erection indicates that he is ready to make love, a woman's readiness is determined by the moistness in her vagina. When she doesn't lubricate, it can be alarming to both partners. Furthermore, if a mother is taking medication for postpartum depression, this too can reduce her sex drive and create physiological barriers to sexual arousal or enjoyment.

"I wish I had known how common a problem this is," Marci said. "I think about the arguments we might have avoided had Joe known that one out of five women has trouble lubricating after she has a baby, and that I really *did* want to make love, that it was *not* a reflection on Joe or his performance, and that I really couldn't help myself: it was a hormonal thing." Marci would have felt better about herself and Joe's ego wouldn't have been crushed if they had known that vaginal dryness after childbirth is a natural but temporary limitation to sexual functioning.

My Breasts Aren't the Same

A woman's breasts play a large part in sexual arousal for husbands and wives. However, after a baby is born, the breasts once associated with sex and romance are often more closely tied to the care and nurturing of a child. "I got my figure back shortly after our baby was born, and since I was breast-feeding, my breasts were larger and fuller than they'd been before," explained Ellen. "I liked my new breasts and I thought Will did, too. Whatever excitement I felt about them, though, quickly disappeared when he told me he no longer looked at them as sensual."

Another new mother stated, "I didn't want my husband to touch my breasts after I had our baby. Before childbirth I liked nipple stimulation, but afterwards my nipples were too sensitive. My breasts became soft and flabby, too, and all but disappeared—and I hadn't even breast-fed! My husband teased me unmercifully until he realized that his comments hurt me. These changes affected my self-esteem and detracted from our love-making."

Some women report that nursing reduces the sensual feelings of their breasts; others report a heightened sensuality and even an occasional orgasm. Nursing a baby is known to fulfill a woman's basic need for intimacy and could actually reduce her desire to be physically close to her husband. This might also bring on bouts of jealousy if a new father feels excluded, or of resentment at the interruption of an otherwise well-tuned household. Feelings such as these undoubtedly transfer to the marital bedroom.

Fear of Conception
One psychological deterrent to an aggressive sex life is the fear of having another baby right away. There are good, physical reasons for concern. A mother's body is usually not fully recovered from giving birth the first time. Furthermore, her emotions are still erratic, and having another baby so soon could be hard on the new baby and its parents, and harder still on their marriage. If a new mother fears conception, lovemaking will not be appealing.

The Priority List
For many new parents, lovemaking tumbles to the bottom of the priority list, edged aside by parental responsibilities, fatigue, and lack of privacy. A new mother who doesn't have time or space for herself is often incapable of experiencing her own sexuality, let alone sharing it. Accustomed to meeting the needs of their new baby and family before their own needs, many new mothers view sex as just one more chore.

"Sometimes we made the effort to make love despite our exhaustion," offered Becky, who received a career-boosting assignment prior to the baby's birth. "Nine times out of ten, the baby interrupted us. There was little spontaneity, and eventually our quickies—just for the sake of making love—weren't fulfilling enough. I didn't have time to become fully aroused, so I seldom relaxed enough to orgasm. Sex became a chore, just one more thing I did for someone else."

"I dreaded making love," admitted another new mother. "I was dead tired. I actually prayed for it to be over, but to protect my husband's ego and my marriage, I usually went along with it. I would have been happier just lying in bed cuddling. To sleep in my husband's arms—now *that* would be pure ecstasy!"

However important sex may have seemed to a marriage, after childbirth, it becomes less so. Many women told me they preferred to express love to their husbands in ways other than sexual intercourse. They wanted to be held and encouraged and emotionally supported. They said they derived a great deal of satisfaction from "being together as a family" and that love-making, though unifying to their marriage and not unpleasant, just sounded less exciting to them than sleep—which is what most new mothers said they would rather do, given the choice.

Just Let Me Sleep!

"There were many nights I crawled into bed, completely wiped out, and my husband wanted to make love. On the one hand, I was thankful that he was interested," said Denise. "On the other, I was so incredibly tired that I just had to say no. I'm convinced fathers don't come close to understanding the physical and emotional exhaustion that accompanies motherhood. More than once we argued when I said no. My husband just couldn't understand how tired I was after being mom all day."

Four out of five new mothers described an "overwhelming fatigue." Over a third said their sex life deteriorated sharply for many reasons, but the main one was that they were just plain "too tired to make love."

Newborns tend to sleep through the night within a month or two of birth, and symptoms of sleep deprivation eventually wane for most new parents. Some babies have erratic sleep patterns for several years, depriving their parents of needed rest. Lack of sleep can make one irritable, nervous, or anxious and often leads to physical and mental exhaustion—or depression—and certainly not to feeling sexual. Caring for a baby is harder work physically and mentally than I ever imagined. The effects of fatigue are even greater for the many women who divide their time and energies between family and the workplace.

13

∾

What Fathers Say About Sex

Many times during the preparation of this book, I had occasion to visit with parents who shed light on valuable aspects of shared parenthood that I had neglected to consider. One area was sex after childbirth from a father's perspective.

Frank, a businessman, was generous in stature, possessed a rich drawl from a long lineage out of Louisiana, proved to have a keen wit about him, and carried himself through life with an abundance of contagious energy. Wading into our interview purposefully, and with a language I'll describe as direct, he proceeded to discuss his marriage with a sensitivity and focus I'd found in few other new fathers. When our conversation veered toward the topic of sex, he leaned toward me. "I finally get to tell *my* side of the story!" His eyes danced. His hearty laughter filled the room. Then in a more subdued tone, he earnestly conveyed what he determined had changed about making love with his wife after they became parents.

"You know," Frank began thoughtfully, "most people think it is just a woman who doesn't want to have sex after childbirth, but I found the idea less appealing, too. Now I didn't have to recover from giving birth, and I didn't experience the hormonal changes my wife talked about, and I can't say my life changed dramatically. I continued to work the same hours and do pretty much the same things I had done before the baby, but I was very tired and emotionally I was tied up with being a father. I dreamed about the ideal father-son relationship, and I felt a huge sense of responsibility. There were some big things going on psychologically that shattered my belief in the myth of male invincibility.

"Margie had delivered this healthy baby boy, and I recall leaving them at the hospital on that first day, walking across the parking lot feeling very happy and grateful that I now had this family to love, and as I maneuvered my car through the exit gates, I knew I had become a different man. I was a father! Becoming a father had somehow authenticated my marriage and made me feel very vulnerable. My wife and I were no longer just playing house. My goodness, somebody seemed to have shaken me at the shoulders and said, 'You're a grown up now, Frank. You've got responsibilities!' I wouldn't have been able to put my finger on the reasons at that particular moment, but I did feel instantly transformed by fatherhood."

Frank told me that this experience impacted every aspect of his life and marriage, and especially how he and Margie related to each other physically and emotionally. "I can't say that sex after childbirth was worse," he said, "but it was different. There were specific reasons. Mostly, I just didn't feel like making love. I wanted to sit and hold the baby. In the evenings, my wife bustled around doing all those mother-things that she hadn't had a chance to do during the day. Although I felt a great deal of love and admiration for Margie, I really wasn't interested in making love. I looked at Margie differently. We were both different. I was a father and she'd become a mother, and that meant a whole slate of new things for each of us. It didn't take long for me to sense changes in Margie, and before long those changes—which we hadn't anticipated or been able to talk about—came between us. I loved my wife, but there was so much going on that I felt out of touch with her, really disconnected. I believe what happened to Margie and me after we became parents was pretty much on par with what happens to other couples after a baby is born."

Frank's candid contribution provides a real-life example of what clinical analysis indicates and is a fairly accurate portrayal of why sex changes for many men after they become fathers. More than half of all new fathers experience some type of psychological reaction to having a baby. This in turn alters their sexual and emotional functioning. Some of the reasons for this change are tied to daily living requirements. Others relate directly to the relationship a man has with his wife. Sometimes it is all the issues outlined in this book rolled into one, which creates a sudden free-fall in the life of a new father.

Fathers Are Tired, Too

"I blame our marital problems on our sleep problems," explained John, a forty-five-year-old physician. "My wife and I didn't have a decent night's rest until our son was three years old. It drove us to counseling, where we determined that our discontent with each other and our marriage was clearly related to our lack of sleep, to a long-term fatigue and continuous broken sleep cycles. Once we corrected our son's sleeping habits, we corrected our own. Our outlook on life improved, as did our relationship and our sex life!"

New fathers are as susceptible to physical and emotional fatigue as are new mothers. They often sleep less, sleep less soundly, and experience an equal number of nighttime interruptions for feedings and diaper changes, even if they aren't getting up to do the work. This leads to broken sleep patterns and the consequences of fatigue.

A psychological fatigue sets in as a man considers the role he plays in supporting his family. Weighing heavily on his mind might be the cost of raising a child to the age of eighteen, estimated to exceed $200,000. Many men fall prey to their own double shift, working harder and longer at the office or plant, then pitching in at home with child care and housework—especially in a two-income family.

Intimacy Needs

The innate need men have for intimacy might be fulfilled by the baby. This happens for a number of reasons. First of all, work schedules often constrict the amount of time fathers are able to spend with their newborn. Most fathers I spoke to looked forward to holding their baby at the end of the workday, and more often than not, they admitted to spending more time with the baby than they did with their wife.

Dr. Jay Belsky studied this phenomenon at the University of Pennsylvania in 1994. He discovered that it was not unusual for couples to make love less frequently after childbirth, cuddle less often, show less overall affection for one another, and eventually experience a physical and emotional distance while the baby became the recipient of the affection that was formerly exchanged between partners. A *Parents' Magazine* survey at about the same time revealed that new parents were more than twice as likely to kiss their new baby as they were to kiss each other. Of course, it could be that a new father develops a close attachment to his baby because he no longer has one with his wife.

Men Feel Differently About New Mothers

Alex looked at Kate differently after childbirth. He viewed her as a mother, not as his sexual partner, nor his sexual equal. He felt guilty and disappointed that he had these feelings, but he couldn't change or conceal them, no matter how much this hurt his wife.

Adjusting to a woman's body and her image as a mother isn't easy for new fathers. "Moms aren't sexy," I heard more than once. "They wear wash-and-wear clothes and are usually too busy or too tired to make love. Mothers are asexual. I mean, how many of us *still* wonder how we ever came to be in this world? Our own parents made love? No way!"

Another new father shared the following thoughts: "I learned from early religious instruction that sex was reserved for 'procreation, recreation, and as an expression of love.' I understood the validity of each, but after childbirth I could only think of sex for procreation. I didn't want another baby right away. Sex as recreation sounded like work, and sex as an expression of love, well, that sounded like work, too."

Each of us, as parents, has conscious and unconscious thoughts that we bring into parenthood about the sexual behaviors we expect of our spouse after we become parents together. Often these ideas are based on what we observed in our own parents' marriage growing up. If we saw our parents being physically affectionate, we associate such intimacy with marriage and parenting. If we never saw our parents kissing—or doubted that they were ever physically attracted to each other, or physically close—it may be difficult for us to integrate sexuality with parenthood.

Breast-feeding is another factor in how new fathers feel about new mothers. Some men find breast-feeding a real turn-on—what could be more feminine? Others find it a turn off sexually. The beauty of the breast is often marred during nursing, when nipples become red, scarred, and gnarled looking, a visual reminder that the breasts, once erotic, are now functional. "We slept apart much of the first year while my wife nursed our baby," explained Dan. "Rachel told me that she actually orgasmed while she breast-fed the baby! Hey, she wasn't interested in making love to me, I thought she could just nurse the baby! I began to think of her breasts as a food supply, leaky and engorged, not too appealing. I had enjoyed foreplay with her breasts and she found it very arousing, but not after the baby was born."

Feelings toward a woman's body and her image as a mother do not have to affect sexual functioning, nor do they cloud the beauty of this intimate exchange for all parents. "My wife's body changed after she gave birth," admitted Steve. "Her breasts sagged, she had scars from her cesarean section, and she just seemed different down there. Was she less physically attractive? Yes, but was I less attracted to her? No! I was every bit as physically and emotionally attracted to my wife *after* she gave birth as I was before."

Men Need Time and Space, Too

Scott crunched numbers all day for a large accounting firm. He had a long commute and his work could be tedious, but he enjoyed his job and it paid well enough that his wife Michelle could stay home with their one-year-old son. "I worked all day, yet when I got home, Michelle expected me to help her with the baby and the housework. She practically threw the baby at me when I walked through the door at night. I barely had a chance to get my coat off before she rambled incessantly about her day," he said.

"Michelle wasn't herself at that time," Scott continued. "She whined about small things that would not have upset her before the baby. Little I did satisfied her. I found no time to replenish my energy or emotional needs at the end of the day. I was exhausted as much as my wife, but that didn't seem to matter to Michelle. *I* hadn't given birth."

Eventually, Scott dreaded going home. "I started to put in longer hours at the office to avoid that scene before mealtime. Our evenings included frequent bouts of criticism, then kindnesses, and other contradictions that overshadowed our happiness about the baby. We became competitive, combative, and frighteningly childish. We'd never acted like this before the baby. Things sure changed quickly and, of course, I blamed my wife."

Many new mothers get so wrapped up with the baby and become overly preoccupied with their own needs that they exhibit traits of neediness or dependency that weren't apparent before they became mothers. A new mother's overdependence can inadvertently drive the new father away.

"My wife *did* drive me away," Scott admitted later. "She was always thinking about herself—*her* needs, *her* feelings, what was going on in *her* little world or with the baby. I became disgusted with this self-absorption. I had needs, too! I know I aggravated the problem. She needed my unconditional love and acceptance, but I was too stubborn to give it to her. She needed and wanted too much from me. I couldn't deal with her dependence and found it a real turn off sexually."

Mom Only

The number one reason men cite for feeling "disconnected" from their wife after childbirth is the perception that she is "just plain too preoccupied with the baby." When feeling disconnected emotionally, one can't help but feel less physically connected, as well as less inclined to engage in sexual activity. Women who see themselves as "mom and mom only" eventually cheat other relationships, especially their marital relationship.

Some women become the household mom as well. "After we had our children, my wife acted like *my* mother, too," one new father complained. "She bossed me around or babied *me* along with the baby. Now, was this what I wanted? Where had the sexy woman gone that I'd married years before? This new behavior took away from our lovemaking."

Slaves to the Baby

Taking care of a baby, the house, careers, and each other is hard work and distracting to a marriage and a sex life, too! For many couples, the intensity of child care and housework leads to disenchantment with each other as sexual partners. Life becomes boring against the backdrop of domestic responsibilities, and without adequate leisure time to enjoy each other and pursuits outside of parenthood, sex can lose its luster altogether.

"We were slaves to the baby, to the house, and each other," Debra recalled. "It was work, work, work. 'Babies are work,' we'd been told, but I don't think we comprehended how *much* work until we became parents ourselves. I felt old and tired—and *sexual*? Far from it!"

Not only do the responsibilities of caring for a child and a home get in the way of lovemaking, but for some couples they get in the way of harmony too. Domestic conflicts reach various levels of intensity and affect more than nine out of ten sets of new parents. Misunderstandings are commonplace, tensions mount, and some parents stop talking altogether. What results? Among other things, a stalemate in the marital bedroom.

Some new parents spend too much time caring for the baby together. Constant togetherness, the loss of separate identities and activities, and fewer interests and associations outside the home can squeeze the life out of a marriage, and certainly out of lovemaking. New parents soon find out that spending time apart is just as important as spending time together.

We're Out of Control!

More often than not, when words fail to describe the reason for the change in intimacy new fathers feel after childbirth, it is due to an "out of control" sensation that comes as they grapple with the newness of responsibilities and adjust to rapid lifestyle changes. New fathers may experience a pervading underlying helplessness and feeling that life is out of control. Some new fathers start to resent their wives and the baby for bringing about the massive changes in their lives and for magnifying differences in the marriage. Anger and resentment become integral in the search for who's to blame.

Under stress from the various consequences of having a baby, some new parents just stop trying. This spells trouble ahead. The marital relationship becomes vulnerable. Couples become too tired to talk, too tired to listen, too tired for sex. Other couples stop making love, not because they are too tired, but because they are too mad. Chronic fatigue often masks anger or resentment or some other festering emotion that gets played out in the marital bedroom. Or the lack of sex drive might indicate some other problems within a marriage. The heart of the matter might not be how often new parents make love, or how angry they are at each other, *but how far they've grown apart.* The following chapter addresses the weakened emotional connection between new parents, the communication gap that widens as children grow.

14

∾

The Severed Connection

What happens in the bedroom of new parents often reflects what is going on in the rest of their relationship. Most thoughtful couples agree that what concerns them most lies not so much in how frequently they make love, as some would believe, but rather in how they communicate as a couple—how well they connect emotionally and spiritually under the sometimes caustic growing pains of parenthood.

Physical obstacles to a fulfilling sex life eventually go away, as do most of the emotional hurdles that initially alter a couple's relationship after their baby's birth. Some conflicts linger, however, and if not addressed, they continue to impact sexual functioning. Unresolved conflicts produce deep emotional scars and lead to long-term emotional estrangement. This chapter explores the weakened emotional connection between new parents. It also discusses the changes in communication that challenge their physical and emotional relationship and describes the reasons many new parents say they don't feel as close to each other after the baby as they did before.

Some new parents continue to make love despite a distance that separates them. "We were making love, but we were missing the connection we'd had before childbirth," explained Kate. "There was a gap between us that widened as our baby and responsibilities grew. Somehow having sex under these circumstances was more alarming than not having sex at all."

One grandfather conveyed the result after years of neglecting the intimate relationship he shared with his wife, most noticeable after their four children left home. "My wife and I became closer at each birth, but as our priorities shifted, out of necessity the babies' needs came first. I became number two to my wife, and felt that way. I responded to the babies' needs before my wife's needs, and over time, instead of being number one to each other, we were number two—then number three, four, and finally number five. We were nearly strangers due to the separation the children created between us. When it was just the two of us again, after the children left home, we hardly knew each other. It may have been a natural progression, but it was nonetheless disturbing and sad," he reflected.

"It is important for young couples to stay both physically and emotionally connected," he added, "so that they aren't totally fractured by their children's lives and someday find themselves strangers."

Most parents don't have to wait until their last child leaves home to feel the emotional gap that stings many marriages after childbirth.

∽ About half of the problems new parents experience tend to revolve around their ability to communicate—to really talk about what is going on in their lives, how it affects them personally, and how it affects their marriage and their feelings for each other.

∽ Seven out of ten couples report a decrease in the level of communication after they have a baby, which for half became permanent. These couples said they talked less, their desires to be physically close decreased, they were together less often, shared fewer common interests and activities, and eventually felt out of touch with each other.

∽ New parents are more troubled by the changes in *how they communicate as a couple* than by the changes they experience in their sexual relationship.

For many new parents, communication becomes awkward and dissatisfying. This leaves them feeling sad and discouraged, distant from one another, and fearful that something is wrong with their marriage.

What Happens When We Don't Talk

Laura and Doug were both about thirty years of age and had become parents for the first time several months before we met. Although I sensed that Laura and Doug loved each other and their baby very much, the distance between them was evident. An uneasy tension hung over our meeting. They glanced back and forth at each other, their exchanges carefully timed so as not to meet each other's eyes and risk revealing what was locked inside. They seemed enthusiastic about being parents, but more so about the opportunity to meet with me that morning and discuss their marriage. I believe they were hoping our exchange would somehow bring them closer together—which it did.

"This feels great," Doug declared only minutes after we began. He leaned back in his chair and stretched his long legs beneath the table, raising his arms high above his head. Relief poured from every muscle in his body. "I am so relieved to talk about everything that's been bottled up for so long. Something happened after our baby was born that changed the way my wife and I talk to each other," he continued. "We stopped talking about the things that really mattered. We discussed the baby and made everyday chitchat the way husbands and wives do, but we stopped telling each other what was going on in our lives and, most importantly, in our hearts. So much was changing around us, I think we felt out of control. We blamed each other for the frustrations and fears we felt as parents—all our inadequacies. Intellectually, everything that was happening to us made sense, but I was surprised that feelings between us changed so rapidly after our daughter's birth. The uneasiness was hard to buy and didn't seem to let up.

"It was a matter of congestion," he concluded. "We were all stopped-up and couldn't figure out how to start talking again without some level of discomfort."

Our meeting was their first attempt.

⤸

The way a couple feels about their marriage and each other really has a lot to do with how they feel about their ability to talk to each other. Can they tell each other what is happening in their lives? Can they say what they are thinking and feeling without the fear of judgment or ridicule? Do they believe they are heard? Does their partner really care?

When couples aren't able to talk freely or suspect that they are not being heard, or that their partner doesn't understand, they often feel emotionally disconnected. This leads, as in Laura and Doug's case, to a myriad of emotions, from sadness and discouragement to anger and resentment. Many interpret the emotional separation as a lack of caring or concern on the part of their spouse. This perception proves to be one of the biggest violations of marital love and trust and does more to alter the marital landscape for new parents than any other issue.

When couples have trouble talking, it often leads to basic unhappiness in their marriage. "I can't talk to him. I'm not being heard. He doesn't care," one mother said. "I don't understand my spouse," a new father lamented. And so it goes. Parents start to feel far apart—not about a single issue, but about every issue in their marriage. Some couples stop talking altogether. Many start to question whether or not they are right for each other. "Are we compatible? Were we ever compatible? Do I really love my spouse? Did I ever really love her?" one new father asked. "Maybe we shouldn't have gotten married in the first place. Look what we've done. We have this baby and now our marriage is falling apart."

Feelings such as these are not uncommon during the first weeks after a baby is born. They generally occur during the discovery zone, smack-dab in the middle of what is considered to be the honeymoon period of childbirth. These feelings occur when men and women are first called upon to deal with the unexpected stresses that come after their baby's birth, and much to their surprise, they are generally unequipped to do so without a lot of conflict in their marriage.

I am familiar with these feelings. About a month after our second son was born, Bruce and I observed our fourth wedding anniversary. I touched up the roots of my hair, had a manicure (my first in months), put on my best black dress, and prepared for a date with my husband. With hearts full of love, we drove downtown for dinner at a lovely new, upscale restaurant. Seated in a remote corner of the room at an intimate table for two, we gazed past the enormous windows to a beautiful park below. We were the only patrons at that early hour (the time when parents with babies eat), and other than the occasional clatter from the kitchen, one could have heard a pin drop. We sat there, all dolled up to celebrate our anniversary— with nothing to say.

Why Does Communication Change?

Some couples don't talk as much after they become parents because there just isn't time. There is a lack of real time together and a lack of quality time. In fact, twice as many new parents said they spent less time with each other after their baby was born than said they spent more time together. Because new parents are so busy with the baby, it is easy to stop expressing their thoughts and feelings and doing those things that maintain a long-lasting connection.

Some parents split child-care responsibilities so that one or the other is with the baby. They go out separately to run errands, exercise at different times, and pursue individual activities in a dramatic attempt to capture some element of the lives they led before they became parents. Some get busy with their own goals and responsibilities—building or resuming a career, caring for the children, maintaining the home. One by one, if a couple doesn't guard against it, another connection is severed, leading to a lack of common ground.

Many new parents find that their basic conversational skills diminish. This includes sharing, healing, inspiring, and nurturing one another. They tend to talk less frequently and find it much less satisfying. They share fewer interests, listen less, and act less interested. My interviews confirmed this.

Self-described yuppies, Sam headed a large real-estate conglomerate and Corinne was a rising star at a national advertising agency. They had been married for three years before their first daughter was born. Within six months of giving birth, Corinne and I met. She was a tired new mother, she told me, yet a happy one. Eventually, though, over several cups of hot black coffee, she revealed the unrest within her as she told me about the distance she felt from her husband as caring for their daughter became her primary mission.

"I was so busy with our baby that when Sam came home from work and told me about his day, I didn't really hear him. I often asked him to repeat himself. This exasperated him. He wanted my full attention. When I was interrupted or distracted by the baby, he became angry and frustrated. Eventually he stopped telling me about his day. Later I might hear him talking to someone else and think, 'Now why didn't Sam tell me about *that*?' I felt disconnected from my husband. I knew less and less about his life. I began to feel that all we had in common was the baby and the responsibilities we shared as parents. I felt very lonely and fearful that our marriage was threatened."

In a later interview, Corinne told me that she and Sam were on two different planes that didn't intersect until they relaxed about child care and led more well-rounded lives.

"I give Sam credit for keeping our marriage intact," she said. "He recognized that we were growing apart, too, but he had the courage to say something. One night he lined up a baby-sitter, and we went out to dinner."

"I don't want us to grow apart and that is what is happening," Sam told her that night. "We have to work on our marriage to keep it alive." Sam's ability to express his commitment to Corinne and their marriage pointed them in the right direction.

"That evening we renewed our love for each other," Corinne related, "and our determination to work on our relationship—to really make it a priority." Several years after the birth of their daughter, they remain physically and emotionally close and tightly united as a family.

"In retrospect, I believe our feelings were a by-product of that specific period in our lives," Corinne noted. "We are one of the lucky couples who saw the warning signs in our marriage soon enough to do something about it. We were also fortunate to have a deep love and commitment which held us together."

The Sex Connection

With less time to talk and enjoy each other, there is also less time to be physically intimate. This, too, causes many couples to feel less connected. Seven out of ten women said they didn't feel as close to their husband after their baby was born because they were no longer making love as often.

"All I could think about was that we were no longer making love, and therefore our marriage was threatened," offered Vanessa. "Somehow, sex was the thread that held us together when all the other fibers seemed weakened. I criticized my husband for the way he took care of the baby. He criticized me for the same. Were there other reasons, too? We argued over everything. Was so much tension accumulating between us because we were not having sex? Or, were we not having sex because we were accumulating so much tension? I didn't know which was the horse and which the carriage."

Lags in communication may be a reaction to unequal sexual interests. Sexual frustrations then become more than just problems with sex; they become marital problems, too. Few feelings disrupt the emotional climate of a marriage as rapidly as sexual rejection. Rejection conjures up anger, resentment, bitterness, guilt, blame, obsession, inadequacy, disappointment, doubt, aggression, and suspicion. Rejection damages egos and diminishes self-esteem. Eventually, rejection weakens the marital union. Perhaps what is needed when couples' sexual appetites don't match up exactly (few of them do!) is the cushioning of the emotional connection. It undoubtedly makes for a softer landing.

We're Just Not as Close

Many reasons explain why couples feel farther apart after the birth of a baby. Chief among them is that parents simply feel "less connected to each other." Mothers and fathers told me that while they loved each other very much and that their feelings for each other were basically unchanged, there seemed to be a gap developing between them—over no single disagreement, just a series of daily living circumstances that built a divisive wall and blocked the emotional and physical intimacy essential to their marriage.

Many couples don't talk as much nor communicate as well after their baby is born because there is so much going on around them that they don't talk about. Afraid to put into words what they are really thinking, new parents let their emotions fester inside. After childbirth might be the first time in their marriage they encounter feelings that they don't know how to deal with.

"We didn't know how to talk about the bad feelings we were having and how they were affecting our marriage," said Doug. "We were afraid they'd lead to conflict, and to me, conflict was one step closer to divorce."

"We were out of kilter," admitted one new mother. "But we were too frightened to express our true feelings. We didn't know how to talk about them. Conflicts could bring improvements and change. They didn't for us because we didn't talk. We just stopped communicating."

After months of bitter wrangling over one or more of the issues outlined in this book, some new parents are left philosophically separated, emotionally divided, questioning what went wrong with their marriage, and doubting that either has the focus or will to restore marital harmony. Too many couples settle into the business of daily living, caring for their baby, going to work, and performing everyday tasks while the gap widens between them. Their struggles become almost routine. Rather than doing something about the distance, they live with it. Committed to averting a major tangle, each partner tries to preserve the calm by sweeping yet another issue under the carpet. Their time together becomes dominated by what's looming below the surface, and the unsettling sensation that something is amiss in their marriage.

When one or the other parent merely shrugs or responds with silence, when both new parents cease to bicker—no longer caring to encounter yet one more battle—that's when I am most afraid for them and for their marriage.

"Arguing with Robert is no longer worth it," Debra declared boldly, resentment evident in each word. "We continue to disagree over the same things. Our battles are tiring, repetitious, and fruitless. Why fight?" There'd been no single run-in, Debra explained, just a series of frequently hostile and uncooperative behaviors that continued to dog their marriage. "Nothing changes anyway," Debra concluded. "Why fight?"

Most threatening to new parents are negative emotions that fail to come to light, even in the midst of marital conflict. Negative emotions are warning signs that mothers and fathers need help. Without these signals, too many couples fail to make the changes that can restore or improve their marriage. Perhaps new parents are overwhelmed by what is happening in their daily lives. Caring for the baby and the home, handling the details of employment and child care, as well as attending to personal needs and caring for their marriage, might be exceeding the resources they have and taxing their ability to cope physically and emotionally. Other parents might be feeling that their rights have been violated—that things aren't fair, as in the cases of child care and housework described in Chapter 8. Negative emotions tell us that some behavior needs correcting. Marital well-being may very well pivot on how well couples express these negative emotions, and whether they have the gumption to tackle the irritations that cause them.

Can It Be Too Late?

Even when we realize what is happening and wish to make improvements in our marriage, it is sometimes hard to stop a downhill slide. Tim and Mindy had three sons under the age of five before they stopped to clear the air. "My husband and I had grown farther and farther apart. He worked long hours. I took care of the children. I tried to ignore the emptiness in our marriage and the loneliness I felt, and I succeeded in doing so until after the birth of our third child," Mindy explained.

"My mother had come to stay with us and help me with the children. Tim was worthless about that time. He offered no help with the children and didn't support me emotionally either. He spent a great deal of time at his office. He seemed to think working was enough justification for his absence from our family."

One morning when the children were installed in front of *Sesame Street,* Mindy's mother drew her into conversation over a pot of steaming black coffee.

"How are you and Tim?" her mother asked abruptly. Heavens, this was big, Mindy thought. She and her mother had never discussed *anyone's* marriage. Mindy outlined every conceivable excuse for why Tim, who was self-employed, was away from home so often: the importance of his work, what a great job he was doing, and how well he supported the family financially.

"He's cold and distant," Mindy's mother interrupted. Her words stung. "He doesn't need to be working so much. It's what he chooses to do. He should be here helping you with these boys. They need him and so do you. I don't like the way he treats you. You deserve better."

Throughout the day, Mindy agonized over her mother's observations. All Mindy's justifying could not conceal the truth. Her mother was right.

"I was so angry at Tim," Mindy told me. "He wasn't being much of a father and certainly not much of a husband. I blamed Tim for everything—the distance between us, the uneasy feelings throughout our household, our boys' lack of obedience, my unhappiness. We were the same couple who had once made love three or four times each week. We never made love now, and there was little affection between us. I was so mad at Tim that I no longer cared about sex; I didn't even care about our marriage. But, well, we had these three kids, so I knew we should work on our marriage for their sake. I wonder how many couples reach this same sad conclusion."

Mindy knew they had to talk. "That evening I asked Tim if we could go out to dinner to discuss our marriage. I stumbled over the words. To my surprise, Tim welcomed the idea. His somber agreement frightened me. If he thought we had problems, then I guess we really did. I could no longer ignore them. I think couples go about their daily lives, ignoring the breadth and intensity of their conflicts until someone or something makes them real. Tim did that, as had my mother earlier in the day.

"Our conversation was way overdue. At first we sat silently, fidgeting over the menus. There was so much to say that we didn't know where to start. I was braced for conflict—and conflict we had! We talked long and hard. Everything poured out. I told Tim how angry I was at him because he had deserted me and our sons—not because he was working hard, but because he had withdrawn from me and the boys, too. I accused him of being childish and selfish. There was venom in my voice.

"After a pause, Tim surprised me by telling me how angry he was at me also. He was angry because he thought I had changed. It had been gradual, he said, but he didn't like the person I'd become since we'd started our family. He missed the old me who was fun-loving, assertive, independent, and carefree. Although he thought I was a good mother, he didn't like who I was as a mom, so he chose to be around me as little as possible. Consequently, he worked. That was his escape. He loved the children, he said, but I drove him crazy. He was perfectly and painfully honest. A knot formed in the pit of my stomach. I defended myself. He defended himself. We sparred for a good hour. Finally, exhausted yet relieved, we left the restaurant in silence. Our conversation came too late. We just couldn't get it together again.

"We had so much at stake—three beautiful sons (our oldest was barely in elementary school). I felt guilty and ashamed. We were both too stubborn to give our marriage another try. We should have talked about our feelings *as they happened.* Instead, we simply stopped communicating."

Tim and Mindy discovered the hard way what many new parents discover in a similar fashion. When conflicts aren't addressed and negative emotions fester, when husbands and wives stop talking, when one or the other ceases to care enough to bring their differences to the forefront, it becomes harder and harder to bridge the gap and make amends that maintain unity within a marriage. Tim and Mindy divorced. Their division seems so tragic, for I recall our first interview. They had been wildly in love, sexually active, and emotionally connected—100 percent committed to each other and their family.

Not all couples grow apart after they become parents together. Many preserve the special connection that attracted them to each other in the first place. Others find a new spark or unity after their children are born. Bruce and I did. Maintaining the emotional bond, though, doesn't always come naturally or easily. Couples need to work on maintaining their communication skills and improving their sexual and emotional union. Many can and do. Both are daily processes. Without consistency and commitment to the intricate details of a marriage, couples too easily get out of practice doing the small, yet significant acts that keep couples close.

POINTS TO CONSIDER

৩ Consider that you may have to increase your efforts to communicate with each other almost immediately after the birth of your baby, to stay abreast of what each of you is thinking or feeling and how it is affecting your marriage and your feelings for each other.

৩ Establish why you feel less connected or out of touch after the birth of your baby. Consider what you might be doing to hinder conversation. Are you using nagging, destructive comments? Are you too "me" oriented? Do you show an interest in your spouse and what your spouse is saying? Are you too busy with work? Are you too focused on the baby? Are you unwilling or unable to talk because you're afraid of what you'd say and where it might lead?

৩ Talk about the changes you're experiencing and how you feel about them. Do you openly discuss the fears and frustrations of parenthood, as well as the joys? Are you not discussing the positive aspects of parenthood, dwelling instead on those things that cause you to feel uncomfortable or unhappy?

৩ Share your feelings. Don't leave your spouse totally in the dark about what you're thinking and feeling. What would you *really* like to say to your spouse at this time?

- Acknowledge that some of the distance you might be feeling is natural for this time in your lives. Understand that the baby will take time and attention away from your marriage. This means you must work harder on your marriage at a time when there is the least amount of time to do so.

- Lighten up on issues that are weighing you down. Are they worth worrying about? Are you taking things too seriously? Are you being overly sensitive? Do you have excessive needs or fears?

- Don't rush to blame your spouse for the distance you might be feeling. Ask yourself, "What can I do to draw us closer again?"

- Consider what kinds of things you did for each other and what you said to each other when you felt closest. Are you doing those things now? How do you show you care? Do your actions reflect your feelings?

- Make your marriage a priority. The baby should not be more important than the couple relationship, despite its needs. Divert part of the attention you are paying the baby toward your marriage. See where it takes you!

- Plan time alone with your spouse. Get involved in your spouse's life. Shared activities increase compatibility. Being physically close also encourages conversation.

- Do you put the same efforts into planning quality time with your spouse as you put into setting up lunch with a friend or arranging an afternoon golf date? Having time and appointments for everyone and everything else but not time for each other sends a very different message from "You are important to me."

- Separate feelings about your spouse from feelings you have about your ability to talk. Rather than dwell on the distance you might be feeling, concentrate on your spouse's good qualities and all the reasons you fell in love with that person in the first place. Consider the things your spouse does well and be liberal with praise.

- Assess mistakes and misunderstandings you've had. Are these keeping you apart? What is your role? Claim fault where you may have been at fault and be willing to apologize.

- Decide what pressures outside your marriage could be fueling the gap between you, such as those related to work or finances.

❧ Give a little. Your spouse may be supporting you in a way that is different from what you need or expect, but it may be the best way he or she knows.

❧ Physically touch. It's a way to connect and show you care. And *smile*. A smile can create an immediate bond.

❧ Set up a ritual to connect. This might be a daily walk around the block, pushing the baby's stroller after a meal, a shared pot of coffee, or a relaxing glass of wine. Keep the ritual simple, cost free, and enjoyable to both.

❧ Look at the distance between you as an opportunity to improve your marriage, to try new things that result in bringing you even closer than you've ever felt before.

❧ Challenge negative thinking. Don't let critical thoughts cloud your view, yet recognize that negative emotions often become stepping stones to larger and more complex obstacles to marital fulfillment. Heed the warning signs. Commit to doing those things *now* which draw you closer together. Above all, remain patient and committed to your marriage.

IV

~

Restoring Sex, Intimacy, and Communication

$\backsim$

A successful marriage is defined in many ways, but some factors prove essential to healthy marriages, such as mutual respect, cooperative spirits, shared power and intimacy, active sexuality, and willing communication. This section addresses these aspects, so often altered after the birth of a child, and touches upon the core ingredients of commitment, using conflict productively, and showing and receiving actions of love.

These chapters offer no magical solutions, but practical, common-sense approaches to improve the daily living arrangements between new parents. Of course, for many couples, the key to marital success will lie beyond the scope of this book. The ideas I've outlined are meant to provide the basic tenets, the cornerstones of successful marriages. Learn these principles. Practice them. You will find that much of this material deals with simple issues that, when neglected, often become stepping stones to larger and more complex obstacles to marital fulfillment.

15

~

Rejuvenating a Withered Sex Life

I don't wish to make light of the sexual concerns shared by new parents, but if "just sex" is the problem, if couples communicate and have not experienced that devastating loss of connectedness, then, I believe their battles are winnable. When couples are open enough to talk frankly about what they believe is wrong and how to fix it, and are willing to explore ways to improve their sexual relationship, chances for success are great. On the other hand, if the emotional bond has been broken and one or the other partner feels trapped in a sexless marriage, frustrated, bitter, or disillusioned, there is much work ahead.

The sexual relationship between my husband Bruce and me is alive and vibrant—and always has been, save for a few excruciatingly long months immediately following the births of our two sons. I credit Bruce for this. His patience through the sexually lean times and his persistence at keeping our sex life alive has done wonders toward building an emotionally intact and strong marriage. I believe that with dedicated focus and effort, new parents can preserve the intimate nature of their union.

Sexual concerns, though, cause tension and unhappiness for many couples. Conflict over sex is frustrating to both partners. Men and women often become angry or resentful. They may feel alienated or rejected. These are natural responses when missing the connection that being physically close provides. Having good sex, or any sex at all, doesn't just happen. Conscious and deliberate actions are needed to really make a difference in what often turns out to be a make-it or break-it aspect of the marriage union.

ﻌ Be realistic. Try not to be discouraged at what you see when you look at your sexual relationship. *All* marriages go through periods when lovemaking lapses. The years when your children are babies and preschoolers form one of the two most stressful periods in a couple's marriage. Sexuality suffers the greatest immediately after the birth of a child and later when that child becomes a teenager.

ⅶ Put your sexual relationship in perspective. The purpose of marriage is to *share life* and to *share life's events.* Sex is a part but not the whole of the marital union. There are other things to enjoy together, especially the new baby.

ⅶ Talk about your sex life with each other. Sexual performance is closely tied to feelings of self-esteem and failure, so be tactful and sensitive to the feelings of your partner. Leave out criticism, blame, or ridicule—these often anger or alienate your spouse. Temper your discussion with genuine concern.

ⅶ Be honest about how you're feeling. If you lack sexual desire, explain why you believe it is so. If you have an increased sex drive, talk about those needs and desires. Having a frank discussion about how you feel about sex *as parents* tends to break down the barriers that separate couples on this issue.

ⅶ Consider why you are not making love. What outside stresses could be affecting each of you individually or together? Is there something your spouse is doing or saying that keeps you from wanting to make love? Are you being critical of your spouse or is your spouse being critical of you? Have you made accusations or demands that are a turn off in the bedroom, or do you appear so overtly uninterested that your spouse dare not make a move?

ⅶ Think about the areas of your marriage you know need work. If you know your wife resents your failure to help with the baby and the house, *help her.* If you know your husband wants you to *be more affectionate,* be more affectionate. Concentrate on the trouble spots. Action outside the bedroom often gets action *inside* the bedroom, too.

ⅶ Acknowledge those valid reasons your spouse might not be sexually motivated. Healing after childbirth is often a lengthy process accompanied by fatigue and a shortage of time, privacy, and spontaneity. The general disenchantment new parents feel toward each other as sex partners could be caused by conflicts over child care and housework. Many new parents are so burdened by added responsibilities that the thought of making love is the last thing on their minds. Lack of sex drive could also indicate other problems within a relationship that are not tied to being parents, such as restlessness, boredom, and growing apart.

❧ Recall that men and women differ in their emotional makeup and sexual needs. Strive to understand how these differences might be affecting your sexual relationship.

❧ Consider how memories of your own parents' marriage might affect your marriage today, then think about what image you would like to portray to your children. If you want them to remember that Mom and Dad had fun and loved each other while they did the parenting routine, try to act that out. Live up to those ideals. Have fun. Show love, be affectionate, and demonstrate this behavior *in front of the kids!*

❧ Bear in mind that a lack of sexual desire could have something to do with problems that lie *within* you. Perhaps excessive needs or worries are affecting the sexual and emotional temperament of your marriage. Don't be too hard on yourself if you find this is so. Nearly *all* new parents question their self-identity or self-worth, and many mothers and fathers suffer from postpartum depression. We need to feel good about ourselves, rested, and energetic to feel lovable, loving, or like making love.

❧ Spell out sensitively how you believe your spouse might have changed and convey specific behaviors you feel have reshaped your marriage or detract from lovemaking.

❧ Develop a self-improvement plan that includes healthier eating habits, plenty of exercise, and a new or more interesting hobby or activity (other than the baby). A man places a great deal of importance on his wife's appearance. He wants and needs to feel physically attracted to her. Make extra efforts in this area—you'll feel better about yourself, too.

❧ Talk about how often you make love and what seems right to you for this time of your life. There are no rule books. Few norms exist for sexual functioning—decide *what seems right for you and what works in your marriage.*

❧ Know that sexual frequency and intensity can be as unpredictable as parenting. You might need to adjust your lovemaking, as well as logistics, to fit into your baby's schedule. Experiment to find the right time and place to be together sexually.

❧ Expect that your sex life will not be perfect. Masters and Johnson point out that more than half of all couples at any given time experience sexual problems, and all of us will have sexual concerns at some point in our marriage.

Sexual dysfunction doesn't have to interfere with marital and sexual happiness. The secret is not letting the lack of sex leave you bitter, angry, or disillusioned. How necessary is lovemaking at this time in your marriage? Do cuddling, holding each other, or talking to each other suffice? Or are you growing apart because you are no longer making love as often?

- Tell your partner you're genuinely too tired, depressed, or hurried to make love, or just plain not in the mood, but be careful how you say it. There is a loving way to communicate "Not tonight, dear."

- Come to an understanding that "maybe tonight isn't the night for lovemaking, but it doesn't mean that I am not interested in you." My husband and I don't always feel like making love at the same time. We compromise. "Let's do it tomorrow, honey," tells me it's the *timing* that's wrong, *not me.*

- Give your sexual relationship the attention it deserves. Sex *is* important to the marital union—and even more so for men than for women. Lovemaking is right at the top of a man's basic needs list. Don't leave your marriage vulnerable in this area.

- Put lovemaking on your priority list. Sacrifice to have sex. Forget golf for an afternoon. Postpone the trip to the office or the mall, or do these things together *after* you've made love! Forget spontaneity; get a sitter. Plan time to reconnect and rekindle sexually. If you've been in the habit of making love on Saturday mornings, for example, don't break it.

- Connect physically and emotionally. Being intimate means emotionally, socially, intellectually, recreationally, and spiritually connected—*as well as sexually close.* Concentrate on these areas of your relationship while you are not sexually active. View the hiatus from lovemaking as an opportunity to learn more about your spouse and to gain deeper insights into your marriage.

- Make your spouse feel loved and wanted by touching and caressing. Be affectionate. Hold hands. Walk and talk. *Spend time together.* Be physically close. For a woman to feel sexually aroused, she must have affection, attentiveness, warmth, kindness, and sensitivity—the things that to her say "He cares." When a marriage struggles sexually, affection is often the missing element. Without it, many women do not feel like making love simply because they do not feel connected to their husbands.

ㄴ Be the sexual organizer in your home. Usually one person in a marriage takes the responsibility to keep it going.

ㄴ Put the romance back in your marriage. It's vital. Consider what kinds of things you did when the romance was strongest. How do you show you care? Does your spouse *really* know the depth of your love?

ㄴ Be creative with time and energy. Change when and where you relate sexually. Masters and Johnson found that changing when as well as where a couple relates sexually has a major impact on sexual satisfaction.

ㄴ Plan time apart from the baby and away from your home and responsibilities. A night or weekend getaway requires arranging reliable child care, but it will be worth the extra efforts needed to make it happen.

ㄴ Don't spend so much time together that you suffocate each other. Maintain meaningful, enriching interests and activities away from the baby, away from the house, away from each other.

ㄴ Take responsibility for your own sexuality and arousal. Gear up for lovemaking. Take a long shower or soak in the tub, or use lotions. Be willing to try new things. The efforts you make to become sexually aroused are pleasing to your spouse as well.

ㄴ Let your spouse know you are interested without pressuring him or her to act. Consider making love even if you don't feel like it.

Most new parents survive the sexual hiatus after childbirth, and for many couples, their sexual relationship improves over time because of the depth of the parenting experience they've shared. Active sexuality is important to adult happiness, and happy couples tend to make better parents. Making love is also a wonderful release from and a balance to all the work and responsibility of raising a family.

A slowdown in lovemaking is often just a consequence of becoming parents and learning to be parents together. Integrating sexuality into the family structure doesn't happen overnight. Be patient with this aspect of your marriage. If you feel your problems need the attention of a sex therapist, seek professional help. Identify a counselor with the proper credentials. Spend time assessing your situation so you can discuss it intelligently with a counselor. This will ensure a positive outcome for your treatment.

Unfortunately, concerns about sex often hint at broader conflicts between new parents. Few couples seek help for sexual dysfunction who are not also out of touch with each other. It is rare, too, that sexual problems do not go hand in hand with the marital problems addressed in the following chapters.

16

∾

When Problems Go Beyond Sex

Roughly three out of four couples who seek help for sexual dysfunction are also out of touch with each other. Not only have they stopped making love; they have stopped communicating, too. Festering inside are unspoken thoughts and feelings that have not only severed the connection between them, but more alarmingly, the very *will* to work at their marriage as they once did.

The following chapters address the broken relationship. These were difficult chapters to write. Couples, I found, want magical solutions, instantaneous results, and concrete assurances. They want to bypass the efforts *and the risks* that are necessary to restore or rebuild a healthy union. This chapter helps couples learn to deal with conflict productively—to talk, fight, and listen artfully. It contains practical approaches that can form the basis of an action plan to change and restore a marriage.

Dealing with Conflict Productively

We all handle conflict differently. I'm not a big one for "face-to-face, let's go to bat and resolve our differences" confrontation. I'd rather ignore any strife between my husband and me, or wish or pray it away. I feel this way because I don't believe that I'm very good at resolving conflict. I hate to blame my parents, but they weren't very good role models in showing me how. There was very little conflict in the home in which I grew up. My parents never argued. To this day, after nearly fifty years of marriage, my father marvels at how few disagreements he and my mother had. In fact, the only memory I have of hearing my parents raise their voices at each other was when my mother collided the family car into my father's truck during a raging snowstorm. "Hey," Mom explained, "the visibility was bad." So never having witnessed my own parents fight, when Bruce and I experience even the slightest marital discord, I think we're one step away from divorce court. It eats me up inside until we're friendly again. I just never learned to handle conflict effectively—which, by the way, is essential to marital longevity: half of all marriages dissolve not because men and women stop loving each other, but because they fail to resolve their conflicts satisfactorily. I've searched for a good way to do so for a long time.

The year was 1986. It was springtime, and I had just received my engagement ring from Bruce. At that time I was a marketing representative for the IBM Corporation, charged with the responsibility of selling data processing systems to some of IBM's largest local customers. The opportunity arose to visit with the head of the Presbyterian Churches Worldwide, who was in town to set up the communications network for his church's annual convocation that would be held in Minneapolis later that summer. Dr. John Martin was a respected author, speaker, and marriage therapist. I flashed my diamond ring under his nose and asked with a great deal of pluck, "What advice might you give me to prevent conflict in my upcoming marriage?" I hadn't really anticipated marital conflict at that time. I asked the question mainly to flatter him.

Dr. Martin paused thoughtfully, then said, "Don't talk too much." I thought this a strange answer until he offered the following explanation. "Many couples come to me, ill will between them, but with the good desire to fix their problems. Many times they come to me, not because they talked too little, as some would suspect, but because they talked too much. It was how they talked rather than what they communicated that made the difference in their marriage. You see, one little argument isn't so bad. But enough of them over several months build a divisive invisible wall. And in their confrontations these couples failed to use any guidelines. What prevailed were blame, accusations, hostility, stubbornness, rebellion, and often an abundance of self-serving initiatives.

"There is a time and a place for talking," he concluded. "Wait until the anger dies down or the baby stops crying or stressful circumstances are eliminated that exacerbate the situation. Take a break. Talk a walk. Exercise. Remove yourself from the heat. Couples need to *think* before they speak and incorporate guidelines into their discussions which bring about a more productive solution."

However many guidelines may exist to help us maneuver through the matrimonial maze, it is rare that couples deal with conflict directly and calmly and in such a fashion that each spouse understands the reasons for discord and is motivated to change so that future confrontations might be avoided. These should be our goals, yet in the heat of conflict, few of us stop long enough to *think* about let alone incorporate the following guidelines, which can lead to more effective problem solving and more satisfying conflict resolution.

Introspection

Taking time for introspection helps you see the whole picture more clearly, as well as each partner's role in creating it. *No party is faultless.* We must be candid about this. Introspection reduces the tendency for partners to blame each other wrongly for conflicts, and it encourages them to choose words and actions that work for rather than against them.

ᴖ Don't just wing it. Prepare for an honest exchange with your mate. Being truthful with yourself about what is happening in your marriage provides the basis from which to work. Keep in mind that truth is the only foundation for effective conflict resolution.

ᴖ Come to grips with how you are feeling. Are you angry? Bitter? Resentful? Sad? Hurt? Frustrated? Why are you having these emotions? Have you shared them with your spouse, or is he or she totally in the dark about what you are thinking and feeling?

ᴖ Consider the reasons for your conflicts and take responsibility for the part you may have played. Are you too quick to blame your spouse—or someone or something else? What could you be doing differently to avoid conflict?

ᴖ Try to see things through your spouse's eyes. What is your spouse feeling? Could these emotions be valid? What pressures outside your marriage could be fueling bad feelings between you, such as work or finances?

꙳ Is your spouse intentionally making you unhappy? Your spouse may believe he or she is doing things that make you happy. Unless you express how you feel, your spouse may not know that what he or she is doing misses the mark.

꙳ Consider your spouse's good qualities and all the good things that have happened in your marriage. Identify areas of agreement and successes you've experienced in your relationship. Keep these in mind as you outline improvements you'd like to see in your marriage. Let them offset any negative emotions you might be feeling at this time.

꙳ Identify problems *specifically.* Little progress can be made if couples sit down to talk about "general unhappiness." There are usually precise areas of focus that are causing unrest. How did you reach this point? Remember to weigh carefully your own part in creating conflict, as well as contributions from outside your marriage.

꙳ Practice saying what you would like to say in words that express how you really feel, in words that are tactful and sound sincere.

Face to Face

After careful introspection, go to your spouse. Timing is everything. Never attempt to address problems when you're in the heat of a disagreement. Wait until tempers have cooled. This makes prospects better for a calm and rational discussion.

꙳ Set up a convenient time to talk in a place with few distractions—*away from the children.* Seeing parents argue is very disconcerting to children, even to very young ones. While boys and girls are generally last to claim blame for taking the last cookie or breaking their mother's favorite vase, they are the first to blame themselves for their parents' disagreements, and certainly for their parents' divorce.

꙳ Express your commitment to your marriage. Lovingly and factually state your goal, which is to improve your union (*not* to change your spouse). Go ahead, say it: "I care enough about our marriage to want to mend and preserve it. I want our marriage to be better. Will you work with me on this?" Let your spouse know that you care and that you want to resolve your differences peacefully. Heartfelt statements, such as "Our marriage is important to me. I love you and I know we'll work this out," increase cooperation and reduce feelings of animosity.

ᔓ Foster a mood to talk. Don't jump right to critical issues. Spend time talking about topics that are neutral, such as how you're feeling about work or what might be happening around the neighborhood. Think how you might bridge to the sensitive issue at hand: how to improve your marriage. Moving into the discussion gradually puts both partners more at ease and in a better frame of mind to tackle the complex issues causing marital unrest.

ᔓ Remind yourself that you are *exchanging information.* You are not fighting a war. There is no contest. No one has to win. Let your discussion be an honest exchange that clears the air and restores intimacy.

ᔓ Walk the fine line of communicating what you believe is wrong without dictating what should be done. Talk in a caring way. Leave out ultimatums, accusations, and destructive comments. Avoid yelling, sarcasm, and put-downs. Most spouses know exactly where to stick the knife. Using a condescending tone or saying hurtful things elicits hostile and defensive responses, making partners less willing to address undesirable behavior. Talk in a way that does not irritate or alienate your spouse. Time spent in preparation helps couples avoid the rhythm of accusation and defensiveness into which many couples fall.

ᔓ If you are angry, express the reasons clearly, precisely, and tactfully. Avoid saying things you'll later regret. This chips away at a good union, wounds your mate, and causes rebellion, defensiveness, and divisiveness. Do not strip your marriage of the dignity it deserves by acting in this way. Angry words can be hurtful and are often remembered long after an argument has been forgotten.

ᔓ Do claim fault when it is your own and apologize. A sincere "I'm sorry" goes a long way, just as "You may be right" can avoid a host of problems.

ᔓ Suggest improvements you would like to see and how they might be made. Practice communicating your expectations, goals, and wishes clearly and tactfully.

꿈 Draw your partner into the solution. Ask for feedback. "What do you think? What might *you* suggest? Which of these points do you agree with? Which do you disagree with? Am I hearing you correctly?" Don't do all the talking. Listen intently to what your spouse is trying to tell you.

꿈 Remember to stick to the facts. Attack the problem, not the person. Fight about the housework or sharing the baby care, but don't assassinate your spouse's character or your spouse's family or friends. Deal with only present issues, not past mistakes. Things that happened months or years before are no longer germane.

꿈 Forget the words "never" and "always" unless they enter the conversation as "I'll never stop loving you" or "I'll always love you." Absolutes are usually overstatements and become stumbling blocks to a fruitful discussion.

꿈 Try not to make assumptions, jump to conclusions, or blow things out of proportion. "Oh, so you want a divorce," he retorted defensively. She replied, "No, I said I wanted you to help me with the dishes." (Big difference.)

꿈 Talk about *feelings* rather than faults. (This technique is outlined in Chapter 9.) "When you spend so much time with the baby, I *feel* that you don't care as much about me," or "I need to tell you how your actions make me *feel*."

꿈 Practice phrases such as "I think you have a point. You may be right. I see what you mean." These demonstrate empathy or that you are listening and trying to understand. An affirming nod helps, too.

꿈 Stay and talk. For confrontations to be constructive, both partners must talk, just as both partners must artfully listen. What matters in most cases is how a problem is discussed and if both spouses are able to voice their concerns and feel they are heard and respected for their views.

Listening Artfully

꿈 Put yourself in your spouse's place. How would you feel in this situation? What is your spouse's perception of the problem or frame of mind? What could be influencing your partner's thoughts or actions at this time? Is your spouse having a bad day? If so, it is also be a bad day to bring up this issue.

ᴖ Give the speaker your undivided attention. Make efforts to connect physically and emotionally. Sit face to face. Lock eyes. Rein in wandering thoughts and focus on what the speaker is saying rather than on your response.

ᴖ Clarify points to make sure you understand what your spouse is trying to say or to confirm that your spouse is hearing you correctly. "What I heard you say is that you become angry when I don't respond to your tears because it makes you feel I don't care. Is that what you mean?" Or "What did you hear me say?" Seek agreement and understanding as you talk. Rephrase key statements to show you are listening and that you are open to discussing ways to resolve your conflicts.

ᴖ Recall that men and women tend to deal with conflict differently. Women grapple with details. They need to talk and are inclined to talk more than men. They also need men to listen. Most men, on the other hand, find talking about relationship issues painful. They eschew details and prefer to skip to solutions. Some men stonewall, too, hoping the discussion will quickly end or that their conflicts will magically disappear. Be respectful of these gender differences.

ᴖ Whatever you do, do not interrupt. You'll eventually get silence.

The Action Plan

The results of a constructive confrontation should be an action plan that brings about change and restoration.

ᴖ Express commitment to your marriage and your desire to improve it. Tell your spouse, "I care enough about our relationship to want to maintain it." You can be stubborn on this point, unwavering in your commitment.

ᴖ Seek agreement that your spouse also wants to improve your marriage. Are you *both* willing to cooperate? Couples will be more successful at making amends if they are motivated.

ᴖ What if your spouse balks at the mere mention of change? What if you get an empty or angry stare? If so, you might want to come up with your own action plan. I believe a marriage can be maintained when only one partner endlessly seeks peace. Be the peacemaker, committed to bringing about change and restoration in your home. In time, your partner may come around and help.

🗷 Be clear about the primary purpose of your action plan. The goal should be that you are friendly again and that harmony is restored in your home.

🗷 With specific issues in mind, state precisely what you would like to see changed or are willing to do in order to preserve or restore family harmony. Don't be nebulous. If you want your wife to be more affectionate, tell her you'd like to have a hand on your shoulder or a goodbye kiss each day. If you want your husband to help you with the baby, outline tasks he can do and how they would help you. Break down your action items into doable tasks.

🗷 Each of you should ask: "What can I do to make this marriage better?" Keep in mind that your spouse's interests and viewpoints are as important as your own. They often shed light on aspects you had perhaps overlooked.

🗷 Be willing to explore new ground, to at least try to incorporate changes and see if they work. Agree to try again in a different way at a later date if the first plans don't succeed.

🗷 Challenge negative thinking. Ask yourself, "Can I change? If not, *why* not? Am I too stubborn to change—even for the sake of my family? *Why* am I afraid of changing? Am I afraid of failure?" Stop thinking of all the reasons that you *can't* change and start concentrating on all the ways you *can* change which will make your marriage better.

🗷 When there are no clear-cut solutions, be willing to give in, to sacrifice some of your own ideas purely for the sake of family harmony. Mature individuals learn to do this. Make trade-offs. If you make a concession, live with it and move on. Don't pick it to death or rehash it over and over.

The Family Plan

There will be times when it is almost impossible to come to terms, when you just can't, for principle's sake, reach a compromise. Then it's best to fashion a plan that is not "his plan" or "her plan" but a "family plan."

ᛣ With personal issues aside, concentrate on the welfare of what links you together, agreeing that you're willing to make sacrifices for the sake of your family.

ᛣ Visualize how you would like your family to be. Do you see family members seated around a dinner table each night? Pleasant conversation? Gatherings for special occasions? Do you see happiness and harmony? How will you make these images a reality? Writing out or describing scenarios such as these encourages you to work together as a couple and determine what needs to be changed in order to meet family goals. "The visual commitment was very helpful for my husband and me," said one new mother, reflecting on the conflict they faced in their marriage and the family plan they'd designed to help them. "I watched my husband scribble his ideas on a legal pad. He was really into it. Seeing how committed he was to working out our problems and making our family better increased my desire to make it work, too. We got excited about all the possibilities of making our family better and found that our irritations with each other faded away."

ᛣ Ask yourself, "What can I do to make our family better?" Chances are that the ideas that make your family better make your marriage better, too.

ᛣ Think of your marriage not as a partnership but as part of a "family team." Stress the importance of a strong family. Do this often. Recognize that respect for the family will sometimes be greater than the love you feel for one another.

ᛣ Keep in mind that even if you can't commit to each other, you *will* commit to your relationship for the sake of the kids.

17

∽

Living Together Each Day

My husband and I never established a formal mission statement for our marriage, but each of us adheres to a code of behavior we designed very early in our lives, if not in the homes where we grew up, long before we met each other. That code includes doing everything in our power to live at peace with one another, or "to do unto others as you would have them do unto you." Our code also includes respecting each other, serving one another, putting the welfare of our family above our own selfish needs or desires, and stepping past daily and vexing irritations to focus instead on the big picture: our desire to have a long, happy marriage and to preserve the family we created together.

Regardless of this code, at times we've found ourselves, like many other couples, hurtling angry barbs and accusations at each other. One time I let Bruce have it in the kidney with a hard-skinned yellow onion I was peeling, which I threw from across the kitchen. We've had our fits of temper, but more often than not, we've set aside our bad emotions and moved on in our marriage, commitment and forgiveness binding us together, choosing to practice the behaviors of love essential to a lasting union.

Behaviors of Love

Happily married couples do certain things each day to live together successfully. These are outlined in this chapter. They are behaviors of love, behaviors of nurturing. They are the common courtesies and everyday exchanges that add sparkle to the marital relationship. They block out what makes couples not love, reminding them instead of the reasons they do.

ৡ Make your marriage a full-time priority. The baby should not be more important than the couple relationship. It is in many families. The relationship between a husband and wife affects every family member. As mentioned in Chapter 16, respect for your family may be greater than the love you feel for your spouse. However, the relationship between a man and woman is intended to be the longest of our relationships and should be treated with the care it deserves.

ৡ Evaluate the amount of time you direct toward the baby or your own needs. Is it too much? Redirect some of your efforts toward your spouse and consider how you might please him or her. Do you have your spouse's best interests at heart, or are your thoughts and actions dominated by self-serving ideas and manipulative power plays that direct things your way? Many conflicts can be resolved or prevented by keeping the best interests of our spouse in mind.

ৡ Control the ordinary moments. These are the daily, minute-by-minute exchanges. You can make giant steps toward marital fulfillment if you succeed in conquering the small details of each day.

ৡ Consider the atmosphere in your home. What does it say? Is it one of acceptance or one of criticism? Are you liberal with praise or stingy? Are you supportive of your spouse? Are you helpful? Are you kind to one another and courteous, or have you ceased using good manners except when you're with others or away from home? The environment in a marriage should say, "I really love you and I know you love me."

ৡ Go out of your way to help your spouse. Don't wait to be asked. Put your efforts where you know they make a difference.

ৡ Listen to your spouse's needs. Be there willingly for each other.

ৡ Be affirming. Touch warmly and affectionately. Touching is an effective way to physically connect and show that you care.

ৡ Smile. In many instances a smile can say much more than words. A generous dose of smiles can change the course of a downhill marriage.

"Smile?" I hear you gasp. Yes, *smile at your spouse.* Studies show that married couples do not often smile at each other, yet when they do it has an amazingly positive effect on their relationship. Smiling helps couples avoid conflict and prevents them from mistaking words or intentions. Consider the following. Three couples were seated at a restaurant. The first was chatting amicably, smiling, laughing, gesturing wildly, actively engaged in conversation and with each other. The second couple, seated close by, was talking to each other but with little emotion in their exchange, and neither was smiling. The third couple shared a table at the far end of the room. Each was reading a book. Who was married? Who was not? The first couple was dating. The second two were married.

Reestablish the Bond

What really makes me sad is when I see couples racing independently through their face-paced lives, meeting the demands of each and every other person or organization in their orbit, yet neglecting the needs of each other. Only making our marriage a priority and setting time aside to be with our spouse will enable us to stay tethered in these rapidly spinning times.

Now I know when two people are estranged, the idea of talking or even spending *time* together can be terribly frightening. There's a great deal of pressure about what to talk about or how to communicate it. Where do you start? A good place to begin is by talking about the things that happen to you each day. Skip the big issues that relate to your marriage or to conflicts between you or your family. Develop casual and pleasant conversation until it seems natural once again to talk to each other without conflict. This daily sharing of the little things also keeps us connected as couples, so that we don't someday reach a point where we no longer have anything to talk about, or cease *wanting* to talk or listen because we no longer care.

A recent study revealed that today's busy couples log less than four minutes in daily conversation. This includes common exchanges at the meal table and in passing. Four minutes is hardly enough time to keep in touch or to pass along what is happening in our lives, let alone how we are feeling inside and how it affects our marriage.

ιɔ Attempt "courting." Think back to how you acted and responded to each other when you dated. What qualities did you like and admire in your spouse? Use memories of when you first met and passions ran wildest to rekindle sparks between you. Schedule an event or activity that you enjoyed together but perhaps haven't done in a long time. Actually have a date.

ιɔ When the time seems right (but not before), make attempts to make love. When there is a history of bad emotions between partners, it's hard to jump right back into lovemaking. Be patient. Most women need to recapture feelings of closeness, to really feel that they click emotionally again. This is accomplished through the behaviors of love. Practice these. They are the greatest aphrodisiacs—for men and women!

ιɔ Stay committed to your marriage. Keep on trying any number of techniques. If one doesn't work, try another. Be patient: healing and restoration do not occur overnight. For some, it's a lifetime process.

ιɔ The Points to Consider at the end of Chapter 14 suggest additional ways to reconnect when the physical and emotional bonds are weak.

The Power of Forgiveness

Too little emphasis is placed on the power of forgiveness, yet it can be the first step in peacemaking. Who of us really enjoys harboring a grudge? Sometimes pride keeps us from claiming our part in the conflicts we have, asking for forgiveness, or saying we forgive. Sometimes we don't *want* to forgive. We don't want to let our partners off the hook for something they've said or done. We don't want them to get by without being punished for the pain they caused or the truly rotten thing they said or did. I don't believe we should totally ignore valid transgressions, but without forgiveness can we really move ahead and heal a broken marriage?

Forgiveness doesn't just happen. It is a decision we make—a choice between hardening the heart or healing our marriage. If we let anger and resentment build, they'll gnaw away at what may have once been a good marriage and could be again. Unforgivingness eats away at our hearts, poisoning every day we're together and influencing the course our marriage will take. Forgiveness means that we wipe the slate clean, that we give up our right to be angry or to get even. Paybacks and tit-for-tat have no place within a marriage. Even if you believe your feelings are justified, sometimes for the sake of the family you must sacrifice your right to feel that way. Forgiveness means letting go of harmful thoughts and reacting in a way you do not feel—which is like forgiving and loving again, and yes, *forgetting*, too, so you can move ahead and have the marriage you'd like to have.

Forgiveness takes courage and practice. It is something we can learn to do, and it is essential that we learn to do it well, for in the shoulder-to-shoulder working relationship of parenting together, there will be one thousand and one occasions calling for this skill. Don't wait for your spouse to make the first move. Be the first to forgive. When at fault, ask for forgiveness: "I'm sorry. Will you please forgive me?" These are simple words. Even if your spouse is at fault, *you still go!* Swallow your pride and say, "I'm sorry we are having this altercation. Can we make amends?" Then *wait for a response.* Asking for and receiving forgiveness are two important steps to the peacemaking process.

Show your spouse you have forgiven by performing the behaviors of love. Forgiveness may be the first action; being sorry enough to change might be the second. Be committed to not doing again those things that caused the problems in the first place. Strong marriage partners learn to do this, and to be the first to do so.

The Decision to Love

It is not always easy to keep on loving when we don't feel like loving, or when we don't feel lovable. I've heard couples whine pathetically, "But I don't *feel* the love. I just don't *feel* it!" Perhaps they are pitted vehemently against each other, enmity molding their history together, caring and intimacy gone from their beleaguered marriage. Perhaps they are waiting for the flame to reignite, counting the days until Cupid reappears. With arms locked, they wait to *feel* love again. I believe we will not feel love unless we choose to. Loving our spouse depends on the *choice* we make to practice the behaviors of love. It is a commitment to love and a decision to keep on loving.

"When someone says he or she no longer loves another person, we often ask when they made the decision to stop loving that person," write David and Jan Stoop in *The Intimacy Factor.* "Usually there was a point at which time the decision to stop loving was made. We believe that decision can be reversed and that is where the commitment to love comes in. The *decision* to love keeps us doing the behaviors of love even when we don't feel like it. And when we act in a loving way, the feelings and emotions of love can and do return."

Sometimes performing the behaviors of love seems almost impossible because we are so terribly at odds with our partner. At such times, we can use several strategies to help us show love when we don't feel like loving. One idea is that we treat our spouse as a friend and as a friend only. Dismiss the fact that you are married to that man or woman—and along with it, all the expectations that come with being married partners. Focus instead on treating your spouse with the common courtesies you might show a very good friend.

Consider this example. A friend is an overnight guest in your home. In the morning you rise from bed before your guest to prepare a pot of hot coffee. When your friend enters the kitchen, you stop reading the newspaper and offer him or her a bright smile and cheery "Good morning."

"How about some of that black coffee I know you like so well?" you ask eagerly. (You've anticipated what they like!) His or her cup is waiting. You pull up a chair alongside your own. You want to please your friend, and you've gone out of your way to do so.

Contrast this scene with how many of us greet our spouse on any given morning. We scarcely lift our eyes from the morning paper and grunt, "Coffee's ready." We resume reading the newspaper in silence. Maybe we went so far as to ask how our spouse had slept, but that is the extent of many morning exchanges. Which scene breeds more good will, cooperation, and communication?

The role of a spouse comes with many expectations and demands that few of us place on even our closest friends. Many marriage conflicts revolve around failed expectations and the disappointment (and consequent anger and frustration) that comes when we aren't treated the way we *expect* to be treated. The above theory assumes, of course, that we are willing to perform the behaviors of love despite how we might be treated in return.

Another strategy to try when you don't feel like loving is to adopt the attitude that "this is my person to love." It is the "possessive" inherent in the marital relationship. Claim your spouse as your person to love. Look upon loving your spouse as *your* responsibility, *your* privilege, *your* goal. Think about it: your spouse is *exclusively* yours to love. This is a powerful charge. Regardless of how little you feel like loving or how little you believe your spouse deserves to be loved, love unconditionally. "This is my person to love. I want to love this person the best way I can. It all depends on me."

I prefer this method in my own marriage, but sometimes performing the behaviors of love seems impossible because I am so angry at Bruce. When this happens, I try the first strategy and force myself to think of Bruce (whom I love dearly all the time, but perhaps do not *like* so well at that particular moment) as my good friend—which he certainly is!

The Element of Commitment

For most of us, plain old love probably isn't going to keep us together for the long haul. Recent studies show that, although feelings of love can and do grow over time, love alone isn't what enables two people to stay married. Commitment is. Couples who are committed to their marriage most often resolve their differences, and love continues to flourish. Those who *aren't* committed let their impulses and desires justify moving on "to find happiness again." This happens one million plus times each year.

Staying married is a choice partners make. Most of us made a commitment to stay married until death parts us. We signed to this vow by placing our signatures on a marriage decree. Many of us forget this. Our marriage vows include loving each other unconditionally—in sickness or in health, for richer or for poorer, for better or for worse—regardless of conflicts, irritations, and transgressions. We kill the notion of commitment because we expect our partner to be perfect and our marriage to be problem free. When we discover our spouse is not perfect or when conflict strikes, we're unwilling to yield or to continue practicing the behaviors of love. We make the decision to stop loving, to stop trying.

Commitment means we'll stick with it. It means, "You can count on me; I can count on you." To me, that promise is worth having in my life. All it might entail—that I forgive my husband when I think he's done me wrong; that I keep performing the behaviors of love when I don't feel like loving; and that I stay committed when I'm tempted to throw in the towel—is worth it to me, because I want someone to count on, and I want someone to count on me.

The decisions to forgive, to love, and to stay married require a great deal of risk. We risk giving of ourselves. We risk hurt, rejection, and failure. I believe that couples, though, need the special gravity that each decision creates. We must cling to our marriage commitment. It's what holds us together when we're spinning through our busy days and tugged into the separate orbits and responsibilities of parenthood.

18

⌒

Seeking Professional Help

The material in this book may not be adequate to deal with some of the deep-seated issues new parents face today. Some couples need the help of a qualified professional. The typical couple in need waits two to five years after the birth of a baby to go to a marriage therapist. By this time their baby is growing and most parents have gotten a handle on the practical management of having a third party in the house. It may be later still, after a second or subsequent birth, that a couple finally seeks solutions to conflicts that were patterned after a first birth or escalated after another. The average couple waits six years before visiting a marriage therapist—six long years of grueling, fruitless fighting or growing estrangement.

Some experts believe that if partners reach the therapist's couch with little love left between them and few positive feelings, there's limited chance for marital survival. Others disagree. "Unless a marriage is 'utterly' destroyed before seeking therapy," writes psychologist John Gottman, "most couples can be helped." I am convinced—and I have seen evidence of this—that when at least *one* spouse endlessly seeks peace and is committed to the marriage, there is at least a fighting chance for survival. What we hope is that partners aren't so totally frustrated in their marriage that they've turned to a third party for love or support. This complicates the situation as well as the process of healing.

Couples who truly want help getting their marriage back on track cooperate honestly and forthrightly in their quest to restore harmony at home and will probably be successful achieving that goal. You'd think that just showing up for couples therapy is a good sign. In most cases it signals that partners, while maybe not ready to *work* on their marriage, are at least willing to examine it. Ideally, showing up indicates that the partners are committed to their marriage and want to make it work, but in real life this isn't always the case. Some men and women are so desperately far apart that by the time they reach a professional's office, one or the other (or both) have already made the decision to split. They arrive seeking permission to end their marriage. They want to hear that it's okay to move out, that they need time to be alone or to sort out their problems, and that yes, the children will be better off if they're apart. These permission seekers probably won't be successful mending their union. They don't want to. They've already cast off the needs of their family and started to concentrate on what's best for them individually.

Sometimes there is someone else involved, and agreeing to therapy is seen as a way to pacify a spouse or a method of getting rid of guilt. "See, I'm here. I tried. I'm not such a creep after all." It's a ruse for appearance sake. In essence, they hope to deposit their spouse at the therapist's office to relieve themselves of the responsibility of picking up the pieces should their spouse totally fall apart. It's then the *therapist's* job to pick up the pieces, *not theirs*. They've made, they believe, the magnanimous gesture of seeing that their spouse gets the help he or she needs.

Not all couples get help when it is needed. Many are not willing to open up to a third party. Some can't withstand the scrutiny. Success rates, however, are high: couples are helped, many marriages are saved. Nevertheless, current statistics are incomplete. Do we measure effectiveness over a year's time, or over five or ten years, or even a lifetime? Isn't "marital happiness" redefined at different stages of the family life cycle? It is tough to measure "happily ever after." However, the general consensus is that all marriages can be improved with the help of a professional.

If your spouse balks at seeking professional help, speak honestly. "Let's give our marriage its best chance. I think our marriage is in trouble. Let's not ignore the reasons. We'd be wrong to do that. Let's go see a counselor who can help us. I want to save our marriage and our family. Will you work with me on this?" It could be that you'll need to give up the counselor you've selected and let your spouse pick one. Make this sacrifice. If you aren't satisfied with the methods or progress made with one professional, try another. Be willing to give it your all to save your marriage and preserve your family. This may mark a turning point within a marriage. Committed couples seek help and attempt improvements. Uncommitted couples think "divorce," the topic covered in Section V.

Sometimes divorced parents experience similar problems in a subsequent marriage and for the first time seek professional help. What they discover in the process is that they might have avoided their first divorce if they'd made the effort to work on that earlier marriage.

How Counseling Helps Couples Get Back on Track

Struggling through one of the toughest times in their fifteen-year marriage and threatened by the vulnerabilities from a recent childbirth, James and Liz gave counseling a try.

"I think it is fair to say that counseling saved our marriage," offered James thoughtfully. "We were locked in a major power struggle. Our marriage was painfully off balance. Our counselor helped us unclog the bottlenecks. We learned to calmly discuss our missteps and find solutions that worked. Once we *began* talking, we wanted to continue. We became excited about the prospects for growth in our relationship. We'd never explored the idea of 'growth' before, which means, we learned, 'positive change.' We became driven by the sense that both of us wanted to make our marriage better—that our marriage was this 'thing' we could mold—and that help was available to help us."

A Counselor Provides a Buffer

Therapy provides a safe environment for discussing sensitive issues and for exchanging information. "It helped us clear the air," said James. "We were able to say things in the presence of a third party that we weren't able to discuss without conflict on our own. We cooperated in the exchange of information. For the first time, we really listened to each other. No one was pronounced guilty, no one proved innocent. Through couples therapy we learned to move past the anger and anxiety that were keeping us apart. We also learned to discuss our conflicts and to handle disagreements in ways that wouldn't destroy each other's self-esteem or our marriage."

A Counselor Helps Couples Reach the Truth Faster

It's easy to get stuck in a rut, rehashing the same issues time and again. We may be capable of telling our spouse exactly what *we believe* the problems in our marriage are, yet we are unsuccessful at resolving them. A professional helps couples dig to the root of discord. "Liz and I were always arguing about sex," explained James. "This was ridiculous—we had a *great* sex life! Our therapist helped us sort through what we were *really* fighting about, which was our inability to tell each other what we needed *as new parents.* Liz felt overwhelmed by motherhood. Not only had I failed to help her with the baby and the housework, she said, but I hadn't paid attention when she explicitly sought my emotional support. Liz became withdrawn and re-sentful. She seldom wanted to make love. I thought she was holding out on me and I didn't know why. Liz later explained that she didn't feel con-nected enough at that point of our marriage to *want* to make love. I'd let her down. Had I realized this? Of course not. I just knew my own frustration: Liz didn't want to make love! Once we narrowed the scope to what we were *really* fighting about, we were able to see our own role in creating or diffus-ing the conflict. We were then able to figure out what to do to make our marriage better. Liz and I resumed lovemaking and I gave her the help and support she needed.

"Our therapist helped us identify our character weaknesses, too, and how they might have played a part in our conflict. I'm a pretty proud guy and sex is important to me. 'Why wouldn't Liz want to make love to *me?*' I thought. Once we understood that *each* of us had a stake in the problem, we recognized how our spouse's complaints might be valid. To move ahead, we had to be willing to see through our spouse's eyes and also appreciate the insights of our therapist."

A Counselor Uncovers the Positive Aspects

"With all our fighting," Alan said, "I'd lost sight of the reasons I'd been at-tracted to my wife in the first place. I was certainly looking past her good qualities and seeing only her bad ones. Our counselor helped me find happy memories of Jan and realize that she was still 'my Jan.' We were *both* struggling through the transition to parenthood, and for the first time in our relationship, we needed someone else to help us along."

Two people are drawn together for specific reasons. When couples are at odds, these reasons can be buried deep inside. With effort, they can be brought to the surface again. "Our therapist helped Jan and me rediscover the respect and attraction we once felt for each other," Alan commented.

Parents of three children under the age of seven, Alan and Jan had been in and out of counseling for nearly as long as they'd been parents. They were preparing to break in their fourth counselor when we met. "Actually," Jan laughed, "we've been in counseling for *ten* years, not seven. We've always believed in the merits of a good therapist, so we met with one before we were even married. I am really optimistic about this new one," she offered enthusiastically. "She'll probably think, 'I can't believe this couple is still together, they've been in counseling for so long.' But I never think about divorcing Alan, and I know he doesn't think about divorcing me, either. *We are committed.* We both have our faults and we may fight—his words sting sometimes, they really do—but we are committed to our marriage. I want to be married to Alan, and he wants to be married to me. I hear him say that each time we see a counselor. Hearing it keeps me loving my husband and increases my desire to resolve our differences."

A Counselor Provides Tools to Work Out Conflicts

Overall, couples who meet with a therapist find that future conflicts are often prevented or delayed, and that when and if conflicts occur, the couples are more optimistic about solving them.

"We learned to compromise and negotiate solutions—ways that weren't 'his way' or 'her way' but 'our way,'" noted James. "Basically, we learned to talk again, which really means, *we learned to listen!*

"Our therapist got us to discuss expectations. Realistically, we knew we were probably going to have some conflicts—most marriages do at some point. Our stumbling block was that we expected each other to be perfect and to have a perfect marriage. We became very unforgiving when we didn't meet each other's expectations. We'd never acknowledged that before. *We were human!* Somehow recognizing our humanness and the frailties that come with it enabled us to be more forgiving of the little—and the big—things that were keeping us apart."

How to Select a Counselor

The best way to find a good marriage counselor is to ask a friend or colleague for a recommendation. "People you know and trust can give you a pretty good idea about a therapist's value system and where that therapist is coming from," offered Dr. Andrea Larsen, a psychologist in family therapy for more than twenty-five years and also my friend and neighbor. "For instance, I am known to exhaust every avenue possible to save marriages, especially when children are involved. So if you were a parent who wanted *out* of your marriage and had pretty much made that decision before meeting with me, you wouldn't want me for your therapist."

Therapists should create an atmosphere that motivates each partner to discuss problems honestly and to cooperate in finding solutions. No two therapists work in the same way. Some may plod along and may not seem to be working fast enough. Others may forge ahead quickly, hastily turning over every stone. They may make you feel you've already done all you could to save your marriage and if you're no closer to making amends, well, maybe there's no hope.

Just as therapists work at different speeds, partners process their emotions at different paces. It may take longer for one of you to feel you've made progress. One partner might feel like giving up. "What's the rush?" James figured. "I saw divorce as our last alternative. We could *always* do that."

Interview several professionals. Counselors are governed by their own set of values and beliefs. You have goals for therapy. What are *their* goals for your therapy? What methods do they employ to reach those goals? How have they helped others? How comfortable are you and your spouse with that professional?

Health care plans often dictate where we can secure professional services. Check with your employer. Is an in-house therapist available at your work? Are those services provided free of charge or for a small fee? Find out, too, if discounts are passed along if you see a therapist who is employer recommended.

Other Sources of Help

A wide range of resources are available to help you mend or enrich your marriage. Take advantage of these. Classes are offered through churches, synagogues, schools, community education centers, and health care facilities. Even corporate America is getting into the business of marriage preservation.

Marriage encounters and marriage enrichment programs originated in the late 1960s and are proliferating today at a rapid rate. More than 80 percent of the couples who attend report positive experiences, believe that the techniques they learned help them to communicate better, and believe that their marriages are improved. Look in your yellow pages for these resources or ask at a local church or synagogue.

Moreover, innumerable self-help books offer useful ideas to help us improve our marriage. See what is available at your local library or bookstore.

V

~

Divorce

∾

Thoughts of divorce prove to be more prevalent after the birth of a baby and when there are preschoolers at home than at any other stage of the family life cycle. Therefore, it would be remiss not to dedicate a section of this book to the fragile and sometimes provocative choice made by many new parents today: marital dissolution. This section discusses the reasons for and ramifications of divorce, and outlines the consequences of divorce on both children and their parents.

19

∽

When Parents Throw in the Towel

Divorce involving the parents of young children is a sober topic many of us prefer not to think about, but that, I believe, would be shortsighted. Too many couples hold the option in reserve until it stands center stage. Waves of conflict start to appear more permanent than temporary. For lack of a better alternative, many couples—without the diehard commitment to stay together—simply declare, "I quit."

While Census Bureau statistics indicate that couples with children are less likely to divorce, each year an estimated 1.2 million children experience marriage dissolution and the devastating consequences of a broken home. Over half of the children born to two parents today can expect to live in a single-parent home by the time they turn eighteen. Most couples, however, throw in the towel long before that. Forty-two percent of divorces involving parents take place before their first child leaves kindergarten, and roughly 15 percent of these parents end their marriage before their children reach even eighteen months of age.

One out of two children can expect to spend an average of five years with either the mother or father absent from their home due to separation or divorce. Many boys and girls have no recollection whatsoever of having lived with both their mother and father. Their memory capacity was simply too underdeveloped at the time of their parents' divorce for them to recall.

The phenomenon of divorce is so widespread that it haunts even children in seemingly healthy families. My husband Bruce taught a Sunday school class comprised of first and second graders, children who were six, seven, or eight years of age. One Sunday, Bruce asked the children to draw pictures or write down what they feared most in life. Expecting to see pages adorned with hideous monsters, ghosts, snakes, or other scary creatures, he was dismayed when more than a third of the class described their greatest fear as that of having their parents divorce. This was quite alarming to my husband and me, for we knew most of these families to be intact. The children's fears reflected an early awareness of divorce. While they maybe failed to comprehend the true impact of their parents' dissolution, they recognized that it would not be good for them, nor for their families.

The Effect on Children

For some parents, the decision to divorce may already have been made, but for their children *it is an issue that may never be resolved.* Marianne Espinosa Murphy, a district court judge, seldom experiences the courtroom drama we've come to savor on network television. She witnesses another kind of drama, much too commonplace, that for many reeks with reality and strikes much too close to home. You see, Judge Murphy is assigned to family court. She maneuvers through tedious divorce proceedings, wrestles with custody issues, and divvies out hard-earned, sought-after assets. Each case chips away a bit more at what has grown to be her tough, yet tender heart, and each piece that falls adds to her heightened conviction to maintain her decades-long marriage "against all odds."

"There's too much at stake," she told me. "I distinctly recall the moment I decided I never wanted to divorce my husband. It was not during a romantic evening warmed by the glow of candlelight. My husband was not even present. I was, instead, a district court judge, assigned to family court, trying to settle a visitation dispute between two divorcing parents."

Each proposed schedule proved unsatisfactory to one or the other parent. Her eyes searched those of the mother, then the father. She knew what was happening. The child had become part of the battleground, part of the same tug-of-war the parents had played long before they stood before her. When she considered the heart of the child, another piece of her own heart broke and she knew, "I could not bear to do this to my children. Children's calendars doom them to living out of duffel bags, always on the move, and on a rigid schedule," she explained sadly.

Children confirm her fears. Many are tired of shuttling back and forth between parents. They are physically and emotionally exhausted children who are caught in the aftermath of their parents' divorce. With little sense that their lives are their own, they go from being individuals to pieces of property with numbered days that belong to a mother or father who "loves them too much not to be a part of their lives," but not enough to preserve the marriage for their sake.

Judge Murphy is not alone in her ability to describe the price children pay when parents decide to throw in the towel. The consequences of divorce on children are well documented. A variety of researchers report that divorce is a stressful "life event" whose ramifications are felt throughout a child's entire lifetime. Poor self-esteem, depression, aggression, sleep disorders, and anti-social behaviors are prevalent among many children of divorced parents. School performance is altered. Children miss school more often, earn lower daily grades and test scores, receive lower approval ratings from peers and teachers, and express less hope of ever going to college.

For many of these children, their parents' divorce is a precursor to still more broken relationships. Temporary relationships are punctuated by starts and stops, hopes and disappointments fostered when mothers and fathers parade suitors in and out of their children's lives, only to have the child's heart open to love again, then shut even tighter when yet another relationship ends. A third of divorced mothers are likely to remarry and an even greater number of divorced fathers tie the knot again. The risk of marital dissolution for these couples is greater than it was for their first union, and divorce, if it does occur, tends to occur more quickly. Thirty-seven percent of remarriages collapse within ten years, and repeat divorces usually magnify the painful consequences of the first. A conservative estimate is that more than 15 percent of all children from divorced families will see the parent they live with remarry and redivorce before turning eighteen. This estimate does not include the many children who live with parents who have elected the alternative of living together rather than marrying.

While the economic picture may brighten for children whose parents remarry, psychologically their world becomes darker than if they were to continue living in a single-parent family. Family life for these kids becomes more complex, uncertain, and potentially conflict-ridden, especially in households attempting to blend children from different families. Most studies show that children in stepfamilies do *not* do better than children in single-parent households, and many researchers indicate that, on average, children in remarriages simply do worse.

Clearly, boys are affected more profoundly than girls are when their parents' marriage breaks up. It could be that they are exposed to more conflict between their parents before and during divorce proceedings or that they receive less coddling and support from their parents and others because, as boys, they are expected to buck up and get on with life. Boys in general might be psychologically more vulnerable and to a wider range of stresses than girls. The estimated negative effects of divorce on social adjustment prove to be stronger for boys than for girls. These include the impact on popularity, loneliness, and cooperativeness. Boys become more aggressive and competitive after their parents divorce, which often results in increased problems at school and with their peers.

The Age of a Child Makes a Difference

A quote from the Carnegie Task Force document *Starting Points* sums it up. "Divorce at any age is devastating to a child, but especially so if it occurs during the very important first years of a child's life, when hopefully and ideally, the child is reared by a few caring, responsive, and dependable adults. This type of environment leads to the development of strong attachments and provides a secure base from which a child can explore its world. Children denied this type of environment are at risk of behavioral, intellectual, and emotional problems."

Preschoolers lack the ability to understand the meaning of divorce and often react with confusion and fear when suddenly one parent disappears. If one parent is gone, what's to stop the other from disappearing, too? Even at a very young age, when their world pretty much revolves around their own wants and needs, preschoolers tend to blame themselves for their parents' divorce. "Daddy left because I was bad." This is a common theme. Preschoolers, too, often regress to earlier behaviors thought to have been previously licked, such as bed-wetting, whining, or thumb sucking.

Children a bit older, of primary school ages, clearly grasp the meaning of divorce. They know it is not good. These children have the ability to grieve for the loss of their family and often feel deep sadness. Depression is not uncommon. Some children see their parents' divorce as a personal rejection. How could Mom or Dad divorce *despite* my feelings and the consequences to *me?* They are not so self-centered to blame themselves for their parents' divorce. They are more likely to place the blame elsewhere, usually on one parent or on both. Consequently, children of this age group may feel a great deal of anger toward one or both parents—and for a very long period of time.

Adolescents struggle less after their parents' divorce than younger children. Generally, teenagers are thought to be most vulnerable; however, they are less dependent on their family at this stage of their lives and more apt to rely on and receive a great deal of support from their friends. This helps them cope. Most are able to find a soul mate among their peers who has experienced parental divorce, and since divorce is so commonplace, junior high schools and high schools often have divorce support groups for students. Becoming unmotivated in studies (and certainly earning lower test scores) is prevalent among teenagers whose parents divorce, as are dropping out of school, having a baby before the age of twenty (often out of wedlock), and marrying. On the whole, a parental divorce often causes teenagers to question whether they have what it takes—or will ever have what it takes—to maintain a long-lasting relationship.

Research by Wallerstein and Kelly suggests that children at every age are affected by their parents' divorce, although the nature of their reactions differ. The bottom line is that broken homes often make broken children and cause them irreparable damage for the rest of their lives.

Don't Kids Get Over It?

I think we underestimate the emotional toll of divorce on our children. We want to believe that, "Hey, within two years most kids are up and at it again." However, current studies show that it takes not just two years for kids to bounce back but, in many instances, a lifetime. In a study of children after divorce, Wallerstein noted that almost eighteen months after a breakup, all of the children she studied thought their parents' divorce was the central event in their life. Even after three years, more than 85 percent of the children still wished for their parents' reconciliation.

The death of a parent is easier for children to accept and get over than is divorce. Death is unavoidable. Accidents do happen, and illness and disease are within the understanding of most young people. Divorce, however, includes a factor that casts a pall over a child's life: parents actually make the choice to divorce. They weigh the pros and cons and make a decision to end their marriage—despite the wails of protest from their offspring. It is hard for children to justify that Mom or Dad decided to leave or that "they thought we'd be better off if they were apart." When all types of stress were studied, the only thing that seemed likely to rattle a child's world more than parental divorce was sexual abuse.

Recent studies tracking adults who were children when their parents divorced find that more than half experience psychological problems which they attribute to their parents' breakup. Forty-one percent are in counseling or therapy, and the majority are crippled in poor relationships with a spouse, father, mother, stepparents, or siblings. Adults who were children when their parents divorced report continued disruption in their interpersonal and intimate relationships. Many remain apprehensive about marriage, fear intimacy, and worry about abandonment and betrayal. Over half of the adults studied failed to attain an equivalent education to their parents, and nearly half fell below their parents' socioeconomic level. These adults were more often underemployed or unemployed and for longer periods of time than children who grew up in stable family environments.

Too often divorce in one generation is introduced to future generations as a viable option to solving relationship problems. A twelve-year study at the University of Nebraska revealed that children of divorce often have poorer quality marriages themselves. Sociology professor Paul Amato found that children of divorce tend to get angry more easily, have problems communicating, and experience jealousy more often, consequently making them behave in ways that just plain make marriage harder. This could possibly result from growing up without good role models who taught them how to behave in a marriage, or from the emotional fallout that occurred years before when their own parents divorced. The children of divorce in Amato's study proved to be harder to get along with and had a 25 percent greater risk of divorcing themselves.

While results vary from study to study about how parental divorce affects children, the best summation comes from Amato and Keith. They pooled results from ninety-two studies that involved 13,000 children, ranging from preschool to college age. After forming their analysis of how kids at these ages were affected, they carried out a second study to see if the differences between children of divorce and children in intact families continued into adulthood. During their second round, they combined results of thirty-seven studies involving 80,000 adults. Their results show that parental divorce has a detrimental impact on children their entire lives.

What Children Say About Divorce

My interviews with divorcing mothers and fathers were not pretty, but those I had with their children were downright ugly. Zach was unable to put into words the desolation he felt when he learned that his parents were divorcing, yet it showed most profoundly in his sad, empty eyes. He hadn't witnessed the verbal lashings exchanged by his parents in private, so when one Sunday afternoon he overheard them quarreling in the darkened garage attached to his house, he was confused—and even more so when he saw his father's right fist jerk back and then strike his mother's face. She hunched over attempting to shield her head from another blow, sobbing, shouting wildly for her husband to stop before the children heard.

Only one such display was needed to cause the cowering eight year old to surmise that his parents would follow the same path as that of countless classmates' parents who had decided to end their union. Zach never told his parents what he had heard or seen that day. Rather, he joined the innumerable children who watch and wait and wonder—usually in silence—as their parents deplete the final reserves of their patience, love, and marital commitment.

Zach's father ended the wait. He came to Zach to explain that he and Zach's mother were divorcing. "For the sake of you kids," his father said levelly, "it is time to end our marriage."

"For *our* sake?" his son cried out. "It's the most *selfish* thing you've ever done!"

◌◌

Selfish, cruel, stupid—these are but a few of the words children use to describe their parents' decision to divorce. Children shared with me the pain, turmoil, loneliness, fear, guilt, resentment, anger, uncertainty, and blame that came in the wake of their parents' decision. Yet these kids were amazingly strong. Few ventured to tell their parents how they really felt. They fettered their emotions to shield their parents from realizing just how shaky their little lives were, hoping that their parents might change their minds. These children didn't want to do *anything* to jeopardize the possibility, however remote, that their parents just *might* make their marriage work again.

I've seen children starved for attention and affection, a gentle touch, or even a few kind words. Some said their parents were simply too tired, too busy, or too "self-centered" to give them a hug or cuddle with them—the reassurance they needed at that time. Others said their parents were too overwhelmed with work, household chores, and the confusion they faced over personal, marital, and financial problems. Some parents spent endless hours watching television, surfing the net, or pumping iron. Too many men and women fail to recognize how much their children need their hugs and kisses, how they hunger for that strong and comforting arm or gentle stroking of their cheeks or hair. For many kids, one of their parents is missing and the other is not there physically or emotionally, either. These children are left with a craving that increases over the years—or a haunting anger that penetrates deeply into every facet of their lives, to show up later in an equally tormented adulthood.

Who Gets the Kids?

Custody battles plague most divorcing parents and implicate wins and losses. The greatest loss—immeasurable—is the loss of the children. Shared custody or not, one parent tends to have less contact than the other with the children, and generally it is the father. In nine out of ten divorce cases, children stay with the mother, uncontested. The perception has been that fathers don't care who gets the kids. This is far from true. Most fathers care deeply. Trends are changing, and an increasing number of divorced fathers seek custody. Those who do can be optimistic: 70 percent of fathers who sue for custody are successful.

Divvying up the furniture, cars, and stock portfolio is easy for most couples compared to deciding which parent gets the kids. The value of the latter cannot be quantified. It is personal and inestimable. For many couples the decision about *who* gets the kids, how *often* they get the kids, *when* they get the kids, and for how *long* becomes a time-consuming, all-consuming, bitter battle.

In half of divorces involving parents, men and women reach a custody agreement without help. Another third is settled without court intervention or its related services even when custody is contested, and other settlements require state-mandated mediation sessions, formal custody evaluations, court trials, or a judge's decision.

Custody is awarded on a case by case determination. Arrangements are usually made keeping in mind what's best for the children. Their physical and emotional well-being takes precedence over monetary concerns or the pride of the parents. Most divorced parents want to continue to see their children. However, many judges, mediators, lawyers, and even parents themselves acknowledge that when parents exercise their right to divorce, they may be giving up some of their rights to parenting.

Making a decision about what's best for the children and carrying it out can be tough. No custody arrangement is perfect or without challenges, and despite the best of intentions, parents often underestimate the emotional toll and logistical nightmares of living apart and parenting together.

The parent who bears the main responsibility for taking care of the children is called the *custodial parent*. In the majority of cases, this is the mother, although most men are perfectly capable of handling parenting tasks. There is little evidence that children are better off with the same-sex parent; however, children tend to do better with their mothers, on the whole.

Physical custody means the children live with you. *Legal custody* involves making decisions that affect their well-being. Physical custody and legal custody can be *joint,* which means the father and mother both play a role; or *sole,* which means the children live with one parent who makes decisions for their well-being. Joint legal custody with the mother having sole physical custody is probably the most common arrangement, followed by sole legal and sole physical custody being awarded to the mother. There is, however, an increase in the award of joint physical custody, by which both parents share legal rights and responsibility.

Children need to spend good chunks of time with both parents. Joint physical custody is intended to ensure this. Mothers and fathers tend to see their children more often under this arrangement; however, it is considered fairly stressful for the children, who divide their time and treasures between two households. Many are confused as they head to Dad's one day, Mom's the next. "Where's my red sweatshirt? My tennis racket? My diary? Call me at Mom's number. Call me at Dad's." It's not only confusing and stressful for the children, but for parents as well. Some men and women complain that they spend too much time shuffling back and forth in the car. Joint custody also means you have to try like the dickens to get along with your ex-spouse, without lambasting him or her in front of the children. Joint physical custody works best when parents cooperate in raising their children. However, if two people didn't see eye to eye *before* their divorce when raising their children together, how easily will they see eye to eye afterwards?

Joint physical custody is especially difficult in divorces that are considered *high conflict*—those in which hostile behaviors and attitudes, physical aggression, and heated disputes are frequent. Hostile parents often attempt to undermine the authority of their ex-spouse, sabotage the other's role as a parent, squelch communication with the child, or block visitation altogether. About one-fourth of couples continue to have high conflict even three to four years after they end their marriage. Most eventually become civil to each other and learn to parent together. However, about 10 to 15 percent of divorced parents continue to do battle, disagreeing about absolutely everything all the days of their lives.

One of the biggest issues between parents after they divorce is their abiding distrust that the other parent "parents" decently. One study showed that 93 percent of disputes regarding custody and visitation mediated during a two-week period were tied to the other parent's parenting habits. Complaints weren't limited to disagreements about whether a child was permitted to play with a wayward friend, use the family car, or see an age-appropriate movie. Three out of four cases referenced child neglect, physical, mental, or sexual abuse, child stealing, or exposure to the other parent's substance abuse or criminal activities.

Moreover, however willingly a parent assumes custody, it's not uncommon for depression to come with the responsibility. A lower emotional state often hinders that parent's ability to care for the children. Many become less affectionate with their children, make fewer demands of them at a time when they need boundaries and restraints, supervise them less but punish them more harshly, and become wishy-washy with discipline or neglect it all together.

Noncustodial Fathers

Most children of a divorced couple live with their mother, and only a little more than half of all divorced fathers are awarded *visitation privileges.* Visitation allows the noncustodial parent a "date" with the kids. These visits can be a stressful, scheduled interface rather than a natural, satisfying experience. Children and their noncustodial parent often feel cut off from each other, missing the day-to-day contact that builds a lasting connection, the kind that also makes a marriage. Included in this contact are the little things, the daily behaviors of love that build strong parent-child relationships, too.

Many parents who divorce try to maintain or repair their relationship with their children. However, studies by Furstenburg and associates show that the relationship between children and their noncustodial parent is often less vital than when the family all lived together. Only a handful of children said they'd seek advice from their noncustodial father on personal or family issues, and another study revealed that only half of children interviewed listed their noncustodial father on their list of family members.

While the amount of time that noncustodial fathers spend with their children is increasing, statistics paint a bleak picture, justifying the term "fatherless America." Only a third of children saw their father at least once a month during the prior year. Fifteen percent saw their father less than monthly, 16 percent had "some contact" in the last one to five years, and 36 percent had not seen their father *at all* in the past five years or knew where he might be living. About one-fourth of noncustodial fathers visit their children weekly. They tackle the challenges and obstacles of fatherhood, doing "the best they can," they said, under the circumstances.

It's more than grumpy ex-wives who keep fathers at bay. Some fathers drop out because they get tired of feeling the frustration and uneasiness that accompany the unnatural arena of visitation. They get tired of the emotional roller-coaster ride and the continuous reminders of their broken family, their terminated or turbulent relationship with their ex-wife, and the questionable and unpredictable relationship they have with their children. Also, geographic barriers—real or perceived—and stepparents, stepsiblings, financial concerns, and the passage of time keep noncustodial dads from being the dads kids want and need.

Child Support

The responsibility to provide practical and emotional support, protection, guidance, and supervision rests with both parents, even when the children live with only one. Money to provide these often comes in the form of *child support*. Unfortunately, child support is not available in all cases. According to the U.S. Bureau of Census, somewhere between 28 and 42 percent of divorced mothers are not awarded child support payments, and of those who are, 62 percent wait for payment and one in four never see a payment at all. Payment patterns tend to be irregular. Furthermore, the amount of the payment may be simply too small to cover the real cost of raising a child. Family income after divorce drops at least 20 percent, and more for women. In 1991, nearly 40 percent of divorced women with children lived in poverty, and 55 percent of those women with children under six years of age were considered poor.

Custodial or noncustodial child support is negotiated by lawyers on a case by case basis. Studies reveal that noncustodial fathers, on average, could afford to pay *three to four times more* than what they're required to pay, and at least two-thirds more than they *do* pay. Financial hardship results for many divorced women and their children. Their standard of living plummets. A child's academic achievement may suffer when the custodial parent is unable to buy books, educational toys, home computers, or other resources that help a child succeed scholastically. (Children from divorced families scored lower than children from intact families on 27 of 34 outcomes.)

Children might also be affected negatively when the parent they live with is unable to meet other financial obligations. Families may have to move to more affordable housing. Children may have to change schools, drop out of extracurricular activities, or eat less nutritiously. For some children, stress accumulates. Their childhood becomes a stress-filled period rather than an era of carefree growth and play.

20

∾

Staying Together for the Children

I was visiting with a minister regarding this chapter when he jumped in and asked if I knew how to spell the word divorce. "It's not spelled how it sounds," he was quick to add, and without waiting for my answer he explained, "It is spelled I-Q-U-I-T." A lump formed in my throat. I hadn't expected an answer so succinct. "Couples," he said flatly, "just give up—they quit."

For many couples, the decision to divorce is not that simple. There are, after all, the children to consider. I do believe that couples from every economic and social stratum enter marriage intending to stay together. I believe they enter parenthood with the same conviction that they will do a good job as parents together. Eventually, though, a series of challenges causes divisiveness and leads to the conclusion that there is no other choice. "We can no longer stay together," they say, and they dissolve their union. The needs of the children become secondary.

Many mothers and fathers justify their decision to divorce with conviction: "The kids will adapt. They're so young, they won't know. Our relationships will be better. There'll be ample financial support. The kids will be better off!" But experts believe differently. Sociologists who once only suggested it now openly declare that staying together for the sake of the children isn't such a bad idea. If there is violence or abuse in a marriage, according to Professor Paul Amato, then children are better off when their parents divorce. "But if parents can get along without a lot of conflict and provide stability for their children and remain even somewhat happy with themselves and each other," he states, "I think it is in the best interests of the children for these parents to stay married."

Some couples are better off apart, and in some cases divorce may be the better of two evils when it comes to the children's well-being. Accounts of spousal and substance abuse, infidelity, financial disarray, conflicts in authority, and just plain incompatibility send plenty of couples to divorce court. Thirty years ago these were considered the obvious or understandable reasons for divorce.

More recent records, however, reflect some dubious rationales behind the dissolution of couples. Sociologists Spanier and Thompson state that today's couples divorce because of differences over the division of labor. They don't work through sexual dysfunction. They choose not to communicate. They don't spend adequate time sharing meaningful activities that nurture the love and intimacy necessary for maintaining a successful marriage. Many new parents are just too busy. Many just don't care enough. Once marriages are molded around the lives of children, though, I believe we need to take a hard look at what's at stake before reneging on our marriage vows.

Changing Attitudes

We are seeing a more concerted effort on many fronts to help curtail the number of divorces when children are expected to suffer from its outcome. One young mother described to me her visit to an attorney when she was considering divorce.

"His thick, white hair hung loosely about his head, and the kindness in his eyes gave him a gentle, grandfatherly look," Dawn began. "The photos displayed around his office supported years of experience. It was time to divorce, and I had confidence that this man, so highly recommended, would ease the burden of ending my troubled marriage. Instead, after hearing my plea, he busily shuffled the papers on his desk, visibly disgruntled. Then he looked up and without meeting my eyes barked, 'You ought to be ashamed of yourself. You have three young children at home who need both a mother *and* a father! Your reasons do not justify this divorce. This isn't what you want to hear, but you go home and make your marriage work.'

"He then rose abruptly, dismissing me. I left his office humiliated, drove home tearfully weighing his words. I was ashamed. I looked at my husband differently that night and reconsidered the needs of our children. Within a week we started therapy with the conviction to stay together.

"My attorney had not made it easy for me to divorce. I credit that gentleman for saving my marriage and my family from the emotional wrenching of a broken home."

I later learned that her attorney's anger was not directed at Dawn alone, but at a whole generation that he believes treats marriage vows too lightly and justifies the dissolution of a family on the belief that divorce will be the answer to all their problems. Perhaps this man represents a new and necessary breed of family law attorney who encourages reconciliation and mediation.

One thing that can reduce the high rate of divorce among parents of young children is fostering the belief "it's gonna hurt my kids. Too many people (including *me*) are going to get hurt in the process, and it's better if I *just don't do it*." Another way to curb high divorce rates is to make marriages better. Few couples divorce if they experience marital happiness or marital stability *consistently* in some form. Staying married is a personal choice, a decision one makes—a commitment to "you can count on me, I can count on you" dependability. In a perfect world marriage partners would have this, just as in a perfect world children would be born to mature, loving, and committed adults who are responsible for their actions and careful enough with their marriages that breaking it is not an option.

The real solution to curbing divorce takes place well outside the bounds of regulation and long before the baby carriage. I believe it starts in our homes and in our hearts. Until we change how we feel about divorce *deep down inside*, any legal restrictions or social opinions against it aren't going to make a big difference.

As parents, we must take responsibility for the most serious and fateful decision we make, that of having a child together. Having a child together means raising a child together, being involved on a sustained basis in the care, nurturing, and growth of that individual for a minimum of two decades, if not a lifetime—not an easy task together, and an even harder task alone.

Again, there are legitimate reasons for divorce. Some couples are better off apart, and some children are better off with one or the other parent. But I hate what happens to children when their parents divorce. I think of the boys and girls who night after night go to bed, longing for the arms of a mother or father who isn't there to tuck them in and who probably won't be there on the following night or on all the nights thereafter. Some children fall asleep cold and hungry; many fall asleep without hope. What turmoil is lodged in their minds? What wrenching emotions sear away at their divided hearts?

Perhaps we all need the guiding light of this principle: "Divorce is *not* the only alternative. There is another way—to use the strength and character of both partners to overcome the trials that are inevitable in any marriage." Staying together requires both parents to make sacrifices for the sake of the children. Children are better off with parents who learn there are alternatives to divorce. Just as the seeds of discord are sown after childbirth, so must we plant the seeds of determination for parents to stay together after the baby, for the latest research confirms what we have known for decades: divorce hurts our children today and affects their world tomorrow.

POINTS TO CONSIDER

ഇ Consider how the relationship you have with your spouse will change after divorce. As parents together, your relationship will not end, nor will many of the conflicts you experienced as married partners disappear. How will you succeed in making your home happy and harmonious post-divorce when it was unhappy and acrimonious before?

ഇ Agree to attend classes to help you understand and ease the process of divorce. Consider participating in mediation and other educational opportunities that help reduce the stress inherent in this type of proceeding.

ഇ Assess how your resources will change and what stress will result in the lives of your children. In what ways will their world be rearranged? Will it be necessary to move, change schools, or cut back on expenditures? What might you do to make it easier? Will your spouse live close by?

ഇ Take into account the timing of divorce. What is in the best interest of your children at their particular stage of development? Consider attachment and separation anxiety that children experience when very young. What about the importance of continuing and nurturing relationships between children and grandparents, aunts and uncles, and extended family? Be honest: *all* relationships will change.

⸱ Assess the impact the divorce will have on your child's academic achievement. What special needs must you consider as a single parent? You might not have the financial resources to purchase books, videos, or educational toys and games that supplement a child's education.

⸱ Reexamine whether your marriage is really dead. What could you do to resurrect it that you haven't yet tried? Have you exhausted every avenue? Has your spouse? Are you satisfied with counseling efforts? What about a weekend retreat?

⸱ Remind yourself that your children's interests (not yours or your spouse's) are the top priority.

⸱ Reassure your children that they are loved by *both* of their parents and that the marital unrest between you and your spouse is *not* caused by them or anything that they've done or said. Children are extremely sensitive to parental discord and often blame themselves for their parents' conflict.

⸱ Come to grips with your role as a spouse or as a parent. Maybe the unhappiness you're feeling has less to do with conditions in your marriage than with personal dissatisfactions or disappointments. Are unresolved emotional issues from childhood affecting your marriage? If so, discuss them with a professional before making a decision to end your marriage.

⸱ Do not draw your children into marital battles by having them serve as a go-between with your spouse, delivering messages and ultimatums. Resist the temptation, too, to tell them *everything* that is happening. Children should not be parental caretakers. Find a friend or adult family member or mental health professional to serve as your sounding board. Refrain from discussing financial concerns in front of or with your children.

• Seek professional help immediately if drinking, drugs, or abuse enter the picture. Don't wait for your spouse to hit you a second time.

• Try not to uproot your children during the decision-making process. Stability in the home and school is very important. Worrying about their parents' marriage is enough, whatever their ages.

• Consider that you and your spouse will be parents together *forever* and will need to make joint decisions that effect your child's well-being. Find a way to put battles behind you. Attend coparenting classes together.

• Know that the actions leading up to a divorce and during divorce proceedings often do a child great psychological harm. Keep a lid on tempers and express anger or frustration far out of earshot of young ears. Witnessing high conflict between parents deprives children of the joys of childhood, and sometimes memories of their parents' disagreements torment them for years, leaving them angry or emotionally shut off later in life.

- Remember that sharing parenthood with someone you're no longer married to can be difficult, but however hard it is, doing it well is one of the best ways to show your children you love them.

- Tell your children about your divorce or separation *before* they hear it from someone else. Don't move out first or get caught in the process. While honesty is usually the best policy, it is better to forgo all the details. There's really no good way or a good time to shatter your children's world, but crucial to conveying the information is being courageous enough to say, "Our lives are going to change, and spending time with the parent you *aren't* living with may not be easy." Encourage your children to talk about their feelings and, if possible, arrange for them to visit with a counselor.

- Keep in mind that if we want to raise happy and competent children who eventually marry for the right reasons and stay married, we need to set an example for them to follow.

- Remember, most children dream of living in a home where the family consists of a mom, a dad, several kids, and a dog or cat. They want this home to be happy and would do just about anything to ensure that it is.

- Send for a free copy of "Stepping Back from Anger," printed by the American Academy of Matrimonial Lawyers, 150 North Michigan Avenue, Suite 2040, Chicago, Illinois 60601, or call toll free, 1-877-4-THE-KIDS. You can also find information at their website: www.aaml.org.

VI

∾

Bringing It All Together

The majority of parents look back on the early years as some of the happiest of their marriage. This section tells what parents learned about themselves and each other as they worked together, struggled together, and lived together to maintain and improve their union, and how each parent grew both individually and as part of a couple.

21

∽

What Makes It All Worthwhile

At this point some of you might be asking, "If having a baby is so hard on a marriage and produces a state of crisis in the lives of new parents, why do so many men and women choose parenthood—in some instances again and again? What makes it all worthwhile?"

The parents I interviewed who had survived twenty, thirty, forty, even fifty-odd years of marriage responded with similar themes. I posed these questions: Was having children worth the hard work, the ups and downs in your marriage, and the sacrifices you made as parents? *What made it all worthwhile?*

When asked if it was all worthwhile, most couples gave a resounding "yes!" Long after conflict and anger had faded from their homes, parents reflected on the years spent under siege, and many said that the transition to parenthood was a defining period in their relationship and for their marriage. It may have been difficult at first, they admitted, for them to adjust their elegant vision of parenthood to awkward reality. Life as parents held oft-threatening moments when dreams and life coalesced in unwanted and unexpected ways. But for the majority of men and women, parenthood proved to be a painfully fantastic journey they made together, leading them permanently from the comforts of childlessness to the rich experience of family life.

I heard many beautiful reflections from mothers and fathers about the emotions they discovered on their journey. The ups and downs were more than balanced by the joys and love—*inestimable* love—their children had brought into their lives. From most couples I heard that all the positives of being parents far outweighed the negatives. I think that many simply forgot whatever bad might have been mixed in with the good.

One mother tried to explain the powerful emotion of parental love. She said, "The love we feel for our children is so great that we forget the ways they might have hurt us or the rocky roads we often traveled as parents. Love is a powerful force. It helps us erase the bad moments and remember only the good."

In my research for this book, I found that parents were more eager to convey why parenthood was worthwhile than to share their marital trials. Many moms and dads referred to the sacrifices they'd made as "opportunities"—chances to give and learn and grow while shaping the life of another. Raising their children wasn't a sacrifice at all for most parents, but a privilege. Some described the work of taking care of a family as "hard work" and making decisions that affected the well-being of the family as "difficult," yet they acknowledged that, while it wasn't easy, they were thankful they'd had the chance to do so, and yes, they'd do it again.

When asked about the high costs of raising a family—both real and psychological—some parents actually chuckled. "The cost? Why, it's incalculable, just as the love you feel for your children is measureless. And the value of a child? Priceless."

The New You

Some believe that becoming a parent blights whatever human growth and development a man or woman might possibly experience, especially in the relationship they share with each other and those they are involved with outside their family. Others avow that being a parent provides *just* that channel for growth and development that is available *only* because of parenthood. Being a parent enables us to discover a new side of ourselves—the loving, nurturing, and caring side. Few roles outside of being a parent do this, just as few roles engage a person so emotionally.

"The selfless side of me surfaced after our daughter was born," said one mother. "Quite frankly, I doubted that that side of me had ever existed. I'd never learned to care for others before in an unselfish way. Most of my motives had been self-serving, and I don't know that I would have made this change without having children. Becoming a mother, however, stirred in me—as I think it must in all parents—certain emotions that were very stimulating and pleasing that made me feel good about who I was and how I treated others. I suppose you'd call it the nurturing side of me, warmth that developed as I grew with the role of mother and gave to my children and others around me. It really is true, the more you give, the more you receive. I saw this change in my husband, too. He became kinder and gentler—larger, in a way, more generous with actions and in spirit."

Looking back, I see that no friend or family member prepared me for what being a parent would mean to me. Those who'd gone before me into this "unknown" watched silently as the world of parenthood opened up to Bruce and me. Later, as I shared with them each small wonder that had seemed so terribly profound to me, they responded with knowing eyes and affirming nods, explaining tenderly that they knew, but they hadn't wanted to spoil the fun for us. They let us discover for ourselves how fulfilling being parents could be.

In retrospect, perhaps they'd been unable, as I am now, to adequately describe the depth of love or emotions one feels as a parent. Emotions run as raw and new as those of an adolescent. One feels *real* and alive. Perhaps our friends were a little afraid, too, to tell us *how* parenthood might change our lives when they knew full well we might not like *all* the changes it would entail. Yet they could have encouraged us by telling us how enriching parenthood would be when and if we made it through the initial quagmire! Lastly, they failed to convey how precious it is, being a parent, although being a parent leaves you so very vulnerable—to the loss of it all.

Yes, it is hard to capture the essence of parenthood for those who've never been there. It's like expounding all the details of an amazing trip down the Amazon, only to have your audience respond blankly to your wild enthusiasm. You're left simply saying, "You've just got to go do it yourself to understand what I am talking about." So it might be with parenthood. We can attempt to explain why it is worthwhile and what makes it so, but no words do justice. No words truly explain the growth one experiences as an individual (or as part of a couple), the powerful connection that unites all other parents, and the almost mysterious oneness you share with your own flesh and blood. You feel for your children, think for them, live for them, yet you know they must feel, think, and live for themselves. So you let them, though reluctantly at first, and it hurts you because you know they will suffer growing pains, question this or that in their lives—as all of us do. You're not sure they'll find the joys and successes and every good thing you want for them so badly. Parenthood entails many uncertainties, but I guess we were willing to accept the unknown risks along with the equally unknown rewards.

Goals change when you become a parent. What may have been important to you *before* the baby might not be important to you afterward. I can now fathom giving up my life for my children, relinquishing my hopes and dreams for theirs. My own mortality comes into focus, too, as I consider the legacy I hope to bequeath at my passing.

As a parent, you aren't locked within the confines of a tiny world that revolves only around your children and their well-being. The world of a parent grows. You feel connected, in a way unimaginable before parenthood, to the institutions of life—the schools, the churches and synagogues, your neighborhood, and the government—the framework of our nation that perhaps stood backstage before you had children.

As a parent, I learned to need others. Having a baby caused me to invest in other relationships because I needed *more* people *more*. I looked to others for help with the kids and our home. I needed my family and friends for support and encouragement—to talk to, learn from, bounce ideas off, and share my hopes, fears, and joys. Men and women who hadn't spoken to Bruce or me prior to our babies' births came out in droves to welcome them with enthusiasm and well-wishes. We felt a rush of love and support at a time, I suppose, when we needed it the most.

Being a parent creates a powerful bond with other parents. As a mom or dad, you become a member of a club you're eligible to join only if you're a parent. Parents tend to understand each other. They share similar experiences and concerns, and many even share similar calendars.

The community treats you differently when you've had a child. That could be because you treat the community differently. Parents look to the community for safety and security for their children.

Nothing unleashes the essence of adulthood like becoming a parent. Personally, I put away my childish behaviors when I became a mother and, as Frank expounded in Chapter 13, felt instantly transformed by childbirth. The responsibilities, while daunting, made me feel more capable, more like a woman than at any other time in my life. Some believe parenthood provides a seal of femininity or masculinity. It does, indeed, propel an individual out of his or her orbit and into that of another. Each parent starts to be-have in a more sensible, mature fashion. Preparenthood behaviors are reined in by a set of new, unspoken parameters. Some welcome this change. Others fight it. Some men and women resent the severe disciplines and duties parenthood imposes.

My childless and single friends sometimes grumble about that other world which includes only parents and children. Some have been a bit per-turbed when Bruce or I turned down an invitation to an elaborate brunch they might have planned or begged-out of an evening at the opera so that we could spend the night huddled on hard, backless bleachers, cheering our sons on in a little league game or clapping wildly in appreciation, cen-ter front, at one of their music recitals. School functions and daily "kids" activities leave us with little time to grab a sandwich with friends or even gab on the phone. But we stay connected the best we can while deeply en-trenched in our world of parents and children.

For many couples, having a baby is not only what pulls them apart, but what binds them together as well. Bearing and rearing kids is no picnic, but parents who take the task to heart find a bond. Some believe unques-tionably that having children is essential for the deepening and strength-ening of a marriage. I know my marriage is richer because of our sons, and I believe the love Bruce and I share is deeper, too, and has far more facets because of what we have shared parenting together.

Some of the men and women I interviewed said that being parents had not been worth it. These parents looked back on a life of heartache and dis-appointment or marital disruption (*because* of the kids, they believe). They recalled the times their children brought them grief and angst. Perhaps their children hadn't grown up to be quite what they'd imagined or wanted them to be. Perhaps they found an empty nest that was empty of love and happy memories, too.

Some parents I spoke with were so deeply in the throes of the transition to parenthood that they had to fight to consider what could *possibly* make being parents worthwhile. Caught in the aftermath of giving birth and just starting their parenting journey, they'd encountered some potholes along the way that were leading them to suspect they shouldn't have ventured down that road at all. Being a family was what they had always dreamed about, but they weren't quite caught up with unbridled enthusiasm. They were fighting like cats and dogs, and while they loved the baby profoundly and unconditionally, they were experiencing the marital havoc that arrives along with the baby. They were unable to imagine that someday they would look back on the early years of parenthood as some of the happiest years in their marriage.

The Core of Being Alive

What makes it all worthwhile? Perhaps nothing I can write could possibly prepare you for what being a parent might mean to you—how it enriches your life in ways you never thought possible, how its rewards go to the very core of being real and alive.

"I experienced everything four-fold," reflected Mary, "because I experienced it through my own eyes and those of each of my children. I learned to delight, as a child does, in simple occurrences. I remember, as a young mother, lying on the beach in the middle of the afternoon with my children, looking full-faced into a turquoise sky and imagining once again that the clouds floating above us were the same cotton balls I'd imagined them to be decades before as a child—or that the angels were resting on those clouds, as they had when I was young and looking up into that same vast sky from atop an old Indian blanket in my own back yard. Another time I watched the children race into the icy-cold lake water, splashing and shivering against an early summer breeze, giddy with laughter. These are memories of being a parent that steal my breath away. They say to me, this is what being a parent—this is what *life*—is all about!"

While the challenges of parenthood prove daunting for some, its rewards go to the core of what it means to be alive, to be human, experiencing life in abundance, the intimacy, growth, learning, and love—even the hard work that being parents entails. Material possessions pale in the face of having children. I reached a point where one more vacation to an exotic island didn't mean much without the kids; a job promotion was empty; attending yet another Saturday-night gala had lost its glitter. I prefer that new release at the video store and the double-cheese pizza, purchased with a two-for-one coupon and gobbled up on the floor of the family room amid wails of "I get the sofa!"

Saying I have a wonderful husband and two great sons sums up the really important things in my life. The rewards of being parents together far outweigh the costs. Being a parent makes all the stress temporary and bearable and someday, I'm sure, forgotten.

∽

Afterword

We've come a long way together. You've read about and dissected the many challenges new parents face on the journey into parenthood. For many couples, it's a long road and a rugged one. Some of you might have just begun your trip and are learning, along with the rest of us, the importance of nurturing your marriage as well as the baby.

This book has been about married life with children. Parents held me spellbound through hours of tales filled with stinging sensations of love and loss. Their vivid accounts of true life were matched with research from experts in psychology, sociology, health care, and family issues.

Perhaps, you say, there are lessons that new parents must simply learn through experience. But I pose these questions: How might our marriages and our early years of parenthood differ if we *did* learn from others? How might our journey be easier for us and for our children if we listened to the experiences of other mothers and fathers? What changes might we make to benefit and protect those we love the most? How might we live together better and longer? How can we keep new parents from dropping out of marriage?

Parents play a great role in molding the next generation. Each future generation depends on our willingness to accept the responsibilities of parenthood and to perform its duties to the best of our abilities. This, most often, means staying together. Our marriages, I believe, will flourish *only* when we are able to learn from and work through the times when we really don't feel like doing those things that make a marriage work. It takes time and energy for individuals to coalesce as parents. Men and women must act on their commonsense and summon their better instincts to do what they know is best for their family. If we don't, someone invariably gets hurt—usually those who did nothing at all to create the problems in the first place, our children. Many of us stumble, not because we want to, but because we just don't know how to help our partners or what to do to support them or love them as they need.

Now I've asked myself, "How do I get the millions of men and women who become parents together each year to do the simple things I've talked about in this book? What more can I say to get them to join hands and hearts and work together to resolve the intrinsic conflicts of early parenthood?"

I believe dealing first with simple issues is the right approach. For if we want civility and human dignity to return to our homes, we must begin by understanding why we might have landed where we have. Then each day we must do those things—the *small* things—that make a difference.

Every couple is different, just as what makes us happy in our relationships varies. What makes children happy, though, wavers little. Children, I found, desire to be a part of and play an active role in a stable family. Too often children become the center of the storm when their parents' marriage teeters precariously. Most mothers and fathers would give their children just about anything, yet some fail to give them the greatest gift of all: a stable marriage.

Being a parent and being the *spouse* of a new parent require hard work, self-discipline, and self-sacrifice in a common project. Marriage is not a simple social institution. Indeed, it becomes even more complex once a baby is born. Marriage can be a trying relationship. It involves commitment, trust, and a willingness to consider the needs—practical and emotional—of our spouse, often before our own needs. After conflict, there must always be an invitation to come back together, to heal and become whole again, preserving the dignity of the family we cherish.

Do you have the staying power? Do you have the fire-in-the-belly conviction to weather the parental and marital difficulties that you will face as parents together? Do you have the stamina to hold fast to the commitment made as two when the going gets tough as three, or four or more?

Staying together after the baby is an assignment of grand scale. It has been my intent in this book to help you understand the missteps that have become a way of life for too many new parents, and to offer a few promising guidelines for staying together as parents after the baby.

Bibliography

Abraham, S., A. Child, J. Ferry, J. Vizzard, and M. Mira. "Recovery after childbirth: a preliminary prospective study." *Medical Journal of Australia* 152 (1990): 9–12.

Alder, E. M. and J. L. Cox. "Breast-feeding and post-natal depression." *Journal of Psychosomatic Research* 27, vol. 2 (1983): 139–44.

Allen, Gina, and Clement G. Martin. *Sensitivity, Sex, and the Art of Love.* Chicago: Cowles Book Company, 1971.

Alpert, J. L., M. S. Richardson, and L. Fodasky. "Onset of parenting and stressful events." *Journal of Primary Prevention* 3 (1983): 149–59.

Amato, P. R. "Children's adjustment to divorce: Theories, hypotheses, and empirical support." *Journal of Marriage and the Family* 55 (1993): 23–38.

Amato, P. R., and B. Keith. "Parental divorce and the wellbeing of children: A meta-analysis." *Psychological Bulletin* 100 (1991): 26–46.

Amato, P. R., and G. Ochiltree. "Child and adolescent competence in intact, one-parent, and stepfamilies." *Journal of Divorce* 10 (1987): 75–96.

"American Council of Education Survey 1988." *American Book Trade Directory.* 38th Edition. New Providence, New Jersey: R. R. Bowker, 1988.

Anderson, S., C. Russell, and W. Schumm. "Perceived marital quality and family life cycle categories: A further analysis." *Journal of Marriage and the Family* 45 (1983): 759–62.

Anthony, E. J., editor. *The Child in His Family: The Impact of Disease and Death.* New York: Wiley, 1973.

Anthony, J. E. "Creative Parenthood." In *Parenthood: A Psycho-dynamic Perspective,* edited by R. S. Cohen, B. J. Cohler, and S. H. Weissman. New York: Guilford Press, 1984.

Antonucci, T. C. , and K. Mikus. "The Power of Parenthood: Personal and Attitudinal Changes During the Transition to Parenthood." In *Transition to Parenthood: Theory and Research,* edited by G. Y. Michaels and W. A. Goldberg. New York: Cambridge University Press, 1988.

Apgar, Sally. "On This Day, the Mother-child Attachment is the Focus." *Minneapolis Star Tribune,* 14 May, 1995.

Arditti, J. A. "Differences between fathers with joint custody and non-custodial fathers." *American Journal of Orthopsychiatry* 62 (1992): 186–95.

Arendell, Terry. *Divorce: Women & Children Last.* Berkeley: University of California Press, 1986.

Arp, David, and Claudia Arp. *The Marriage Track.* Grand Rapids, Michigan: Zondervan Publishing, 1992.

———. "Love, Sex, and the Very Married Parent." *Christian Parenting Today,* January/February, 1993.

Ball, F. L. J. "Understanding Problem-solving in Couple Relationships: Individual and Couple Satisfaction During the Transition to Parenthood." Paper presented at the symposium of the American Psychological Association, Anaheim, California, August 1983.

Ball, F. L. J. "Understanding and satisfaction in marital problem solving: A heremeneutic inquiry." In *The Transition to Parenthood: Current Theory and Research,* edited by G. Y. Michaels and W. A. Goldberg. New York: Cambridge University Press: 1988.

Ballinger, Barbara C., Dorothy E. Buckley, Graham J. Naylor, and David A. Stansfield. "Emotional Disturbances following childbirth: Clinical findings and urinary excretion of cyclic AMP." *Psychological Medicine* 9 (1979): 292–300.

Barrett, N. *I Wish Someone Would Have Told Me.* New York: Fireside, 1990.

Behrman, Richard E., editor. *Future of Children: Children and Divorce.* vol. 4 (1). Los Altos, California: Center for the Future of Children, The David and Lucile Packard Foundation, 1994.

Belsky, J. "The determinants of parenting: A process model." *Child Development* 55 (1984): 83–96.

———. "Exploring individual differences in marital change across the transition to parenthood: The role of violated expectations." *Journal of Marriage and the Family* 47 (1985): 1037–46.

———. "Early human experience: A family perspective." *Developmental Psychology* 17 (1981): 3–23.

Belsky, Jay, and John Kelly. *The Transition to Parenthood: How a First Child Changes a Marriage. Why Some Couples Grow Closer and Others Apart.* New York: Delacourte Press, 1994.

Belsky, J., M. Lang, and M. Rovine. "Stability and change in marriage across the transition to parenthood: A second study." *Journal of Marriage and the Family* 47 (1985): 855–66.

Belsky, J., M. Perry-Jenkins, and A. C. Crouter. "The work–family interface and marital change across the transition to parenthood." *Journal of Family Issues* 6, vol. 2 (1985): 205–20.

Belsky, J., and M. Rovine. "Patterns of marital change across the transition to parenthood: Pregnancy to three years postpartum." *Journal of Marriage and the Family* 52 (1990): 5–19.

Belsky, J., G. Spanier, and M. Rovine. "Stability and change in marriage across the transition to parenthood." *Journal of Marriage and the Family* 45 (1983): 567–77.

Benedek, T., and E. J. Anthony, editors. "Parenthood during the life cycle." In *Parenthood: Its Psychology and Psychopathology.* Boston: Little, Brown, 1970.

Bennett, V. R., and L. K. Brown, editors. *Myles Textbook for Midwives.* United Kingdom: Churchill Livingstone, 1989.

Berglund, R., H. Flodh, and P. Lundborg. "Drug use during pregnancy and breast-feeding." *Obstetricia et Gynecologica Scandinavica* 126 (1984): 1–55.

Berstrand, H. and L. K. Rosenblood. "Stripping out pus in lactational mastitis." *Canadian Medical Association Journal* 145 (1991): 229–306.

Blankenhorn, David. Fatherless America: Confronting *Our Most Urgent Social Problem.* New York: Basic Books, 1994.

Block, J. H., J. Block and P. F. Gjerde. "The personality of children prior to divorce: A prospective study." *Child Development* 57 (1986): 827–840.

Block, J. H., J. Block, and A. Morrison. "Parental agreement-disagreement on child-rearing orientations and gender-related personality correlates in childcare." *Child Development* 52 (1981): 965–974.

Blum, M. E. "A longitudinal study of transition to parenthood in primiparous couples." Paper presented at the meeting of the American Psychological Association, Anaheim, California, August 1983.

Bombardieri, M. *The Baby Decision: How to Make the Most Important Decision of Your Life.* New York: Rawson Associates, 1981.

Bowker, R. R., editor. *Broadcasting and Cable Yearbook.* New Providence: A Reed Reference Publishing Co., 1993.

Bowman, M., and C. R. Ahrons. "Impact of legal custody status on fathers' parenting postdivorce." *Journal of Marriage and the Family* 47 (1985): 481–88.

Bradburn N., and D. Caplovitz. *Reports on Happiness.* Chicago: Aldine, 1965.

Bradley, R. A. *Husband Coached Childbirth.* 3rd edition. New York: Harper and Row, l981.

Brandt, Henry, with Phil Landrum. *I Want My Marriage to Be Better.* Grand Rapids, Michigan: Zondervan Publishing, 1976.

Braver, S. L., P. J. Fitzpatrick, and R. C. Bay. "Noncustodial parents report of child support payments." *Family Relations* 40 (1991): 180–85.

Braverman, J., and J. F. Roux. "Screening for the patient at risk for postpartum depression." *Journal of Obstetrics Gynecology* 52 (1978): 731–6.

Bray, James. Interview by Katie Couric. *The Today Show.* National Broadcasting Corporation, 30 June 1995.

Brockington, I. F., K. R. Cernik, E. M. Schofield, et al. "Puerperal psychosis: phenomena and diagnosis." *Archives of General Psychiatry* 38, vol. 7 (1981): 829–33.

Brody, G. H., E. Neubaum, and R. Forehand. "Serial Marriage: A heuristic analysis of an emerging family form." *Psychological Bulletin* 103 (1988): 211–22.

Bronson, W. "Antecedents of emotional expressiveness and reactivity control." *Child Development* 37 (1966): 793–810.

Brown, Jeanette S., and William Crombleholme, editors. *Handbook of Gynecology and Obstetrics*. Norwalk, California: Appleton & Lange, 1993.

Brownstein, Ronald. "Candidates Unfurl Morality Banner." *Minneapolis Star Tribune*, 3 August 1994: 4a.

Buchanan, C. M., E. E. Maccoby, and S. M. Dornbusch. "Adolescents and their families after divorce: Three residential arrangements compared." *Journal of Research on Adolescents* 2 (1992): 261–91.

Bumpass, Larry. "Children and marital disruption: A replication and update." *Demography* 21 (1984): 71–82.

Bumpass, L., and R. R. Rindfuss. "Children's experience of marital disruption." *American Journal of Sociology* 85 (1979): 49–65.

Carnegie Task Force. *Starting Points: Meeting the Needs of Our Youngest Children*. Carnegie Corporation of New York, April 1994.

Carnes, J. W. "Psychosocial disturbances during and after pregnancy: Helping the patient cope with prenatal stress and postpartum blues." *Postgraduate Medicine* 73, vol. 1 (1983): 135–145.

Carter, Les. *Broken Vows*. Nashville: Thomas Nelson Publishers, 1992.

Chadwick, Bruce A., and Tim B. Heaton, editors. *The Statistics Handbook on the American Family*. 1st ed. Phoenix: Oryx Press, 1992.

Chadwick, Bruce A., and Tim B. Heaton, editors. *The Statistics Handbook on the American Family*. 2nd ed. Phoenix: Oryx Press, 1999.

Chambers, D. L. *Making Fathers Pay: The Enforcement of Child Support*. Chicago: University of Chicago Press, 1979.

Cherlin, A. "The effect of children on marital dissolution." *Demography* 14 (1977): 264–72.

Cherlin, A. J., and F. F. Furstenberg. "Step families in the United States: A reconsideration. *Annual Review of Sociology* 20 (1994): 359–381.

Chilman, C. S. "Parent satisfactions, concerns, and goals for their children." *Family Relations* 19 (1980): 339–45.

Chira, Susan. "Kids May Suffer in Multiple Breakups." *New York Times,* 19 April 1995.

Cleek, M., and T. Pearson. "Perceived causes of divorce: An analysis of Interrelationships." *Journal of Marriage and the Family* 47 (1985): 180.

Cochran, Moncrieff M., and Jane Anthony Brassard. "Child development and personal social networks." *Child Development* 50 (1979): 601–6.

Cohen, R. S., B. J. Cohler, and S. H. Weissman, eds. *Parenthood: A Psychodynamic Perspective*. New York: Guilford Press, 1984.

Coleman, A., and L. Coleman. *Pregnancy: The Psychological Experience*. New York: Seabury Press, 1971.

Cooney, T. M., and P. Uhlenberg. "Divorced men and their adult children after midlife." *Journal of Marriage and the Family* 52 (1990): 677–88.

Cowan, C. P., Carolyn Pape, and Philip A. Cowan. *When Partners Become Parents: The Big Life Change for Couples.* New York: Basic Books, 1992.

Cowan, C. P., Philip A. Cowan, L. Coie, and J. D. Coie. "Becoming a family: The impact of a first child's birth on the couples' relationship." *The First Child and Family Formation,* edited by W. B. Miller and L. F. Newman. Chapel Hill: University of North Carolina, Carolina Population Center, 1978.

Cowan, C. P., Philip A. Cowan, G. Heming, E. Garrett, W. S. Coysh, H. Curtis-Boles, and A. J. Boles. "Transitions to parenthood: His, hers, and theirs." *Journal of Family Issues* 6 (1985): 451–481.

Cowan, Philip A. "Becoming a Father: A Time of Change, An Opportunity for Development." In *Fatherhood Today: Men's Changing Role in the Family,* edited by P. Brownstein and C. P. Cowan. New York: Wiley, 1988.

Cowan, Philip A., C. P. Cowan, M. Schulz, and G. Heming. "Prebirth to preschool family factors predicting children's adaptation to kindergarten." In *Exploring Family Relationships With Other Social Contexts: Advances in Family* Research 4, edited by R. Parke & S. Kellam. Hillsdale, NJ: Lawrence Erlbaum Associates, 1992.

Cronenwett, L. R. "Elements and outcomes of a postpartum support group program." *Research in Nursing and Health* 3 (1980): 33–41.

Cunningham, F. H., P. C. MacDonald, and N. F. Gant. Williams Obstetrics. 18th ed. East Norwalk, Connecticut: Appleton and Lange, 1989.

Cutrona, C. E. "Nonpsychotic postpartum depression: A review of recent research." *Clinical Psychology Review* 2 (1982): 487–503.

Cutrona, C. E. "Social support and stress in transition to parenthood." *Journal of Abnormal Psychology* 93 (1984): 378–90.

Cutrona, C. E., and B. R. Troutman. "Social support, infant temperament, and parenting self-efficacy: A mediational model of postpartum depression." *Child Development* 57 (1986): 1507–18.

Cypress, B. K. "Patterns of Ambulatory Care in Obstetrics and Gynecology: The National Ambulatory Medical Care Survey." Series 13, No. 76. Department of Health and Human Services Pub. No. 84-1737. Washington, D.C.: United States Government Printing Office, 1984.

Daniels, Peggy Kneffel, and Carol A. Schwartz, editors. *Encyclopedia of Associations* 1, Part 2, 28th ed. Detroit: Gale Research, 1984.

Davis, T. F., and R. Cobin. "Thyroid disease in pregnancy and the postpartum period." *Mt. Sinai Journal of Medicine* 52, vol. 1 (1985): 59–77.

Dentsch, Cynthia. "Love and Marriage." *Parents Magazine* (April 1982): 52.

Diagnostic and Statistical Manual of Mental Disorders. Washington, D.C.: American Psychiatric Association, 1980.

Diehr, Price & Williams. "Factors related to the use of ambulatory mental health services in three provider plans." *Social Science Medicine* 23 (1986): 773–780.

Dillow, Linda. *How to Really Love Your Man.* Nashville: Thomas Nelson Publishing, 1993.

Dix, Carol. *New Mother Syndrome.* New York: Doubleday, 1985.

Doering, Susan G., and Doris R. Entwisle. "Preparation During Pregnancy and Ability to Cope with Labor and Delivery." *American Journal of Orthopsychiatry* 45 (1975): 825–837.

Downey, D., and B. Powell. "Do children in single-parent households fare better living with same-sex parent?" Journal of Marriage and the Family 55 (1993): 55–71.

Duncan, S. W. "The transition to parenthood: Coping and adaptation of couples to pregnancy and the birth of their first child." *Dissertation Abstracts International* 45 (1984): 1600.

Duncan, S. W., and H. J. Markman. "Intervention programs for the transition to parenthood: Current status from a prevention perspective." In *Transition to Parenthood: Theory and Research.* Edited by G. Y. Michaels and W. A. Goldberg. New York: Cambridge University Press, 1988, 270–310.

Dyer, E. D. "Parenthood as Crisis: A study." *Marriage and Family Living* 25 (May 1963): 196–201.

Eakins, Pamela S., editor. *American Way of Birth.* Philadelphia: Temple University Press, 1986.

Eheart, Brenda Krause, and Susan Karol Martel. *The Fourth Trimester, On Becoming a Mother.* Norwalk: Appleton-Century-Crofts, 1983.

Elliott, S. A. "Pregnancy and after." In *Contributions to Medical Psychology,* vol. 3, edited by S. Rachman. New York: Pergamon Press. 1984.

Emery, R. "Interparental conflict and the children of discord and divorce." *Psychological Bulletin* 92 (1982): 310–30.

Entwisle, S., and S. Doering. *The First Birth: A Family Turning Point.* Baltimore: Johns Hopkins University Press, 1981.

Erikson, E. "Identity and the life cycle." *Psychological Issues* 1 (1959): 1–171.

———. *Identity, Youth and Crisis.* New York: W. W. Norton, 1968.

———. *Childhood and Society.* New York: W. W. Norton, 1950.

Extner, Max Joseph. *The Sexual Side of Marriage.* New York: W. W. Norton, 1932.

Fargo, J., K. Tokuno, and M. A. Migan. "Comfort/discomfort in the parenting role: Implications for the provision of child rearing information." *Family Perspectives* 15 (1981): 63–71.

Fawcett, J. T. "The value and cost of the first child." In *The First Child and Family Formation,* edited by W. B. Miller and L. F. Newman. Chapel Hill: University of North Carolina, Carolina Population Center, 244–265.

———. "The value of children and the transition to parenthood." In *Transitions to Parenthood,* edited by Robin J. Palkovitz and Marvin B. Sussman. New York: Haworth Press, 1988, 11–34.

Fedele, N. M. , E. R. Golding, F. K. Grossman, and W. S. Pollack. "Psychological issues in adjustment to first parenthood." In *The Transition to Parenthood: Current*

Theory and Research, edited by G. Y. Michaels and W. A. Goldberg. New York: Cambridge University Press: 1988.

Feldman, H. "The effects of children on the family." In *Family issues of employed women in Europe and America,* edited by A. Michel. London: Brill, 1971, 114–125.

Feldman, Harold, and Margaret Feldman. *Current Controversies in Marriage and Family.* Beverly Hills: Sage Publications, 1985.

Feldman, S. S., and B. Aschenbrenner. "Impact of parenthood on various aspects of masculinity and feminity: A short-term longitudinal study." *Developmental Psychology* 19 (1983): 278–89.

Feldman, S. S., and S. C. Nash. "Antecedents of parenting." In *Origins of Nurturance,* edited by A. D. Fogel and G. F. Melson. Hilldale, New Jersey: Earlbaum, 1984, 209–32.

———. "The transition from expectancy to parenthood: Impact of the firstborn child on men and women." *Sex Roles* 111 (1984): 84–96.

Finkelhor, David, Gerald Hotaling, and Kersti Yllo. *Stopping Family Violence: Research Priorities for the Coming Decade.* Beverly Hills: Sage, 1988.

Fischman, S. H., E. A. Rankin, K. L. Soeken, and E. R. Lenz. "Changes in sexual relationship in postpartum couples." *Journal of Obstetrics and Gynecology Neonatal Nursing* (January/February 1986): 58–63.

Folberg, J. *Joint custody and shared parenting.* 2nd ed. New York: Guilford Press, 1991.

Fraiberg, S., E. Adelson, and V. Shapiro. "Ghosts in the nursery: A psychoanalytic approach to the problems of impaired infant-mother relationships." *Journal of Child Psychiatry* 14, vol. 3 (1975): 387–421.

Frank, Anderson and Rubenstein. *Journal of Professional and Personal Enrichment* (Summer 1994): 9.

Frate, D., J. Cowen, and A. Rutledge. "Behavioral reactions during the postpartum period: Experiences of 108 women." *Women's Health* 4, vol. 4 (1979): 355–371.

Friedman, James T. *The Divorce Handbook.* New York: Random House, 1982.

Fuller, Elizabeth. *Having Your First Birth After Thirty.* New York: Mead and Company, 1983.

Furstenburg, Frank, and Andrew Cherlin. *Divided Families: What Happens to Children When Parents Part.* Cambridge, Massachusetts: Harvard University Press, 1994.

Furstenburg, F. and C. Nord. "Parenting apart: Patterns of child-rearing after marital disruption." *Journal of Marriage and the Family* (1985) 47:893–904.

Furstenburg, Frank, C. Nord, J. Peterson, and N. Zill. "The Life course of children and divorce, marital disruption and parental contact." *American Sociological Review* 48 (1983): 656–68.

Galinsky, Ellen. *Between Generations: The Stages of Parenthood.* New York: Berkley Books, 1981.

Galinsky, Ellen, and Judy David. *The Preschool Years.* New York: Ballantine Books, 1988.

Gaines, Susan. "And Baby Makes . . . Marital Conflict." *Minnesota Parent* (October 1994): 46–47.

Garfinkel, I. *Assuring child support: An extension of Social Security.* New York: Russell Sage Foundation, 1992.

Garvey, M. J., and G. D. Tollefson. "Postpartum depression." *Journal of Reproductive Medicine* 29, vol. 2 (1984): 113–6.

Genasci, Lisa. "Your Child or Your Job." *Minneapolis Star Tribune,* 19 March 1995: 1E.

Genevie, Louis, and Eva Margolies. *The Motherhood Report.* New York: MacMillan, 1987.

Gerstein, H. C. "How common is postpartum thyroiditis?" *Archives of Internal Medicine.* 150 (1990): 1397–1400.

Gjerdingen, Dwenda K., and Debra G. Froberg. "The fourth stage of labor: The health of birth mothers and adoptive mothers at six weeks postpartum. " *Family Medicine* 23 (1991): 29–35.

Gjerdingen, Dwenda K., Debra G. Froberg, Kathryn M. Chaloner, and Patricia M. McGovern. "Changes in women's physical health during the first postpartum year." *Archives of Family Medicine* 2 (March 1993): 277–283.

Gjerdingen, Dwenda K., Debra G. Froberg, and Patricia Fontaine. "The effects of social support on women's health during pregnancy, labor and delivery, and the postpartum period." *Family Medicine* 23 (1991): 370–5.

Gjerdingen, Dwenda K., Debra G. Froberg, and Diane L. Wilson. "Postpartum mental and physical problems: How common are they?" *Postgraduate Medicine* 8 (December 1986): 133–145.

Gleick, E. "Making Marriage Stick." *Time* (27 February 1995): 50.

Glenn, N. D. "Further discussion of the effects of no-fault divorce on divorce rates." *Journal of Marriage and the Family* 61 (1999): 800–802.

Glenn, N. D., and S. McLanahan. "Children and marital happiness: A further specification of the relationship." *Journal of Marriage and the Family* 44 (1982): 63–72.

Glick, P. C., and S. Lin. "Recent changes in divorce and remarriage." *Journal of Marriage and the Family* 48 (1986): 737–747.

Gold, J. S., and H. A. Wissinger. "Carpal tunnel syndrome in pregnancy." *Southern Medical Journal* 71 (1978): 144–145.

Gold-Bilkin, Lynn. Phone interview. "Preserving Marriage Project." Norristown, Pennsylvania: American Bar Association Family Law Division, May 1995.

Goldberg, W. A., and G. Y. Michaels, editors. *The Transition to Parenthood: Theory and Research.* New York: Cambridge University Press, 1988.

Goldberg, W. A., G. Y. Michaels, and M. E. Lamb. "Husbands' and wives' adjustment to pregnancy and first parenthood." *Family Issues* 6 (1985): 485–503.

Gordon, R. E., and K. K. Gordon. "Social factors in the prediction and treatment of emotional disorders of pregnancy." *American Journal of Obstetrics and Gynecology* 77 (1959): 1074–83.

Gottlieb, B. H., and S. M. Pancer. "Social networks and the transition to parenthood." In *The Transition to Parenthood: Current Theory and Research,* edited by G. Y. Michaels and W. A. Goldberg. New York: Cambridge University Press: 1988.

Gottman, J. *Why Marriages Succeed or Fail.* New York: Simon and Schuster, 1994.

Gottman, J. M., H. Markman, and C. Notarius. "The topography of marital conflict: A sequential analysis of verbal and nonverbal behavior." *Journal of Marriage and the Family* 39 (1977): 461–77.

Gottman, J. M., and L. J. Krokoff. "Marital interaction and satisfaction: A longitudinal view." *Journal of Consulting and Clinical Psychology* 57 (1989): 47–52.

Gottman, J. M., and R. W. Levenson. "The social psychophysiology of marriage." In *Perspectives on Marital Interaction,* edited by Patricia Noller and Mary Anne Fitzpatrick. San Diego: College Hill Press, 1989.

Gray, John. *Men are from Mars, Women are from Venus,* New York: Harper-Collins, 1992.

Greif, G. "Fathers, children and joint custody." *American Journal of Orthopsychiatry* 49 (1979): 311–19.

Greenberg, Susan H. "A Place for Kids . . . and Help for Their Parents." *Minneapolis Star Tribune,* 6 June 1994.

Greenblat, Cathy Stein. "The salience of sexuality in the early years of marriage." *Journal of Marriage and the Family* 45 (May 1983): 289–299.

Grossman, F. K., with L. S. Eichler, L. S. Winickoff, M. K. Anzalone, M. Gotseyeff, and S. D. Sargent. *Pregnancy, Birth, and Parenthood.* San Francisco: Jossey–Bass, 1980.

Gruis, M. "Beyond maternity: Postpartum concerns of mothers." *American Journal of Maternal Child Nursing* 2 (1977): 182–183.

Grych, J. H., and F. D. Fincham. "Marital conflict and children's adjustment: A cognitive-contextual framework." *Psychological Bulletin* 108 (1990): 267–90.

Guidubaldi, J., H. K. Cleminshaw, J. D. Perry, et al. "The role of selected family environment factors in children's post-divorce adjustment." *Family Relations* 35 (1986): 141–51.

Gutman, H. G. "Parenthood: A key to the comparative study of the life cycle." In *Life-span Developmental Psychology: Normative Life Crisis,* edited by N. Datan and L. Ginsberg. New York: Academic Press, 1975.

Hall, R. C., and T. P. Beresford. "Physical illness in psychiatric patients: Areas of inquiry." *Psychiatric Medicine* 2, vol. 4 (1984): 401–415.

Hardin, Jerry D., and Diane C. Sloan. *Getting Ready for Marriage: How to Really Get to Know the Person You're Going to Marry.* Nashville: Thomas Nelson Publishers, 1992.

Harley, Willard F. *His Needs, Her Needs.* Grand Rapids, Michigan: Fleming H. Revell, 1988.

Hayslett, J. P. "Postpartum renal failure." *New England Journal of Medicine* 32, vol. 24 (1985): 1556–9.

Heinicke, C. "Impact of pre-birth parent personality and marital functioning on family development: A framework and suggestions for further study." *Developmental Psychology* 20 (1984): 1044–53.

Heming, G. "Predicting adaptation in the transition to parenthood." Ph.D. diss. University of California, Berkeley, 1987.

Herzog, A., and T. Detre. "Psychotic reactions associated with childbirth." *Diseases of the Nervous System* 37, vol. 4 (1976): 229–35.

Hill, R. *Families Under Stress.* New York: Harper, 1949.

Hobbs, Daniel F. "Parenthood as crisis: a third study." *Journal of Marriage and the Family* 27 (1965): 367–72.

Hobbs, Daniel. F. Jr., and Susan Peck Cole. "Transition to parenthood: A decade replication." *Journal of Marriage and the Family* 38, vol. 4 (1976): 723–31.

Hochschild, Arlie, with Anne Machung. *The Second Shift: Working Parents and the Revolution at Home.* New York: Viking/Penguin, 1989.

Hodges, W. F., C. W. Tierney, and H. K. Buchsbaum. "The cumulative effect of stress on preschool children of divorced and intact families." *Journal of Marriage and the Family* 46 (1984): 611–20.

Hoffman, L. W., and M. L. Hoffman. "The value of children to parents." In *Psychological Perspectives on Fertility* edited by J. T. Fawcett. New York: Basic Books, 1973.

Hoffman, L. W., and J. Manis. "Influences of children on marital interaction and parental satisfaction and dissatisfaction." In *Child Influences on Marital and Family Interaction: A Life-span Perspective,* edited by R. M. Lerner and G. W. Spanier. New York: Academic Press, 1978.

Holmgren, Kristine M. "Laws Aren't Best Way to Deter Divorce." *Minneapolis Star Tribune* (16 August 1993): 9A.

Hopkins J., M. Marcus, and S. B. Campbell. "Postpartum depression: A critical review." *Psychological Bulletin* 95, vol. 3 (1984): 498–515.

Hotchner, Tracy. *Childbirth and Marriage.* New York: Avon Books, 1988.

Howard, Philip K. *The Death of Common Sense: How Law Is Suffocating America.* New York: Warner Books, 1994.

Huber, Joan, and Glenna Spitze. *Sex Stratification: Children, Housework, and Jobs.* New York: Academic Press, 1983.

"Husband and Wife for Life, What are the Odds?" *Minneapolis Star Tribune* (9 July 1994): 9.

Huston, T. M., S. M. McHale, and A. C. Crouter. "When the Honeymoon is Over: Changes in the Marriage Relationship Over the First Year." In *The Emerging Field of Personal Relationships,* edited by R. Gilmour and S. Duck. Hilldale, New Jersey: Erlbaum, 1986.

Ihinger-Tallman, M., and K. Pasley. *Remarriage.* Newbury Park, California: Sage, 1987.

Iosif, S., and L. Henriksson. "Postpartum incontinence." *Urology International* 36 (1981): 53–58.

Johnson, C. L. *Ex familia: Grandparents, Parents, and Children Adjust to Divorce.* New Brunswick: Rutgers University Press, 1988.

Johnston, J. R., M. Kline, and J. M. Tschann. "Ongoing divorce conflict: effects on children of joint custody and frequent access." *American Journal of Orthopsychiatry* 59 (1989): 576–92.

Johnston, J. R. "Family transitions and children's functioning: The case of parental conflict and divorce." In *Family, Self and Society: Toward a New Agenda for Family Research* edited by Philip A. Cowan, D. Field, and D. A. Hansen. Hillsdale, NJ: Lawrence Erlbaum Associates, 1993.

Johnston, J. R. "High conflict and violent parents in family court: Findings on children's adjustment and proposed guidelines for the resolution of custody and visitation disputes." Final report to the Judicial Council of the State of California, Statewide Office of Family Court Services. San Francisco: Judicial Council, 1992.

Kach and McGhee. "Adjustment to early parenthood: The role of accuracy of pre-parenthood expectations." *Journal of Family Issues* 3 (1982): 375.

Kalmuss, D., A. Davidson, and L. Cushman. "Parenting expectations, experiences, and adjustment to parenthood: A test of the violated expectations framework." *Journal of Marriage and the Family* 54 (1992): 516–26.

Karney, B. R. and T. N Bradbury. "The longitudinal course of marital quality and stability: A review of theory, method, and research." *Psychological Bulletin* 118 (1995): 3–34.

Kaslow, Florence W., and Lita Linzer Schwartz. *Dynamics of Divorce/A Life Cycle Perspective.* New York: Brunner/Mazel, 1987.

Kelly, J. "Current research on children's post-divorce adjustment: No simple answers." *Family and Conciliation Courts Review* 31 (Jan. 1993): 29–49.

Kelly, J. B. "Developing and implementing postdivorce parenting plans: Does the forum make a difference?" In *Nonresidential Parenting: New Vistas in Family Living,* edited by C. Depner and J. Brays. Newbury Park, California: Sage, 1993.

Kendall-Tackett, D. A., L. M. Williams, and D. Finkelhor. "Impact of sexual abuse on children: A review and synthesis of recent empirical studies." *Psychological Bulletin* 113 (1993): 164–80.

Kent, Debra. "Sex and Housework." *Working Mother Magazine* (September 1992): 18–24.

Kitzinger, Sheila. Giving Birth: How it Really Feels. New York: The Noonday Press/Farrar, Straus and Giroux, 1989.

Kligman, A. M. "Pathologic dynamics of human hair loss." *Archives of Dermatology* 83(1961): 175–185.

Kline, M., J. R. Johnston, and J. M. Tschann. "The long shadow of marital conflict: A family process model of children's adjustment postdivorce." *Journal of Marriage and the Family* 53 (1990): 197–309.

Kline, M., J. M. Taschann, J. R. Johnston, and J. S. Wallerstein. "Children's adjustment in joint and sole physical custody families." *Developmental Psychology* 25 (1989): 430–38.

Kochakian, Mary Jo. "Children of Divorce Can Be Just Hard to Get Along With." *Hartford Courant*, August 13, 1995.

Kruk, E. "Psychological and structural factors contributing to the disengagement of non-custodial fathers after divorce." *Family and Reconciliation Courts Review* 30 (1992): 81–101.

Kumar, R., and K. M. Robson. "A prospective study of emotional disorders in child-bearing women." *British Journal of Psychiatry* 144 (1984): 35–47.

Ladies' Home Journal, editors. "Can This Marriage Be Saved? Don't Ignore Resentment Over Home Tasks." Minneapolis Star Tribune, August 13, 1996.

Lang, Susan S. *Women Without Children*. New York: Pharos Books, 1991.

LaRossa, R. "The transition to parenthood and the social reality of time." *Journal of Marriage and the Family* 45 (1983): 579–87.

LaRossa, R., and M. M. LaRossa. *Transition to Parenthood: How Infants Change Families*. Beverly Hills: Sage, 1981.

Laumann, Edward O. , John H. Gagnon, Robert T. Michael and Stewart Michaels. *The Social Organization of Sexuality in the United States*. Chicago: University of Chicago Press, 1994.

Lazarus, R. L. *Emotion and Adaptation*. Oxford: Oxford University Press, 1991.

Lazarus, R. and S. Folkman. *Stress, Appraisal, and Coping*. New York: Springer, 1984.

Leach, Penelope. Interview. Minneapolis, Minnesota, May 1994.

Leach, Penelope. *Children First: What Our Society Must Do — And Is Not Doing For Our Children Today.* New York: Knopf, March 1994.

Lee, Cy, B. Madrzo, and B. H. Drukker. "Ultrasonic evaluation of the postpartum uterus in the management of postpartum bleeding." *Journal of Obstetrics and Gynecology* 58 (1981): 227–232.

Left Side Lines. Laguna Beach, CA: Side Lines National Support Network. Ongoing.

Leifer, M. "Psychological changes accompanying pregnancy and motherhood." *Genetic Psychology Monographics* 95 (1977): 55–96.

LeMasters, E. E. "Parenthood as Crisis." In *A Sourcebook in Marriage and the Family*, 2nd Edition, edited by Marvin B. Sussman. Boston: Houghton Mifflin, 1963.

Levenson, R. W., and J. M. Gottman. "Physiological and affective predictors of change in relationship satisfaction." *Journal of Personality and Social Psychology* 49 (1985): 85–94.

Lewis, R. A., and G. B. Spanier. "Theorizing about the quality and stability of marriage." In *Contemporary Theories About the Family* 1, edited by W. R. Burr, R. Hill, F. I. Nye, and I. Reiss. New York: Free Press, 1979, 269–294.

Lieberman, A. F. "Infant-parent psychotheraphy during pregnancy." In *Infants and Parents*, edited by S. Provence. New York: International Universities Press, 1983.

Lieberman, M. A. "The effects of social support in response to stress." In *Handbook of Stress*, edited by Goldgerger and Breznitz. New York: Free Press, 1981, 764–781.

Lopata, H. *Occupation: Housewife.* New York: Oxford University Press, 1972.

Luckey, E., and J. Bain. "Children: A factor in marital satisfaction." *Journal of Marriage and the Family* 32 (1970): 43–54.

Maccoby, E. E., and R. H. Mnookin. *Dividing the Child: Social and Legal Dilemmas of Custody.* Cambridge, MA: Harvard University Press, 1992.

MacDermid, S., T. Huston, and S. McHale. "Change in marriage associated with the transition to parenthood: Individual differences as a function of sex-role attitudes and changes in the division of household labor." *Journal of Marriage and the Family* 52 (1990): 475–86.

Markman, H. J., F. Floyd, and F. Dickson/Markman. "Towards a model for the prediction and primary prevention of marital and family distress and dissolution." In *Personal Relationships for Dissolving Personal Relationships,* edited by S. Duck. New York: Academic Press, 233–61.

Markman, H. J., S. M. Stanley, and S. L. Blumberg. *Fighting for Your Marriage: Positive Steps For A Loving and Lasting Relationship.* San Francisco: Jossey Bass, Inc.

Markman, H. J., F. Floyd, S. M. Stanley, and R. A. Lewis. "Prevention." In *Clinical Handbook of Marital Therapy,* edited by N. S. Jacobson and A. S. Gurman. New York: Guilford Press, 1986, 173–95.

Markman, H., and C. Notarius. "Coding marital and family interaction." In T. Jacob (Ed.) *Family Interaction and Psychopathology.* New York: Plenum, 1987, 329–390.

Marut, J. S., and R. T. Mercer. "Comparison of primiparas perception of vaginal and c/s births." *Nursing Research* 28 (1979): 260–6.

Masters, William H., Virginia E. Johnson, and Robert J. Levin. *The Pleasure Bond: A New Look at Sexuality and Commitment.* New York: Bantam, 1975.

Masters, William H., Virginia E. Johnson, and Robert C. Kolodny. *Human Sexuality.* Boston: LittleBrown, 1982.

McGinnis, Alan Loy. *The Friendship Factor.* Minneapolis: Augsburg Publishing House, 1979.

McHale, Susan, and Ted Huston. "The effect of the transition to parenthood on the marriage relationship: A Longitudinal Study." *Journal of Family Issues* 6, vol. 4 (1985): 409–33.

McLanahan, S. "Family structure and the reproduction of poverty." *American Journal of Sociology* (1985) 873–901.

McLanahan, S., and K. Booth. "Mother only families: Problems prospects, and politics." *Journal of Marriage and the Family* 51 (1989): 557–80.

McLeod, J. D., and M. J. Shanahan. "Poverty, parenting, and children's mental health." *American Sociological Review* 58 (1993): 351–66.

McLaughlin, S., and M. Micklin. "The timing of the first birth and changes in personal efficacy." *Journal of Marriage and the Family* 45 (1983): 47–55.

McNeil, T. F. "Women with non-organic psychosis; psychiatric and demographic characteristics of cases with versyus without postpartum psychotic episodes. *Acta Psychiatricia Scandinavica* 78, 603–609, 1988.

Melvin, J. L., C. N. Burnett, and E. W. Johnson. "Median nerve conduction on pregnancy." *Archives of Physical and Medical Rehabilitation* 50 (1969): 75–80.

Michael, Robert T., John H. Gagnon, Edward O. Laumann, and Gina Kolata. *Sex in America: A definitive survey.* Boston: Little, Brown, 1995.

Michaels, G. Y., and W. A. Goldberg, editors. *The Transition to Parenthood: Current Theory and Research.* New York: Cambridge University Press, 1988.

Miller, B. C., and D. H. Olson, editors. *Family Studies, Review Yearbook*, Vol. 3. Beverly Hills: Sage Publications, 1985.

Miller, N. B., Philip A. Cowan, C. P. Cowan, E. M. Hetherington, and G. Clingempeel. "Externalizing in preschoolers and early adolescents: A cross-study replication of a family model." Paper presented to the American Sociological Association, Cincinnati, Ohio, August 1991.

Miller, B., and D. Sollie. "Normal stresses during the transition to parenthood." *Family Relations* 29 (1980): 459–65.

Mills, Beverly. "Child Life." *Minneapolis Star Tribune* (12 June 1994): 3e.

Minirth, Frank, Mary Alice Minirth, Dr. Brian Newman, Dr. Deborah Newman, Dr. Robert Hemfelt, and Susan Hemfelt. *Passages of Marriage.* Nashville: Thomas Nelson Publishers, 1992.

Mira, M. "Recovery after childbirth: A preliminary prospective study." *Medical Journal of Australia* 159 (1990): 9–12.

Morgan, S. P., D. M. Lye, and G. A. Condran. "Sons, daughters, and the risk of marital disruption." *American Journal of Sociology* 94 (1988): 110–129.

Munk, Nina. "The Child is the Father of Man." *Forbes* Magazine, August 16, 1993, 88–93.

Murphy, Marianne Espinosa. "Divorce Stinks: A Judge's View." *Redbook Magazine* (April 1995): 39.

Myers, Michael F. *Men and Divorce.* New York: Guildford Press, 1989,5–9.

National Center for Health Statistics. *Health and Selected Socioeconomic Characteristics of the Family*: United States, 1988–1990. (PHS) 97-1523. Washington D.C.: General Printing Office, 1997.

National Center for Health Statistics. *Vital Health Statistics.* Series 24, No. 1. "Compilations of data on natality, mortality, marriage, divorce, and induced termination of pregnancy." Washington D.C.: General Printing Office, 1997.

Navonezny, P. A., R. D. Shull, and J. L. Rodgers. "The effect of no fault divorce law on the divorce rate across 50 states and its relationship to income, education, and religiosity." *Journal of Marriage and the Family* 59 (1995): 477.

Nock, Steven L. "The family life cycle: Empirical or conceptual tool?" *Journal of Marriage and the Family* 52 (1990).

Norbeck, J. S., and V. P. Tilden. "Life stress, social support, and emotional dis-equilibrium in complications of pregnancy: A prospective, multivariate study." *Journal of Health Social Behaviors* 93 (1983): 378–90.

Nordby, Daniel, Ph.D. Interview with the author. Minneapolis, Minnesota, Summer 1989.

Notman, M. T, and C. C. Nadelson. *The Woman Patient: Medical and Psychological Interfaces.* New York: Plenum, 1978.

Nott, P. N., M. Franklin, and C. Armitage, et al. "Hormonal changes and mood in the puerperium." *British Journal of Psychiatry* 118 (1976): 379–83

Nuckolls, K. B., J. Cassell, and B. H. Kaplan. "Psychosocial assets, life crisis, and the prognosis of pregnancy." *American Journal of Epidemiology* 95 (1972): 431–41.

Ogle, K. S., and S. Davis. "Mastitis in lactating women." *Journal of Family Practice* 26, vol. 2 (1988): 139–44.

O'Hara, M. W. "Social support, life events, and depression during pregnancy and the puerperium." *Archives of General Psychiatry* 43 (1986): 569–73.

O'Hara, M. W. "A prospective study of postpartum depression: A test of cognitive and behavioral theories." Ph.D. diss., University of Pittsburgh, 1980.

O'Hara, M. W., D. J. Neunaber, and E. M. Zekoski. "Prospective study of postpartum depression: Prevalence, course, and predictive factors." *Journal of Abnormal Psychology* 93, vol. 2 (1984): 158–71.

O'Hara, M. W., L. P. Rehm and S. B. Campbell. "Postpartum depression: A role for social network and life stress variables." *Journal of Nervous Mental Disorders* 171 (1983): 335–41.

Olson, David H., and Brent C. Miller. *Family Studies*, Review Yearbook, Vol. 1. Beverly Hills: Sage Publications, 1983.

Osofsky, J. D., and H. J. Osofsky. "Psychological and developmental perspectives on expectant and new parenthood." In *Review of Child development Research: The Family,* vol. 7., edited by R. D. Parke. Chicago: University of Chicago Press, 1984, 372–97.

Parke, R. D. "Perspectives on father-infant interaction." In *Handbook of Infant Development,* edited by J. D. Osofsky. New York: Wiley, 1979.

Paschall N., and N. Newton. "Personality factors and postpartum adjustment." *Primary Care* 3, vol. 4 (1976): 741–50.

Pasley, K., and M. Ihinger-Tallman, editors. *Remarriage and Step-parenting: Current Research and Theory.* New York: Guilford Press, 1987

Passmore, C. M., J. C. McElnay, and P. F. D'Arcy. "Drugs taken by mothers in the puerperium: Inpatient survey in Northern Ireland." *British Medical Journal* (1984): 289.

Paxson, David. President, World Population Balance. Interview with the author. Richfield, Minnesota, June 1995.

Paykel, E. S., E. M. Emms, J. Flectcher, and E. S. Rassaby. "Life events and social support in puerperal depression." *British Journal of Psychiatry* 136 (1980): 339–46.

Peale, Ruth Stafford. *Secrets of Staying in Love.* Carmel: Guideposts, 1994.

Pearsall, Paul. *Super Marital Sex/Loving for Life.* New York: Doubleday, 1987.

Pederson, F. "Change in positive marital sentiment during the transition to parenthood." Poster presented at the Conference on Human Development, Richmond, Virginia, 1990.

Pernoll, Martin L., editor. *Current Obstetrical and Gynecologic Diagnosis and Treatment.* Norwalk, California: Appleton & Lange, 1991.

Peterson, K. "New Moms in Work Force Now the Norm." *USA Today* (16 June 1988): 1A.

Peterson, J., and C. Nord. "The regular receipt of child support: A multi-step process." *Journal of Marriage and the Family* 52 (1990): 529–52.

Peterson J. L., and N. Zill. "Marital disruption, parent-child relationships and behavior problems in children." *Journal of Marriage and the Family* 48 (1986): 295–307.

Piaget, J. *Six Psychological Studies.* Edited by D. Elkind. New York: Random House, 1967.

Pistang, N. "Women's work involvement and experience of new motherhood." *Journal of Marriage and the Family* (May 1984): 433–47.

"Postpartum Education for Parents." *Journal of Professional and Personal Enrichment* (1994): 9.

Power, T. B., and R. D. Parke. "Social network factors and the transition to parenthood." *Sex Roles* 10 (1984): 949–72.

Radloff, L. "Sex differences in depression: The effects of occupation and marital status." *Sex Roles* 1 (1977): 429–265.

Rausch, H. L., W. A. Barr, R. K. Hertel, and M. A. Swain. *Communication, Conflict and Marriage.* San Francisco: Jossey-Bass, 1974.

Reamy, K. J., and S. E. White. "Sexuality in the puerperium: A review." *Archives of Sexual Behavior* 16 (1987): 165–186.

Resnick, R. "E-Mail Goes Female." *Ladies' Home Journal* (May 1994): 100.

Rhodes, Sonya, and Joslen Wilson. *Surviving Family Life: the Seven Crises of Living Together.* New York: G. P. Putnams Sons, 1981, 72, 73.

Riley, Glenda. *Divorce, An American Tradition.* New York: Oxford Press, 1991.

Roberts, G., H. H. Block, and J. Block. "Continuity and change in parents' child rearing practices." *Child Development* 55 (1984): 586–97.

Robins, P., and K. Dickinson. "Receipt of child support by single-parent families." *Social Science Review* 58 (1984): 622–41.

Robson, K. M., H. A. Brant, and R. Kumar. "Maternal sexuality during first pregnancy and after childbirth." *British Journal of Obstetrics and Gynecology* 88 (1981): 882–889.

Romalis, Shelly, ed. "An Overview." *Childbirth: Alternatives to Medical Control.* Austin: University of Texas Press, 1981.

Roper Storch Organization. "Virginia Slims Opinion Poll: A 25-Year Perspective of Women's Issues." New York: Phillip Morris, 1995.

Rosen, Mortimer, and Lillian Thomas. *The Cesarean Myth.* New York: Viking/Penguin, 1989.

Roth, A. "The tender years presumption in child custody disputes." *Journal of Family Law* 15 (1976–77): 423–61.

Rubin, Nancy. "When Kids See You Fight." *Parents Magazine* (July 1989): 73–8.

Rubinstein, Carin. "The Baby Bomb." *New York Times Good Health Magazine* (8 October 8, 1988): 34.

Russell, C. "Transition to parenthood: Problems and Gratifications." *Journal of Marriage and the Family* 36 (1974): 294–302.

Rutter, M. "Sex differences in children's responses to family stress." In *The Child in His Family*, vol. 1, edited by E. J. Anthony and C. Koupernik. New York: Wiley, 1970.

Sarbin, T. R., and V. L. Allen. "Role Theory." In *The Handbook of Social Psychology*, 2nd ed., vol. 1, edited by G. Lindzey and E. Aronson. Reading, Massachusetts: Addison Wesley, 1968. 488–567.

Schram, R. W. "Marital satisfaction over the family life cycle: A critique and proposal." *Journal of Marriage and the Family*, 1979.

Schrof, Joanne M., with Betsy Wagner. "Sex in America." *U.S. News and World Report* (17 October 1994): 74.

Schumacher, H. R. Jr., B. B. Dorwart, and O. M. Korzeniowski. "Occurrence of de Quervain's tendinitis during pregnancy." *Archives of Internal Medicine* 145, vol. 2 (1985): 2083–84.

Schwartz, P. J. *Peer Marriage: How Love Between Equals Really Works.* New York: Free Press, 1994.

Selbert, Kim. *Childbirth Choices in Mothers' Words.* Bedford, Massachusetts: Mills and Sanderson, 1990.

Seltzer, J. A. "Relationships between fathers and children who live apart: The father's role after separation." *Journal of Marriage and the Family* 53 (1991): 79–101.

Shereshefsky, P. M., and Leon J. Yarrow. *Psychological Aspects of a First Pregnancy and Early Postnatal Adaptation.* New York: Raven, 1973.

Sirignano, S. W., and M. E. Lachman. "Personality change during the transition to parenthood: The role of perceived infant temperament." *Developmental Psychology* 21, vol. 3 (1985): 558–67.

Slater, E., K. J. Steward, and M. W. Linn. "The effects of family disruption on adolescent males and females." *Adolescence* 18 (1983): 931–42.

Spanier, Graham B., and Linda Thompson. In *Dynamics of Divorce: A Life Cycle Perspective*, edited by Florence W. Kaslow and Lita Linzer Schwartz. New York: Brunner/Mazel, 1987.

Snowden, L., T. Schott, S. Auolt, and J. Gillis-Knox. "Marital satisfaction in pregnancy: Stability and change." *Journal of Marriage and the Family* 50 (1988): 325–333.

Spiegel, J. S., B. Leake, T. M. Spiegel, et al. "What are we measuring? An examination of self-reported functional status measure." *Arthritis Rheumatoid* 31, vol. 6 (1988): 721–728.

Stanley, Charles. *How to Keep Your Kids on Your Team.* Nashville: Thomas Nelson Publishers, 1986.

———. *The Making of a Marriage.* Nashville: Thomas Nelson Publishers, 1993.

Steffensmeier, R. "A role model of the transition to parenthood." *Journal of Marriage and the Family* 43 (1982): 319–34

Stewart, Felicia H., Felicia Hance Stewart, Gary Stewart, and Robert A. Hatcher. *Understanding Your Body: Every Woman's Guide to a Lifetime of Health.* New York: Bantam Doubleday, 1990.

Stewart, Mary, and Pat Erickson. "The Sociology of Birth: A critical assessment of Theory and Research." *Social Sciences Journal* 14 (April 1977): 33–47.

Stolberg, A. L., and J. M. Anker. "Cognitive and behavioral changes in children resulting from parental divorce and consequent environmental changes." *Journal of Divorce* 7 (1983): 23–37.

Stoop, David, and Jan Stoop. *The Intimacy Factor.* Nashville: Thomas Nelson Publishers, 1993.

Talley, James, and Leslie Stobbe. *Reconcilable Differences.* Nashville: Thomas Nelson Publishers, 1991.

Tannen, D. *You Just Don't Understand.* New York: William Morrow, 1990.

Teachman, J. D. "Who pays? Receipt of child support in U.S." *Journal of Marriage and the Family* 53 (1991): 759–72.

Thompson, Anthony P. "Extra marital sex: A review of the research literature." *Journal of Sex Research* 19, vol. 1 (1983): 1–22.

Thompson, R. A. "Fathers and the child's 'best interests': Judicial decision-making in custody disputes." In *The Father's Role: Applied Perspectives,* edited by M. Lamb. New York: Wiley, 1986.

Tulman L., and J. Fawcett. "Recovery from childbirth, looking back six months after delivery." *Health Care Women International* 12 (1991): 341–350.

Turner, R. H. "The Role and the Person." *American Journal of Sociology* 84, vol. 1 (1978): 1–23.

"Two Studies Paint a Bleak Childhood." Gallup Organization Study from August and September 1995 in the *New York Times,* as cited in the *Minneapolis Star Tribune,* 7 December 1995.

Uhlenberg, P. "Death and the family." *Journal of Family History* 5 (1980): 313–20.

Ulbrich, Patricia M. "Work at home and on the job: role overload reconsidered." Paper presented at the Annual Meeting of the American Sociological Association, Los Angeles, CA, 7 August 1994.

United States Bureau of the Census. Current Population Reports, Series P-60, Nos. 173 and 181, *Poverty in the United States.* Washington D.C.: United States Government Printing Office, 1992.

United States Bureau of Census. *Child Support and Alimony.* Washington, D.C.: United States Government Printing Office, 1989.

United States Bureau of Census. Current Populations Reports, P23-180, *Marriage, di-*

vorce, and remarriage in the 1990s. Washington D.C.: United States Government Printing Office, 1992.

United States Congress, House Committee on Ways and Means, Subcommittee on Human Resources. *The child support enforcement policy program: Policy and practice.* WMCP 101-19. Washington, D. C.: Congressional Research Service, 1989.

United States Congress. Mathematica Policy Research. *Income withholding, medical support, and services to non-AFCD cases after the Child Support Enforcement Amendments of 1984.* Princeton, New Jersey: Mathematica Policy Research, 1991.

United States Department of Health and Human Services, *Vital Statistics Report,* Vol. 42, No. 3. Washington D.C.: U.S. Government Printing Office, 1993.

United States Department of Health, Education and Welfare. *Divorce and Divorce Rates,* US 1978,. Pub. No. (PHS)78-1907. Washington D.C.: U.S. Government Printing Offices, 1993.

United States Department of Health and Human Services, *Vital Statistics Report, Final Divorce Statistics 1976.* Washington D.C.: U.S. Government Printing Offices, August 16, 1978.

United States Department of Health and Human Services. *Monthly Vital Statistics Report, Provisional Data.* Washington D.C.: National Center for Health Statistics, Volume 40, No. 1, May 16, 1991.

Vanton, Monte. *Grounds for Divorce.* Burbank: Victoria Press, 1977.

Veroff, J., E. Douvan, and R. Kulka. *The Inner American: A Self-portrait From 1957 To 1976.* New York: Basic Books, 1981.

Wainwright, W. H. "Fatherhood as a precipitant of mental illness." *American Journal of Psychiatry* 123 (July 1966): 40.

Walbroehl, G. S. "Sexuality During Pregnancy." *American Family Physician* 29, vol. 5 (1984): 273–5.

Waldron, H., and D. K. Routh. "The effect of the first child on the marital relationship." *Journal of Marriage and the Family* 43, vol. 4 (1981): 785–8.

Waldron, I. "Employment and women's health: An analysis of causal relationships." *International Journal of Health Services* 10, vol. 3 (1980): 435–54.

Wallace, P., and I. Gotlib. "Marital adjustment during the transition to parenthood: Stability and predictors of change." *Journal of Marriage and the Family* 52 (1990): 21–29.

Wallerstein, Judith S. "Children of divorce: Preliminary report of a ten-year follow up of young children." *American Journal of Orthopsychiatry* 54 (1984): 444-58.

———. "Children of divorce: Preliminary report of a ten year follow up of young children." *American Journal of Orthopsychiatry* 24 (1985): 545–53.

———. "Children of divorce: Preliminary report of ten year follow up of young children." *American Journal of Orthopsychiatry* 57 (1987): 119–212.

Wallerstein, Judith S., and Sandra Blakeslee. *Second Chances: Men, Women, and Children a Decade After Divorce.* New York: Ticknor & Fields, 1989.

———. *The Good Marriage: How and Why Love Lasts.* New York: Warner, 1995.

Wallerstein, Judith S., and S. Corbin. "Father-child relationship after divorce: Child support and educational Opportunity." *Family Law Quarterly* 20 (1986): 109–28.

Wallerstein, Judith S., and J. B. Kelly. *Surviving the Breakup: How Children and Parents Cope With Divorce.* New York: Basic Books, 1980.

Walter, Carolyn Ambler. *The Timing of Motherhood/Is Later Better?* Lexington, Massachusetts: Heath Company, 1987.

Wandersman, L. P. "Parent-infant support groups: Matching programs to needs and strengths of families." In *Research on support for parents in the postnatal period,* edited by C. F. Zachariah Boukydis. Norwood, NF: Ablex, 1987.

Wangerin, Walter Jr. *As For Me and My House.* Nashville: Thomas Nelson Publishers, 1990.

Warner, H. *The Comparative Psychology of Mental Development.* New York: Follett, 1948.

Wenner, N. K., M. B. Cohen, E. V. Weigert, R. G. Kvarnes, E. M. Ohaneson, and J. M. Fearing. "Emotional problems in pregnancy." *Psychiatry* 32 (1969): 389–410.

Werner, H. *The Comparative Psychology of Mental Development.* New York: Follett, 1948.

Wetzler, H. P., and R. J. Ursano. "A positive association between physical health practices and psychological well-being." *Journal of Nervous and Mental Disorders* 176, vol. 5 (1988): 280–83.

Whelan, E. M. *A Baby? Maybe: A Guide to Making the Most Fateful Decision of Your Life.* New York: Bobbs-Merrill, 1975.

White, Lynn. Sociologist, University of Nebraska: The National Institute on Aging, 1982.

Wile, D. B. *Couples Therapy: A Nontraditional Approach.* New York: Wiley, 1981.

Williams, H. E., and A. Carmachael. "Depression in mothers with infants and young children: Its social origins and effects." *Australian Paediatrics Journal* 17, vol. 2 (1981): 126.

Wolkind, S., E. Z. Coleman, and M. Ghodsian. "Continuities in maternal depression." *International Journal of Family Psychiatry* 1 (1980): 167–81.

Wright P., S. Henggeler, and L. Craig. "Problems in Paradise? A longitudinal examination of the transition to parenthood." *Journal of Applied Developmental Psychology* 7 (1986): 277–91.

Yalom, I. D., D. T. Lunde, and R. H. Moos. "'Postpartum blues' syndrome: A description and related variables." *Archives of General Psychiatry* 18, vol. 1 (1968): 16–27.

Zajicek, E. "The experience of being pregnant." In *Pregnancy: A Psychological and Social Study,* edited by Eva Wolkind and Stephen and Zajicek. New York: Academic Press, 1981.

Zaslow, M., F. Pedersen, E. Kramer, R. Cain, J. Suwalsky, and M. I. Fivel. "Depressed mood in new fathers: Interview and behavioral correlates." 1981.

Ziglar, Zig. *Courtship After Marriage.* New York: Ballantine Books, 1991.

———. *Raising Positive Kids* in a Negative World, New York: Ballantine Books, 1985.

Index

Action plan, 157–158
Amato, Paul, 182–183, 190
American Academy of Matrimonial
  Lawyers, 195
American Medical Association, 115
The American Way of Birth (Eakins), 20

Baby
  attention given to, 26–28
  becoming slaves to, 127–128
  birth of. *See* Childbirth
  blame and, 6–7
  caring for. *See* Baby care
  having
    decision regarding, 37–38
    rewards of, 199–205
  sex of, 40–41
  See also Child, children
Baby blues, 66–67, 75
Baby care, 81–82, 83–84
  battle for time and, 84, 87–89
  becoming slaves to baby and, 127–128
  expectations regarding, 20
  mother's demand for more help and,
    90–92
  postpartum depression and, 71
  responsibility for
    division of labor and, 83–84, 91
    fairness and, 84–87
    squabbles about, as smoke screen,
      102–103
    working toward change and, 96–102
  tag-team parenting and, 89
Barr, Maxwell, 6

Behaviors of love, 160–162
  choosing to practice, 164–166
Being alive, core of, 204–205
Belsky, Jay, 86–87, 124
Breast(s)
  concerns about, during
    physical healing, 58
  feeding baby and, 71, 78, 88, 120, 125
  lovemaking and, 119–120, 125–126
  prolactin and, 75

Career, choices regarding,
  postpartum depression and, 72–73
Carnegie Task Force, 180
Census Bureau, 21, 177
Child, children
  birth of. *See* Childbirth
  care of, choices regarding, postpartum
    depression and, 72–73. *See also* Baby
    care
  child support and, 188–189
  custody of, 184–188
  divorce and. *See* Divorce, children and
  staying together for, 190–195
  See also Baby
Childbirth
  bad experience during, postpartum de-
    pression and, 72
  conflicts after. *See* Conflicts after child-
    birth
  crisis after, 11–12
  depression after. *See* Postpartum depres-
    sion
  episiotomy during, 56

229

❧
Acknowledgments

I would like to thank my literary agent, Jane Dystel, and her editorial assistant, Susanna Kirk.

I would also like to thank the following parents who opened up their hearts and homes to me: Jeannie and Tom, Carol and Ted, Neil and Anne, Paul and Teresa Kruse, Don and Mary, Lisa and Rick, Dr. Arnold, Jack and Denise, Peter and Monica, Bill and Linda, Lisa and Rod, Judy, Becky and Mark, John, Christopher, Patty and Jon, Connie and Brad, Mary and Steve, Jane and Ben, Ellen and Will, Janet and Matt, Edward, Jerry and Suzie, Nancy and Roger, Susan and Michael, Philip and Jennifer, Rachel and Dan, Mindy and Tim, Karen and Jim, Marci and Joe, Pam, Frank and Margie, Kate and Alex, Scott and Michelle, Laura and Doug, Corinne and Sam, Debra and Robert, Deb and Terry, Cari and Jeff, Joleen and Jeff, Connie and Steve, Cara and Jeff, Nancy and Marty, James and Mary, Barbara and John, Marilyn Miller, Kaye Peters, Wheelock Whitney, Rita and Bob; as well as countless others I interviewed but do not name specifically.

A special thank you for the support from Dr. Andrea Larsen; Shirley Dixon; Dr. Daniel Nordby; Linda Kleven; Dr. John Martin; Pastor John Crosby; Marianne Espinosa Murphy; Dr. William Galston; Carol Linkins; Tom Pritchard; Morgan Brown; Sylvia Hewlett; Peggy Shiller; Dr. David Walsh; Misti Snow; Wade Horn, Ph.D., President of the National Fatherhood Initiative; as well as many others, unnamed, who lent me their ears and their expertise.

I would like to thank my parents, Leslie and Gertrude Kruse. They created the home that provided the basis of comparison for the material in this book. I also thank my sister and brother and their families, my "in-laws" who ceased being "out-laws" years ago, and the countless friends who offered their support and listened patiently as I rambled incessantly about a topic that grew to be an integral part of my life.

Lastly, I thank my editor, Camille Cline, and her associates at Taylor Publishing—Tonya Curtis, Eileen Smith, Anita Edson, Jim Green, Barbara Werden, Julie Kacala, and Delia Guzman. Thanks also to Janis Owens for the book design and to Mike Stromberg for the cover design. I will be forever grateful for their contributions and their faith in my work.

~

About the Author

Rhonda Kruse Nordin is an advocate for the well-being of today's families. Through *Children First,* a community-wide partnership dedicated to helping children build developmental assets, Rhonda interfaces with community and business leaders, health care workers, educators, and parents to create initiatives that strengthen families. She is responsible for bringing *Partners for Students* (a ten-week curriculum designed by the American Bar Association) into area high schools. Rhonda frequently speaks at religious, community, and corporate events. She lives with her husband Bruce and their two sons in Minneapolis, Minnesota.

Dr. Dwenda K. Gjerdingen has served as medical advisor for this book. A doctor, researcher, author, and teacher, Dr. Gjerdingen's focus for over two decades has been women's prenatal and postpartum physical and mental health. She is Associate Professor in the Department of Family Practice and Community Health at the University of Minnesota Medical School and is on staff at Bethesda Clinic; both institutions are in St. Paul, Minnesota. Dr. Gjerdingen lives with her husband and two sons in St. Paul, Minnesota.

HE DID IT
ALL FOR
YOU

KENNETH & GLORIA COPELAND

KENNETH
COPELAND
PUBLICATIONS

Unless otherwise noted, all scripture is from the *King James Version* of the Bible.

Scripture quotations marked *The Amplified Bible* are from *The Amplified Bible, Old Testament* © 1965, 1987 by the Zondervan Corporation. *The Amplified New Testament* © 1958, 1987 by The Lockman Foundation. Used by permission.

Scripture quotations marked *New King James Version* are from the *New King James Version* © 1982 by Thomas Nelson Inc.

He Did It All for You
A compilation of five previously published books:
Welcome to the Family
God's Will Is the Holy Spirit
Now Are We in Christ Jesus
The Force of Righteousness
Love—The Secret to Your Success

ISBN-10 1-57562-814-7   30-0739
ISBN-13 978-1-57562-814-1

15 14 13 12 11 10   10 9 8 7 6 5

Kenneth Copeland Publications
Fort Worth, TX 76192-0001

For more information about Kenneth Copeland Ministries, call 800-600-7395 or visit www.kcm.org.

Table of Contents

chapter 1

WELCOME TO THE FAMILY

by Kenneth Copeland

Welcome to the Family

God loves you and cares for you

...so much that He sent His only Son, Jesus, to be a sacrifice for you.

...so much that He sent His precious Holy Spirit into the earth to be your comforter and teacher.

...so much that He has provided for you to live free from sickness and disease.

God desires the very best for you! You can begin today to receive His best in your life.

God's Word says it's yours, so get ready to receive!

How to Become a Christian

Do you know where you stand with God?

If you have never made Jesus the Lord of your life, then you are separated from God by sin. You are the reason God sent Jesus to the cross. John 3:16 says, "For God so loved the world, that he gave his only begotten Son, that whosoever believeth in him should not perish, but have everlasting life." God loved you so much that He gave His only begotten Son for you.

Second Corinthians 5:21 says that God made Jesus, who knew no sin, to be sin for us. Jesus was the spotless Son of God. Sin was the reason He came to earth. He died on the Cross and went to hell for one reason: to pay the price for sin. Once that price was paid, Jesus was raised from the dead, triumphant over Satan, and the sin problem was taken care of.

God does not hold your sin against you. The only thing keeping you from becoming a child of God is failure to turn from your present world and your present god—Satan—and make Jesus the Lord over your life.

When Jesus paid the sin price for you, He became your substitute. Heaven has it recorded that you died on that cross over 2,000 years ago. You have been set free. But that doesn't mean you will automatically go to heaven. Even though God sent Jesus to pay for your sin—even though He holds nothing against you—you can still go straight to hell. Why? Because you have not made the choice to receive Jesus as your personal Lord and Savior—to accept His sacrifice as yours.

You have a free will—the right to choose your own destiny. God will not force you to receive salvation. The choice is yours. You can go straight to hell and God will not lift a finger to stop you. He did all He is going to do when He sent Jesus into the world.

The choice is set before you.

If you do choose to make Jesus your Lord, God will receive you as His very own child. You will become a part of His family. He will be your Father and you will be His child. This is not just a theological idea. It is a fact. It actually happens.

Jesus actually walked the earth as a man, went to the cross, died there, was raised from the dead, and is alive today. He is seated at the right hand of God in heaven.

When you become a Christian—or born again—you take on His nature, the nature of God, your heavenly Father. The nature of sin and Satan is death but the nature of God is life. Jesus spoke to the people of His day saying, "Ye are of your father the devil..." (John 8:44). When you accept Jesus as your Lord, you are turning your back on your father the devil, or on "the god of this world," as Satan is called (2 Corinthians 4:4). You take on a new Father, a heavenly Father, and you are born again—not physically, but spiritually. Your spirit is reborn in the likeness of God.

You see, you are a threefold being: You are a spirit, you have a soul (mind, will, emotions), and you live in a body. Jesus referred to this in a conversation with Nicodemus (John 3:3-7). Jesus said to him, "You must be born again."

Nicodemus replied, "What do you mean? Do I have to go back again into my mother's womb?" Jesus answered, "No. What is born of the flesh is flesh. What is born of the Spirit is spirit."

Being born again is a spiritual rebirth. You are born of the Spirit of God. The Holy Spirit was sent into the earth to carry out this new birth. When you make Jesus the Lord of your life, the Holy Spirit comes to indwell you and causes your own spirit to be re-created. According to 2 Corinthians 5:17, when you accept Jesus as your Lord, you become a new creature, or new creation—old things pass away and all things become new. As far as God is concerned, at that moment you stand before Him as a brand new person. You are reborn from sin and death to righteousness and new life. First John 5:1, 4 says, "Whosoever believeth that Jesus is the Christ is born of God.... For whatsoever is born of God overcometh the world: and this is the victory that overcometh the world, even our faith."

I want you to realize what happens the moment you make Jesus Christ the Lord of your life. In the eyes of God, you become a world overcomer. Sin no longer reigns over your life. It is no longer your lord. Jesus is your Lord, and you can live above the satanic forces in the world.

After Jesus was raised from the dead, He stood before His disciples and said, "All power is given unto me in heaven and in earth" (Matthew 28:18). Then He delegated that power to His people, saying, "Go ye into all the world, and preach the gospel to every creature" (Mark 16:15). What is the gospel? The good news that God is no longer holding your sins and trespasses against you.

The Bible gives some specific instructions you are to follow to become a Christian, or in order to be born again. Look at Romans 10:8-11:

> The word is nigh thee, even in thy mouth, and in thy heart: that is, the word of faith, which we preach; that if thou shalt confess with thy mouth the Lord Jesus, and shalt believe in thine heart that God hath raised him from the dead, thou shalt be saved. For with the heart man believeth unto righteousness; and with the mouth confession is made unto salvation. For the scripture saith, Whosoever believeth on him shall not be ashamed.

Jesus said, "...Him that cometh to me I will in no wise cast out" (John 6:37). No matter what kind of sinner you are, no matter what you have done, you can come to Jesus and He will accept you. He will cause you to be born again—to be re-created. And that sin which has been plaguing you will be a thing of the past—gone. You'll be accepted before God as if you had never sinned!

To be born again, you must use your mouth and your heart. First, believe in your heart that God's Word is true. Then confess it with your mouth because you believe it (see Romans 10:9-10).

I want you to realize one very important fact: You don't confess you're saved because you feel saved. Feelings have absolutely nothing to do with salvation. Let me give you an example.

Suppose someone says to you, "I went to the bank this morning and deposited $1,000 in your account." How do you know they actually did what they said? You don't believe they did it because you feel $1,000 richer, and you don't doubt them just because you don't feel any different. Your feelings really have nothing to do with it. If that person's word is good, you'll believe him. If his word is bad, you won't.

When your salvation is involved, you are relying on God's Word—and He doesn't lie. He means what He says. If He said it, then you can believe it. He has said that if you believe in your heart and confess with your mouth that Jesus is Lord, you will be saved. You don't base your salvation on the way you feel. You base it on the pure, unadulterated Word of Almighty God.

God's Word is the only evidence you have that you are saved, but that's all the evidence you need!

Several days or weeks from now, you may not feel very saved. You may begin to wonder if you were ever really saved to start with. You will have doubts—Satan will see to that! But when those thoughts and feelings come, just go back to the Word of God. You'll see that it still says the same thing. God never changes and His Word never changes. It is just as true today as when it was first spoken. People may try to convince you that it didn't work. Temptations may come to convince you that it didn't work. Doubts may come to your mind. But none of those things alter the fact that God's Word is true.

Jesus said, "...I am come that they might have life, and that they might have it more abundantly" (John 10:10). The moment you make Jesus the Lord of your life will be the moment you have a desire to live and not die.

I can testify to that fact in my own life. Before I accepted Jesus as my Lord, I was headed straight for hell. Everything I liked to do was bad for me. The habits I had formed for 25 years were destructive to my body and my mind. But when I made Jesus the Lord of my life, all those desires changed. I suddenly had a desire to get rid of my filthy habits. I wanted to get rid of tobacco, alcohol, immoral thoughts and behavior, profanity, etc. Why? Because I was changed. The real me, my spirit, was reborn. The change in my spirit brought changes to my mind and body.

These changes are available to you, too. God is right there, ready to accept and change you. You don't have to live in sin any longer. You don't have to live a defeated life any longer. You don't have to be anything except God's child. You can walk the road of life victoriously with Jesus as your Lord and Savior. You don't have to take a back seat to Satan ever again. You can be the head and not the tail!

I want you to join me now in praying this prayer for salvation. Don't just read it. Make a conscious effort to speak these words from the very depths of your being. When you finish this prayer, you will be born again:

> Heavenly Father, in the Name of Jesus, I present myself to You. I pray and ask Jesus to be Lord over my life. I believe it in my heart, so I say it with my mouth: "Jesus has been raised from the dead." This moment, I make Him the Lord over my life. Jesus, come into my heart. I believe this moment that I am saved. I say it now: "I am reborn. I am a Christian. I am a child of Almighty God."

Now, thank God for making you His child. Colossians 1:12 says, "Giving thanks unto the Father, which hath made us meet to be partakers of the inheritance of the saints in light." You have just been made a partaker of an inheritance from God. *You have just inherited the kingdom of God!*

You don't have to wait until you die to receive your inheritance. You are a child of God right this very moment, and you can receive all that belongs to you right now! First John 3:2 says, "Beloved, *now* are we the sons of God." You have been delivered from darkness into the kingdom of God.

Jesus said, "Fear not, little flock; for it is your Father's good pleasure to give you the kingdom" (Luke 12:32).

I welcome you into the family of God!

Now as part of the family, you'll need to know more about your Father—the One who has changed you and made you new through the power of His Spirit. You'll want to find out what's yours and how to walk in it.

In the next chapter, Gloria will show you how you can receive one of His greatest blessings, the same power and anointing that was on Jesus Himself, to empower you to be a success in your new life. You'll be full of His joy and overcoming power—victorious in all you set your hand to do.

GOD'S WILL
IS THE
HOLY SPIRIT

by Gloria Copeland

God's Will Is the Holy Spirit

You have been involved with the Holy Spirit since you first heard the good news that Jesus took your place and bore the penalty for your sins. It was the Holy Spirit, through the Word, who made the truth that Jesus was raised from the dead a reality in your heart.

Romans 10:9 says, "That if thou shalt confess with thy mouth the Lord Jesus, and shalt believe in thine heart that God hath raised him from the dead, thou shalt be saved." First Corinthians 12:3 says that no man can say Jesus is Lord except by the Holy Spirit.

Jesus came to make it possible for man to receive the nature of God—eternal life (John 10:10). A man could not be born again while Jesus was on the earth. He had power to forgive sins, but there could be no new creatures until He paid the sin price at Calvary and became the firstborn from the dead.

> Nevertheless I tell you the truth; It is expedient for you that I go away: for if I go not away, the Comforter will not come unto you; but if I depart, I will send him unto you…. I have yet many things to say unto you, but ye cannot bear them now. Howbeit when he, the Spirit of truth, is come, he will guide you into all truth: for he shall not speak of himself; but whatsoever he shall hear, that shall he speak: and he will show you things to come. He shall glorify me: for he shall receive of mine, and shall show it unto you. All things that the Father hath are mine: therefore said I, that he shall take of mine, and shall show it unto you (John 16:7, 12-15).

Jesus told the men who walked by His side for three years that it was more profitable for them if He went away and sent them the Holy Spirit.

It was the miraculous work of the Holy Spirit that made you a new creature. When you made Jesus Lord over your life, the Holy Spirit came on you and overshadowed you, just as He did Mary when there was conceived in her a "holy thing" (Luke 1:35).

You were born again to a new life, a new spirit. Spiritual death was eradicated from your spirit. You were literally born of God. "Beloved, *now* are we the sons of God" (1 John 3:2). "Whosoever believeth that Jesus is the Christ is born of God" (1 John 5:1). God became your Father by spiritual birth.

The miracle of the new birth should never become commonplace to you. It is not a theological idea, but a fact. The Holy Spirit personally carries out this miracle when you make Jesus Christ your Lord. He takes a sin-ridden, selfish man and re-creates his spirit in God's image. This change in a man's nature is a great, miraculous and supernatural event in the realm of the spirit causing all of heaven to rejoice (Luke 15:7, 10).

The Spirit Within

After you make Jesus Lord, the Holy Spirit comes to live in you. Jesus told the disciples: "If ye love me, keep my commandments. And I will pray the Father, and he shall give you another Comforter, that he may abide with you for ever; even the Spirit of truth; whom the world cannot receive, because it seeth him not, neither knoweth him: but ye know him; for he dwelleth with you, and shall be in you" (John 14:15-17). The Holy Spirit had been working *with* the disciples as they had been preaching, healing the sick and casting out devils. But Jesus said when the Holy Spirit came to abide forever, He would live on the *inside* of them.

The ministry of the Holy Spirit is not only to impart the nature of God to the spirit of man, but also to live in the new creature and to reveal to him the exact knowledge of God. The Spirit within enables the new creature to walk in newness of life. One writer said that the Spirit that gives us life must also sustain that life.

Ezekiel 36:26-27 says, "A new heart also will I give you, and a new spirit will I put *within* you: and I will take away the stony heart out of your flesh, and I will give you an heart of flesh. And I will put my spirit within you, and cause you to walk in my statutes, and ye shall keep my judgments, and do them."

After Jesus had been raised from the dead, He appeared to the disciples. They were born again as He breathed the life of God into them, saying, "Receive the Holy Spirit." (Compare with Genesis 2:7.) Eternal life came into them. They could not have been born again until after Jesus paid the price for sin. As they received the life of God, the Spirit who gave that life began to dwell in them.

The Spirit Upon

From that moment they were changed. They were no longer troubled, afraid or sad. Luke's account lets us know of the change: "And it came to pass, while he blessed them, he was parted from them, and carried up into heaven. And they worshipped him, and returned to Jerusalem with great joy: and were continually in the temple, praising and blessing God. Amen" (Luke 24:51-53).

Where there had been sadness, now there was great joy—fruit of the spirit. Where there had been fear and confusion, now there was continual praise and blessing of God. And they were obedient. They went to Jerusalem and waited for the enduement of power from on high expecting to receive the promise of the Father (Acts 1:4-5).

This promise was for yet another wonderful event to come. Just before Jesus blessed the disciples and was carried into heaven He gave these instructions: "And, behold, I send the promise of my Father upon you: but tarry ye in the city of Jerusalem, until ye be endued with power from on high" (Luke 24:49). The account of this event in Acts says:

And, being assembled together with them, commanded them that they should not depart from Jerusalem, but wait for the promise of the Father, which, saith he, ye have heard of me. For John truly baptized with water; but ye shall be baptized with the Holy Ghost not many days hence.... Ye shall receive power, after that the Holy Ghost is come upon you: and ye shall be witnesses unto me both in Jerusalem, and in all Judea, and in Samaria, and unto the uttermost part of the earth (Acts 1:4-5, 8).

He said they were to be baptized with the Holy Ghost and receive power! They had already received the Holy Spirit within. Now Jesus was instructing them what to do to receive the power of God *upon* them. Acts 10:38 says Jesus was anointed with the Holy Ghost and power. The disciples were to receive that same power of the Holy Spirit!

Jesus said in our everyday speech, "Don't leave town without it!" This enduement of power was necessary in order to carry out the work Jesus set before them. (See Mark 16:15-20; Matthew 28:18-20.) Nothing has changed. The Body of Christ today is still under the same mandate.

Jesus had taught them about these works in John 14, talking to them about the Holy Spirit. He said,

Believest thou not that I am in the Father, and the Father in me? the words that I speak unto you I speak not of myself: but the Father that dwelleth in me, he doeth the works.... Verily, verily, I say unto you, he that believeth on me, the works that I do shall he do also; and greater works than these shall he do; because I go unto my Father (John 14:10, 12).

The disciples were to continue doing the same works Jesus Himself had been doing. It would take the same power and anointing of the Holy Spirit that was on Jesus Himself. (See Acts 10:38; Matthew 3:16-17; John 14:12; Luke 4:18-21; Acts 5:12-16.)

This power came on the Church on the Day of Pentecost. The

Holy Spirit is still assigned to the Church to help us fulfill our commission. Didn't Jesus say He would abide with us forever?

Jesus said it was not Him but the Father in Him who did these works. When He said, "But *ye* shall receive power, after that the Holy Ghost is come upon *you...*" (Acts 1:8), they knew what He meant!

The Greek word *dunamis,* translated *power,* means "ability and might." When you receive the Baptism in the Holy Spirit, you receive the ability of God to do His work on the earth. The Spirit within is for fruit bearing—for your own personal life (Galatians 5:22-23). Jesus talked about this in John 4:14. He called it: "...a well of water springing up into everlasting life." But the Spirit *upon* is for service. Jesus talked about this in John 7:38-39. He described it as rivers of living water. The well is for your own life and the rivers flowing out of you are for others.

The dictionary says a *witness* is "evidence or confirmation." This power of the Holy Spirit living in you can transform your life into evidence for the world that Jesus has been raised from the dead and is alive today. Jesus said, "But ye shall receive power, after that the Holy Ghost is come upon you: and ye shall be witnesses unto me..." (Acts 1:8).

The traditions and doctrines of men have robbed many believers of this power to be a witness with evidence that Jesus has been raised from the dead. The world is not only supposed to hear words but see proof that Jesus is alive today. New converts should be taught to receive the Baptism in the Holy Spirit—the enduement of power to reveal Jesus to lost humanity.

Many believe He is automatically received at the time of salvation—that there is nothing more. It is certainly true that if you are born again, the Holy Spirit has come to live in you and endeavors to work in your life. I had been born again and the Holy Spirit lived inside me, but the power Jesus spoke of was not evident in my life until after I received the Baptism in the Holy Spirit. I wanted to do right, follow God and be a strong Christian, but outwardly I didn't change much until after I received the Baptism in the Holy Spirit and began to speak in other tongues. Then, the combination of the power of God upon me and the Word of God in my heart began to change weakness to victory. As I learned truth from God's Word and acted on it, the Spirit of God upon me enabled me to overcome in my own life and to help others overcome.

Learn to continually pray this prayer from Ephesians for yourself:

> For this cause I bow my knees unto the Father of our Lord Jesus Christ, of whom the whole family in heaven and earth is named, that he would grant [me], according to the riches of his glory, to be strengthened with might by his Spirit in [my] inner man; that Christ may dwell in [my heart] by faith; that [I], being rooted and grounded in love, may be able to comprehend with all saints what is the breadth, and length, and depth, and height; and to know the love of Christ, which passeth knowledge, that [I] might be filled with all the fulness of God. Now unto him that is able to do exceeding abundantly above all that [I] ask or think, according to the power that worketh in [me], unto him be glory in the church by Christ Jesus throughout all ages, world without end. Amen (Ephesians 3:14-21).

According to the power that worketh in us! His unlimited ability to work in your life is according to the power working in you. God designed that He would abide continually inside your spirit and then come upon you in power to carry out His work.

In the early Church, much of the time people were born again and received the Baptism in the Holy Spirit at the same time. In Acts 8, however, we can clearly see the two separate experiences. It tells us that Philip, while in Samaria, preached the things concerning the kingdom of God and the Name of Jesus. Verse 12 says they believed, and both men and women were baptized. These people were believers.

Later, Peter and John came to pray for them that they might receive the Holy Ghost. "(For as yet he was fallen upon none of them: only they were baptized in the name of the Lord Jesus.) Then laid they their hands on them, and they received the Holy Ghost" (Acts 8:16-17).

The term "receiving the Holy Ghost" is also correct in speaking about the Baptism in the Holy Spirit. Later, in chapter 19, Paul asked men at Ephesus, "Have ye received the Holy Ghost since ye believed? And they said unto him, We have not so much as heard whether there be any Holy Ghost" (verse 2).

These men had been baptized into John's baptism. Paul told them that John had said to believe in Jesus. "When they heard this, they were baptized in the name of the Lord Jesus. And when Paul had laid his hands upon them, the Holy Ghost came on them; and they spake with tongues, and prophesied" (Acts 19:5-6). In this instance they were baptized in water and then Paul laid hands on them to receive the Holy Ghost.

From these references we can see that the apostles laid their hands on men who were already believers to receive the Holy Spirit. These scriptures reveal that the enduement of power called the Baptism in the Holy Spirit is not the same experience as the new birth. In these two examples, this enduement of power came as hands were laid on them.

On the Day of Pentecost, however, at the house of Cornelius, the Spirit of God came on the people and they began to speak with other tongues. They received the new birth and the enduement of power simultaneously.

The Baptism in the Holy Spirit is received by faith the same way you receive Jesus as Lord (Galatians 3:14). Christians should be taught to believe for and to receive it. The disciples in the upper room on the Day of Pentecost had already been taught about receiving the Holy Spirit by the Master Himself (Luke 24:49; John 14-16; Acts 1:1-9).

The entrance of God's Word gives light or understanding (Psalm 119:130). The disciples knew that they were waiting for the Holy Spirit to baptize them with His power and were expecting it just as Jesus had told them.

We receive blessing from God by believing what we hear from Him. That is faith. For example, healing belonged to you the moment you were born into God's family, but if you never get into the Word and see that divine health is yours, you will continue to be sick.

To walk the faith walk and be pleasing to God, His Word must be the authority in your life—not what men or traditions say!

Learn to Depend on the Holy Spirit…He Will Guide You Into All Truth

"But as it is written, Eye hath not seen, nor ear heard, neither have entered into the heart of man, the things which God hath prepared for them that love him. But God hath revealed them unto us by his Spirit: for the Spirit searcheth all things, yea, the deep things of God" (1 Corinthians 2:9-10).

Who can know what is on the inside of a man except the man's own spirit, and who can know what is on the inside of God except the Spirit of God? (verse 11). The Spirit of God living within your spirit can reveal to you the inside of God—the heart of the Father. The Holy Spirit, who knows all the deep things of God, desires to come and live in you to teach you the profound and unsearchable wisdom of God.

No man knows the things of God because they are spiritually discerned (1 Corinthians 2:14). "But God hath revealed them unto us by His Spirit" (1 Corinthians 2:10). These deep things of God can enter into the heart of man only by the Spirit of God.

His Word must be revealed to you by His Spirit before you can walk in it because your spirit alone cannot comprehend or see into these deep things. But Jesus said that the Holy Spirit would teach you all things (John 14:26). He told the disciples, "I have yet many things to say unto you, but ye cannot bear them now. Howbeit when he, the Spirit of truth, is come, he will guide you into all truth: for he shall not speak of himself; but whatsoever he shall hear, that shall he speak: and he will show you things to come" (John 16:12-13).

Remember, Jesus told the disciples that the Holy Spirit was *with* them now, but later would be *in* them? He told them He had many things to say to them that they could not bear, or grasp, now, but when the Spirit of truth came, He would open all things to their understanding. Without the Holy Spirit living in their spirits to reveal the truth to the disciples, even Jesus could teach them no more.

They were limited in their ability to understand spiritual things.

He was telling them now that when the Holy Spirit came there would be no limit to spiritual knowledge. He said the Holy Spirit would show them all things that the Father has— even things to come.

Now can you see the limitless knowledge and understanding available to Spirit-filled believers? The Holy Spirit has been given to teach you how to be a success in this life. In the light of these truths from the Word of God, it is unthinkable for anyone to refuse God's offer of His Spirit.

I Will Send Him Unto You

"Nevertheless I tell you the truth; It is expedient for you that I go away: for if I go not away, the Comforter will not come unto you; but if I depart, I will send him unto you" (John 16:7). Jesus has personally sent the Holy Spirit to you. He arrived in the fullness of His ministry on the Day of Pentecost and is still here.

"And, behold, I send the promise of my Father upon you: but tarry ye in the city of Jerusalem, until ye be endued with power from on high" (Luke 24:49). Jesus told His disciples to wait until they were furnished with power. When you made Jesus Lord, you became His disciple, and you should not do another thing until you are endued with the same power that was in and upon Him.

Jesus said, "I will pray the Father, and he shall give you another Comforter, that he may abide with you for ever" (John 14:16).

On the Day of Pentecost, Peter told the people, "This Jesus hath God raised up, whereof we all are witnesses. Therefore being by the right hand of God exalted, and having received of the Father the promise of the Holy Ghost, he hath shed forth this, which ye now see and hear.... For the promise is unto you, and to your children, and to all that are afar off, even as many as the Lord our God shall call" (Acts 2:32-33, 39).

This promise of receiving the Holy Spirit is to all. It is to you and your children. God has already given the Holy Spirit to the Body of Christ. You, as a member of the Body, must individually receive what He has already given. He has been sent to endue you with power. You don't have to be a weak Christian. Provision of power has been made for you.

If there has ever been a day when believers need the power of God manifest in their lives, it is today. Don't try to get by on your own strength any longer. Set your faith to receive this enduement of power without delay.

You can have hands laid on you by a believer or by someone in the ministry, or you can receive in your own place of prayer alone with God.

Study the following scriptures about receiving the Holy Spirit so that you will believe and act in line with God's Word.

Be Filled With the Spirit

Ephesians 5:18 simply says, "...be filled with the Spirit." Since you know that the Bible is God speaking to you and the Word of God is the will of God, then it is God's will for you to receive the Baptism in the Holy Spirit!

And I say unto you, Ask, and it shall be given you; seek, and ye shall find; knock, and it shall be opened unto you. For every one that asketh receiveth; and he that seeketh findeth; and to him that knocketh it shall be opened. If a son shall ask bread of any of you that is a father, will he give him a stone? or if he ask a fish, will he for fish give him a serpent? Or if he shall ask an egg, will he offer him a scorpion? If ye then, being evil, know how to give good gifts unto your children: how much more shall your heavenly Father give the Holy Spirit to them that ask him? (Luke 11:9-13).

First, we see that you, as a son, are to ask the Father for the Holy Spirit. Even though He has already been given to the Church, you are inviting Him to come upon you and endue you with power. Ask for the Baptism in the Holy Spirit.

We are told that if we ask, we will receive. The Word assures you that you will receive the good gift—the Holy Spirit—and not a counterfeit. Therefore, ask expectantly and without fear, knowing that your Father gives only good gifts to His children. Jesus said ask and you would receive the Holy Spirit.

Let's look at more instances where believers received the Holy Spirit:

And they were all filled with the Holy Ghost, and began to speak with other tongues, as the Spirit gave them utterance (Acts 2:4).

While Peter yet spake these words, the Holy Ghost fell on all them which heard the word. And they of the circumcision which believed were astonished, as many as came with Peter, because that on the Gentiles also was poured out the gift of the Holy Ghost. For they heard them speak with tongues, and magnify God...(Acts 10:44-46).

And when Paul had laid his hands upon them, the Holy Ghost came on them; and they spake with tongues, and prophesied (Acts 19:6).

In each account of believers receiving the Holy Spirit, they began to speak with other tongues. Nowhere in the New Testament does it say the Holy Spirit does the speaking. The believer speaks as the Holy Spirit gives him utterance.

You supply the sounds as the Holy Spirit supplies the words. These words will be unknown to you. The Scripture teaches that in the spirit we speak mysteries to God. "For he that speaketh in an unknown tongue speaketh not unto men, but unto God: for no man understandeth him; howbeit in the spirit he speaketh mysteries.... He that speaketh in an unknown tongue edifieth himself; but he that prophesieth edifieth the church" (1 Corinthians 14:2, 4). You are not speaking to man but to God.

One translation says we speak divine secrets. You can pray beyond your natural knowledge when you pray in other tongues.

So too the [Holy] Spirit comes to our aid and bears us up in our weakness; for we do not know what prayer to offer nor how to offer it worthily as we ought, but the Spirit Himself goes to meet our supplication and pleads in our behalf with unspeakable yearnings and groanings too deep for utterance. And He Who searches the hearts of men knows what is in the mind of the [Holy] Spirit [what His intent is], because

the Spirit intercedes and pleads [before God] in behalf of the
saints according to and in harmony with God's will (Romans
8:26-27, *The Amplified Bible*).

The Holy Spirit comes to our aid to help us in prayer when we
don't know how to pray as we ought to and gives us utterance in
other tongues, praying the perfect will of God. We need this help.
So much of the time we know so little. We may only see a symptom
of a much deeper problem, but the Holy Spirit goes right to the root
and prays the perfect will of God for us in each situation.

Look at Jude 20, *The Amplified Bible:* "But you, beloved, build
yourselves up [founded] on your most holy faith [make progress,
rise like an edifice higher and higher], praying in the Holy Spirit."
Praying in tongues edifies you. It builds you up or charges you as you
would charge a battery.

I am so grateful to be able to pray in the spirit by the Holy Spirit.
This will be a great blessing to you, too. After you receive your prayer
language, pray in the spirit every day. This helps your spirit to be
strong and to keep rule over your life.

First Corinthians 14:14 says, "For if I pray in an unknown
tongue, my spirit prayeth, but my understanding is unfruitful." *The
Amplified Bible* says, "...my spirit [by the Holy Spirit within me]
prays." The Holy Spirit gives your spirit the prayer or praise. Your
voice is giving sound to this spiritual language.

The Amplified Bible says that Cornelius and his household
spoke in unknown languages, extolling and magnifying God.
Extol means "to praise enthusiastically."

When you receive the indwelling of the Holy Spirit, your spirit
will immediately have a desire to express itself in praise to God.
How could you help but pour forth praise after having the Holy
Spirit, who proceeds directly from the Father God, come upon you
in power? Your well begins to overflow and rivers are the result!
(John 4:14, 7:37-39).

There may be no unusual feeling physically. Spiritual blessings are received by faith—not by sight or feeling. Your lips may flutter and your tongue feel thick, or you may hear supernatural words forming down inside your being. Or none of the above may be evident.

The lips and tongue are the organs we use to form words. Your physical instruments of speech—lips, tongue, vocal cords—must cooperate with your spirit to give sound to prayer or praise that the Holy Spirit has given. Immediately upon receiving, spiritual language is ready for you to speak.

Remember, you have nothing to fear. God has already said you would receive the real thing. Isaiah 57:19 tells us that God created the fruit of the lips. Do not be concerned with what it sounds like to you. God will perfect your praise. Matthew 21:16 says, "...Out of the mouth of babes and sucklings thou hast perfected praise."

Mark 16:17 says, "And these signs shall follow them that believe... they shall speak with new tongues." Jesus said that the believer would speak with new tongues. You are a believer.

When you pray in tongues, you are praying in the spirit. Just as your native language, such as English, is the voice of your mind, praying in tongues is the voice of your spirit. Therefore, after you ask, speak no more in your native language. You cannot speak two languages at once.

Expect the Holy Spirit to come on you just as He came on the believers on the Day of Pentecost, then at Samaria, Cornelius' home and at Ephesus. You will begin to speak with other tongues as the Spirit gives *you* the words.

Ask and Receive!

Lord Jesus, I come to You in faith to receive the Baptism in the Holy Spirit. I ask You to fill me to overflowing with the Holy Spirit—the same enduement of power that happened on the Day of Pentecost. Cause rivers of living water to flow out of me as I give utterance to my spiritual language. I receive now in Your Name. (Now begin to speak in tongues in praise and adoration as the Spirit gives you words.)

Rely on Your Comforter

Jesus called the Holy Spirit the Comforter (John 14:16). The word used for *comforter* means "counselor, helper, intercessor, advocate, strengthener, standby." Learn to rely on the Holy Spirit in all these areas of His ministry. He is the Great Enabler!

Jesus said the Holy Spirit is given to teach you, not just some things, but *all* the truth.

"Ye are of God, little children, and have overcome them: because greater is he that is in you, than he that is in the world" (1 John 4:4). Meditate on this verse and confess it with your lips until your spirit sings with its reality.

There is One on the inside to guide you who knows everything from beginning to end.

Rely on His guidance and direction in every decision. Expect His power to aid you in everyday life as well as in crisis. He is more powerful than the enemy. Satan is no match for Him.

This Great One has been instructed to lead you into all the truth. He will lead, so be quick to follow. He will not only tell you what to do, but will also help you to do it. He will empower you.

The Spirit who created the universe now dwells in you. Allow your mind to grasp what your spirit is telling you. Remember, this Great One lives in you!

"But ye shall receive power, after that the Holy Ghost is come upon you…" (Acts 1:8). Something wonderful has happened to you today. Power! Power! Power! You have been endued with God's power and ability! "And ye shall be witnesses unto me…." Dare to believe for this truth and power to be displayed in your life and you will be a witness to men that JESUS IS ALIVE!

As you read the next chapter, allow the Holy Spirit, the Great Teacher who now lives in you, to teach you the truth of who you are in Christ Jesus. He will reveal what the Word has to say about your inheritance in the kingdom. You have been delivered out of the power of darkness and translated into the kingdom of God's dear Son (Colossians 1:13). This Great One, the God of the universe, has given you His righteousness and made you a king and a priest—a joint heir with Jesus!

chapter 3

NOW ARE WE
IN
CHRIST JESUS

by Kenneth Copeland

Now Are We in Christ Jesus

I...cease not to give thanks for you, making mention of you in my prayers; that the God of our Lord Jesus Christ, the Father of glory, may give unto you the spirit of wisdom and revelation in the knowledge of him: the eyes of your understanding being enlightened; that ye may know what is the hope of his calling, and what the riches of the glory of his inheritance in the saints.... For we are his workmanship, created in Christ Jesus unto good works, which God hath before ordained that we should walk in them. Wherefore remember, that ye being in time past Gentiles in the flesh, who are called Uncircumcision by that which is called the Circumcision in the flesh made by hands; that at that time ye were without Christ, being aliens from the commonwealth of Israel, and strangers from the covenants of promise, having no hope, and without God in the world: But now in Christ Jesus ye who sometimes were far off are made nigh by the blood of Christ (Ephesians 1:15-18, 2:10-13).

When you made Jesus the Lord of your life, something happened to you. You were re-created in Him. You were given an inheritance. Now, you are in Christ Jesus. You are born of God.

In the physical realm, you weren't created, you were born of your mother. But in the spiritual realm, when you were "born of God," you were re-created by Him. A change took place. You were *re*born. The Bible says in 2 Corinthians 5:17 that you became a new creature—a new creation. "Therefore if any man be in Christ, he is a new creature: old things are passed away; behold, all things are become new." One translation says that any man who is in Christ Jesus is "a new species of being that never existed before."

When you accepted Jesus as your Lord, an actual creation took place. The old man—your unregenerated spirit man—was replaced by a new man, created in Christ Jesus. Old things passed away and all things became new. The new birth that took place in you was done by the creative power of God. It took place inside you—in your spirit.

The "creation" that occurs at the new birth is the same type of "creation" that took place in Genesis 1. The word translated *created* in Genesis 1:1 gives the impression that before God brought heaven and earth into existence, there was nothing like it anywhere else. The same is true with the "new creation in Christ Jesus." You are a "new species of being that never existed before."

Being in Christ

You are a unique individual. There has never been, and never will be, another person just like you. When you received Jesus as Lord, God brought you into existence by His creative power. You were born of the Spirit of God. A seed was sown in your heart—the incorruptible seed of God's Word—and you were placed *in Christ Jesus.*

You need to know and understand the reality of being in Christ. It is an outstanding revelation from God's Word that will affect your thinking, your believing, your actions and your speech.

Ephesians 2:13 says, "But now in Christ Jesus ye who sometimes were far off are made nigh by the blood of Christ." When? *Now.* When are you in Christ Jesus? The moment you make Jesus your Lord.

Who is in Christ Jesus? Ephesians 1:10 says, "That in the dispensation of the fulness of times he might gather together in one all things in Christ, both which are in heaven, and which are on earth; even in him." So it's not just those who have died and gone to heaven who are in Christ Jesus, but also believers who are here on earth.

Notice, this scripture says, "…all things *in Christ,* both which are in heaven, and which are on earth; even *in him.*" Verse 13 says, *"In whom* ye also trusted, after that ye heard the word of truth, the gospel of your salvation: *in whom* also after that ye believed, ye were sealed with that holy Spirit of promise."

The most effective way I have found to develop the reality of being in Christ is to begin with the book of Romans and search through all the letters of the New Testament for the phrase, "in Christ." For example, as we have read in 2 Corinthians 5:17, "Therefore if any man be *in Christ,* he is a new creature." Scriptures that refer to being "in Christ," "in Him" or "in whom" occur 134 times in the Bible. Find those scriptures and read them carefully. Study them and run cross-references on them. You can be sure that whatever the Word says about being "in Christ," belongs to you because you are in Christ Jesus.

Being in Christ means that you are "the saved." Why? Because you have confessed with your mouth that Jesus is Lord and have believed in your heart that God raised Him from the dead (Romans 10:9).

Being in Christ means that you are "the healed." Why? Because Jesus went to the cross, bore the curse of the Law, and broke the power of sickness and disease. He was made sick with your sickness; but He didn't stay sick. Today, He is healed; and because you are in Him, you are healed, too!

Being in Christ means you are "the delivered." Why? Because Colossians 1:13 says God has delivered you from the power of darkness and has translated you into the kingdom of His dear Son. Jesus said He was sent to preach deliverance to the captives (Luke 4:18).

All the power it takes to save any human being, to heal any human being, to deliver any human being, came into this earth on the Day of Pentecost. When Jesus walked into a place, the power was there to heal the people. Why? Because the power was in Him. He said, "The Father that dwelleth in me, he doeth the works" (John 14:10). Now, that power is in you because you are in Him. Because you are in Christ Jesus, you can live like Him, talk like Him and act like Him. The Word of God will change you—spirit, soul and body.

The Bible says that God sent Jesus that He might become the firstborn of many brethren (Romans 8:29). God planted the seed of His Son, Jesus, in order to get a harvest, and He reaps that harvest as new souls are added to the kingdom of God. The hundredfold principle is now in operation.

You are called a joint heir with Christ Jesus. The Word says that when you made Jesus your Lord, you became one spirit with Him. God sees you in Jesus. He not only came inside you, but you went inside Him. We have preached that Jesus comes inside a person, but we have thought very little about the fact that we have entered into Him. You are the Body of Christ. Jesus said, "If ye abide in me, and my words abide in you, ye shall ask what ye will, and it shall be done unto you" (John 15:7). You are abiding in Him.

Ephesians 1:4 says, "According as he hath chosen us in him before the foundation of the world, that we should be holy and without blame before him in love."

You are holy and without blame before Him in love. Jesus provided for God to be your own heavenly Father. You are no longer without hope and without God in the world (Ephesians 2:12). You have been accepted in the beloved (Ephesians 1:6). The letter Paul wrote to the Ephesians was also written to you because you are in Christ Jesus. It's a letter from God to you saying, "I have accepted you in My Son. You are in the Beloved. You are Mine."

Have you ever heard the phrase: "But I'm so unworthy"? That was true before you got saved. You were not worthy to receive what Jesus did for you. But He did it anyway! Because He died for you, you can live in Him. He *made* you worthy. You have been created in Christ Jesus and there is nothing unworthy in Him. You are not worthy because of anything *you* did, but because of Jesus and what He did for you.

Some people say, "Brother, I know we're in Christ Jesus, but I just can't stand up and say that I'm healed. I don't deserve to be healed." None of us deserve it in ourselves, but God knew that. If you have sin in your life, get it out. If you can't receive healing from God because of the way you have been living, quit living that way! Repent and get rid of it! The Word says that God is faithful and just to forgive us of our sins when we confess them (1 John 1:9). When you confess the sin, He will forgive you. Don't rebel against God. Don't run *from* God when you sin, run *to* Him! If you have to rebel, then rebel against the devil, not God. The Bible says, "Awake to righteousness, and sin not" (1 Corinthians 15:34).

As a born-again believer, sin has no dominion over you. It can't dominate you. It has to leave you. Satan is a defeated foe—he is not your god. James 4:7 says if you resist him, he will flee from you.

You need to see yourself "in Christ" and know the reality of it. If you ask some people today, "Are you a son of God?" they'll say, "Who, me? Certainly not!" When you ask, "Are you saved?" they'll say, "Oh yes, thank God, I'm just an old sinner, saved by grace." No, you are not! You *were* a sinner; you got saved by grace! You can't be both at the same time. You are a new creation in Christ Jesus. You have been born into the kingdom of His love. As far as God is concerned, you are holy, blameless and beyond reproach. So quit thinking, speaking and acting like the world. Let go of all those religious "sin tags." Begin confessing that you are the righteousness of God in Christ.

Your Inheritance

What does it mean to obtain an inheritance? Acts 20:32 says, "And now, brethren, I commend you to God, and to the word of his grace, which is able to build you up, and to give you an inheritance among all them which are sanctified." The Word will build you up and give you your inheritance.

Ephesians 1:11 says, "In whom also we have obtained an inheritance, being predestinated according to the purpose of him who worketh all things after the counsel of his own will." This doesn't say you are going to obtain your inheritance. It says you have already obtained it. This verse of scripture is past tense. You *have obtained* an inheritance. You *have been accepted* in the beloved. Part of your inheritance includes your family position with God in heaven after you lay down your body, but you have entered into your inheritance in Him right now here on this earth. You have the right to operate in that inheritance today.

Colossians 1:12 says, "Giving thanks unto the Father, which hath made us meet to be partakers of the inheritance of the saints in light." The word *meet* is an Old English word that means "able." God has made you able to be a partaker of the inheritance of the saints in light. Verses 13-14 say, "Who hath delivered us from the power of darkness, and hath translated us into the kingdom of his dear Son: in whom we have redemption through his blood." You are "the redeemed." Jesus has made you able to be a partaker of that inheritance. It's yours! You are able to receive it and walk in it because God has said you are able. A literal translation of verse 12 is: "Who has made us able to enjoy our share of the inheritance." You are to give thanks to the Father, who has made you able to enjoy your share of the inheritance. So thank God for it! Praise and thanksgiving to the Father play a big part in receiving your inheritance.

What did you inherit in Him? Did you just inherit heaven as your home? No. Hebrews 1:4 says, "Being made so much better than the angels, as he hath by inheritance obtained a more excellent name than they." You have inherited Jesus' Name as well as His authority. You have inherited the kingdom of God. Colossians 2:9-10 says, "For in him dwelleth all the fulness of the Godhead bodily. And ye are complete in him, which is the head of all principality and power." There is embodied in you all that is in the Godhead—Jesus, the Spirit of God, the heavenly Father, the mind of Christ, the faith of God, the love of God. You have in you the very life of God, because you are in Christ Jesus.

Everything Jesus received when He was raised from the dead and everything that has happened to Him since then is yours— not just part of it, all of it!

When Jesus was raised from the dead, He received a glorified body. You will get one, too.

Where did Jesus go when He was raised? To the right hand of the Father. That's where you are now! Ephesians 2:6 says, "And hath raised us up together, and made us sit together in heavenly places in Christ Jesus." Jesus was raised from the dead by the mighty power of God and was seated at God's own right hand in the heavenly places. That same mighty power of God worked in you when you made Jesus the Lord of your life, raising you up and seating you in heavenly places in Christ Jesus.

He is in you and you are in Him. *His inheritance and your inheritance are one and the same.* You are a joint heir with Him.

The Apostle Paul prayed that the eyes of our understanding would be enlightened to know the glory of our inheritance in the saints and the exceeding greatness of God's power toward us who believe (Ephesians 1:18-19).

The exceeding greatness of His power. What does His power mean to the believer? Let's read on in Ephesians 1:20-23:

> Which he wrought in Christ, when he raised him from the dead, and set him at his own right hand in the heavenly places, far above all principality, and power, and might, and dominion, and every name that is named, not only in this world, but also in that which is to come: and hath put all things under his feet, and gave him to be head over all things to the church, which is his body, the fulness of him that filleth all in all.

The Body of Christ is "the fullness of Him." He is not full and complete without you and you are not full and complete without Him.

Colossians 1:21-23 says, "And you…hath he reconciled in the body of his flesh through death, to present you holy and unblameable and unreproveable in his sight: If ye continue in the faith grounded and settled, and be not moved away from the hope of the gospel, which ye have heard." Don't be moved away from the gospel. Don't be moved away from the things the Word is telling you. Don't think: *That couldn't be for me.* Don't allow the devil or anyone else to move you away from the inheritance that rightfully belongs to you in Christ Jesus. When the Word says you are holy, unblamable and unreprovable in the sight of God, then receive it.

We see from God's Word that *in Him* you are holy and without blame before God. Philippians 2:15 says, "That ye may be blameless and harmless, the sons of God, without rebuke, in the midst of a crooked and perverse nation, among whom ye shine as lights in the world." We shine as lights. Where? *In the world.*

You are in the Body of Christ here on earth. If you are in His Body, then you are in Him. You are His workmanship, created in Christ Jesus. In the eyes of God you are holy and blameless, beyond reproach and without rebuke. You, as a believer, are to hold forth the Word of life in the midst of a crooked and perverse generation.

If you have a working revelation of your redemption in Christ Jesus, there is not one prayer that needs to go unanswered nor any need that has to go unmet. When you see that your inheritance contains a complete redemption from the curse of the Law, you will want to close the door to Satan and to the things of this world. You are redeemed from the curse, so don't allow it to operate in your affairs.

Isaiah 54:17 says, "No weapon that is formed against thee shall prosper; and every tongue that shall rise against thee in judgment thou shalt condemn. This is the heritage of the servants of the Lord, and their righteousness is of me, saith the Lord." You need to see yourself in Him, the way the Word says you are.

John said, "Beloved, now are we the sons of God" (1 John 3:2). When? *Now!* Paul wrote in Galatians 4:7, "Wherefore thou art no more a servant, but a son; and if a son, then an heir of God through Christ."

God's Word has the power to give you an inheritance. Ephesians 1:3 says, "Blessed be the God and Father of our Lord Jesus Christ, who hath blessed us with all spiritual blessings in heavenly places in Christ." God has already unleashed in your life all the blessings heaven has to offer. They are already yours! But He won't force them on you. You have to accept your inheritance in Christ Jesus and allow it to be a part of your life before you will be able to walk in it.

Living in Righteousness

Therefore if any man be in Christ, he is a new creature: old things are passed away; behold, all things are become new. And all things are of God, who hath reconciled us to himself by Jesus Christ, and hath given to us the ministry of reconciliation; to wit [or to know], that God was in Christ, reconciling the world unto himself, not imputing their trespasses unto them; and hath committed unto us the word of reconciliation.... For he [God] hath made him [Jesus] to be sin for

us, who knew no sin; that we might be made the righteousness of
God in him (2 Corinthians 5:17-21).

When you become a new creature, your spirit is completely re-created.
Old things are passed away, all things become new, and all things are of
God. You need to realize that you are not a spiritual schizophrenic—half
God and half Satan—you are all God. The problem area is not in your
spirit but in your mind and body. It is every believer's responsibility to
renew his mind with God's Word, and then use that Word to control his
body. Look at Ephesians 4:20-24:

But ye have not so learned Christ; if so be that ye have heard him,
and have been taught by him, as the truth is in Jesus: that ye put off
concerning the former conversation the old man, which is corrupt
according to the deceitful lusts; and be renewed in the spirit of your
mind; and that ye put on the new man, which after God is created
in righteousness and true holiness.

In Paul's letter to the Ephesian church, he explained that they had
been delivered from their sinful flesh and re-created in righteousness.
It was now their responsibility, as an act of their will, to put on
the new man in Christ and stop the works of the flesh. The same
principle applies to you and me as believers today. We have been re-
created by God in the spirit, but we must take the Word of God and
use it to renew our minds and control our flesh.

Just knowing that you have been made the righteousness of God in
Christ is not enough. You need to have a full understanding of what
righteousness is and what it means to you as an individual believer.
Many sincere Christians are living far below their privileges in
Christ simply because they do not understand their place as a child
of God. Righteousness is one of the most vital areas in the Christian
walk. Without a knowledge of righteousness, you will never obtain
all that is yours in God.

The word translated *righteousness* literally means "to be in right-standing." When a person receives Jesus as Lord of his life, he is made righteous. By being brought into right-standing with God, every believer is given certain privileges or rights as God's child.

Some people confuse righteousness with holiness, but righteousness has nothing to do with the way you act. Holiness is your conduct; righteousness is what you are—the nature of God. You didn't come into right-standing with God by being good or acting right. It was faith in Jesus Christ and His redemptive work at Calvary that brought you into right-standing with God.

Your position in the Body of Christ can be compared to the position of a citizen of the United States. An American citizen has certain rights outlined in the Constitution called "The Bill of Rights." Had the American forefathers been using Old English terminology, they would have called it, "the Bill of Righteousness." As long as you are obedient to the laws of the land, you are a citizen in right-standing with the United States government.

The same principles apply to you as a child of God. Being a believer (being in Christ Jesus) makes you a citizen of the kingdom of God and entitles you to everything in that kingdom. The Bible is your spiritual "bill of righteousness," outlining all the rights and privileges available to you. Whether or not you partake of your rights is another matter. Ignorance will rob you of the abundant life that is freely available to you.

The best illustration of this is the story of the man who saved for years to be able to buy a boat ticket to America. Once he had saved enough, he bought his ticket and boarded the ship. Since he didn't have any money left for food, he brought along some crackers and cheese. Every evening at mealtime, he would look into the dining room at the other passengers enjoying their food, then he would return to his cabin and eat his crackers and cheese. The day the ship docked in New York harbor, a steward came to him and said, "Sir, have we offended you in any way? I noticed that you didn't eat any of your meals in our dining room." The man answered, "Oh, no! You see, I didn't have enough money for meals so I ate in my room." Then the steward said, "But sir, your meals were included in the ticket!"

As Christians, we have an abundance of privileges available to us. They were bought and paid for by Jesus at Calvary. But if we don't know it, how can we take advantage of them?

In Ephesians 6:10-17, the Apostle Paul is describing the armor of God. *One of the most important pieces of this armor is the breastplate of righteousness.* A breastplate covers the vital parts of a soldier's body. Your right-standing with God acts as that breastplate. It covers the vital part of a Christian's identity—his right to the authority provided for him in Jesus Christ. You need to put on your breastplate of righteousness and wear it victoriously. It will bring the force of righteousness into operation on your behalf.

One of your rights in the kingdom is answered prayer. According to 1 Peter 3:12, "The eyes of the Lord are over the righteous, and his ears are open unto their prayers." James 5:16 says, "The effectual fervent prayer of a righteous man availeth much." When you pray in faith, you have a right to expect your heavenly Father to answer.

Developing what I call a "righteousness consciousness" will cause you to live an overcoming, victorious life. Jesus was in right-standing with the Father during His earthwalk and the results He obtained were outstanding. As a child of God and with Jesus, you should expect to receive the same results. Jesus Himself said, "He that believeth on me, the works that I do shall he do also; and greater works than these shall he do; because I go unto my Father" (John 14:12).

Spend time in God's Word and find out for yourself what rights you have. When you do, righteousness will become an active, powerful force in your life.

Standing in a Position of Authority

One of the hardest things for people to understand and receive is living from a position of authority.

When you made Jesus the Lord of your life, Colossians 1:13 says you were delivered from the power of darkness. The word *power* is literally translated *authority*. You have been delivered from the power, or authority, of darkness and placed into God's kingdom. The kingdom of God includes both heaven and earth. Jesus said, "All power is given unto me in heaven and in earth. Go ye therefore" (Matthew 28:18-19). That power was given to you as part of your inheritance in Christ Jesus. You have entered into this position of authority because you are in Him.

The Word says that righteousness has come upon all men (Romans 5:18). You may ask, "Then why don't all men become righteous?" Because in order to receive it, you have to act on righteousness from the position of authority.

On November 2, 1962, I used my authority as a human being and made a choice. I made the decision to receive Jesus as Lord of my life. At that moment, the righteousness that had been upon me came inside me. I was *made* the righteousness of God in Christ. Second Corinthians 5:21 says, "He hath made him to be sin for us, who knew no sin; that we might be made the righteousness of God in him."

Because you have made Jesus your Lord, the new birth is now a reality in your spirit. You have been made the righteousness of God in Him. God wants to treat you like that. He wants to treat you as if you had never sinned. He sent Jesus to the cross to bear your sin, to completely wash away the sin that had been in you. Because you are in Jesus, God sees you the same way He sees Jesus. He wants to treat you like He treats Jesus—so let Him!

God's power is in His Word. He is upholding all things by the word of His power (Hebrews 1:3). You need to learn to minister and walk from a position of authority. In His earthwalk, Jesus said such things as, "Be thou made whole. Take up your bed and walk." Then to a lame man Peter said in Acts 3:6, "In the name of Jesus Christ of Nazareth rise up and walk." He, too, ministered and spoke from a position of authority.

It's time for you as a believer to begin to act that way. You have obtained an inheritance, and in that inheritance you have been given all authority.

The God of the universe lives inside you! He lives and walks in you. Become God-inside-minded and you will begin to walk in this point of authority.

Keep right on building yourself up in your inheritance. You live in a world that is full of evil influences. Satan wants to see to it that you forget the reality of being born again. When you see in the Word who you are in Christ Jesus, then confess it with all of your heart. Then you will be strong, standing in a point of authority and operating in your inheritance in Him.

Let This Mind Be in You

Philippians 2:5-6 says, "Let this mind be in you, which was also in Christ Jesus: who, being in the form of God, thought it not robbery to be equal with God." You are to think the way Jesus thought. He didn't think it robbery to be equal with God.

Then verse 8 says, "He humbled himself, and became obedient unto death, even the death of the cross." You have to humble yourself. No one else can humble you. You are to humble yourself under the mighty hand of God, and at the same time, keep in mind that you are a joint heir with Jesus (1 Peter 5:6; Romans 8:17).

Kings and Priests

According to Romans 8:29, Jesus is "the firstborn among many brethren." Glory to God! Jesus is no longer the only begotten Son of God. Revelation 1:5-6 describes Jesus as "the prince of the kings of the earth. Unto him that loved us, and washed us from our sins in his own blood, and hath made us kings and priests unto God and his Father; to him be glory and dominion for ever and ever." You have been made a king and a priest unto God because of Jesus and the inheritance that He provided for you.

From the book of Acts to the Revelation of John, Jesus is known as *the first begotten from the dead*. If there is a firstborn, then there has to be a second born, a third born, a fourth born, etc. Every believer is counted as a child of God. We are members of God's family and heirs to all He has.

Jesus has made you a king and a priest. He has made you the righteousness of God in Him. In Him, you are *the accepted*. In Him, you are *the beloved*. You are His chosen and His elect—a royal priesthood that has been bought with His blood and made His own child.

First John 4:17 says, "Herein is our love made perfect, that we may have boldness in the day of judgment: because as he is, so are we in this world." As He is, so are you in this world! Because you have accepted the sacrifice of Jesus at Calvary and received Him as your Lord, you have the power and the authority to walk in the inheritance that He made available to you. But if you don't know what is yours and what belongs to you, you won't be able to enjoy the benefits of it. Find out what is included in your inheritance in Christ Jesus and then resist any influence that would try to convince you otherwise.

Luke 12:31-32 says, "Seek ye the kingdom of God; and all these things shall be added unto you. Fear not, little flock; for it is your Father's good pleasure to give you the kingdom"—the whole kingdom! When the reality gets down in your heart that you are an heir of Almighty God, that He has given you the whole kingdom and has instructed you to seek first that kingdom, then all the benefits of your inheritance will be added to you and you will grow and develop in God's Word.

However, you will never receive any portion of your inheritance until you begin to acknowledge it. With your thoughts, your words and your actions, you acknowledge the fact that you are in Christ Jesus, that you have received an inheritance, that you have the right to walk in all the blessings and promises of God's Word. Acknowledge the things of God and allow the assurance of them to enter into your heart. Then see them become a part of your life in every area.

How have you been approaching God...on the level of a king or a beggar? Are you backing your way into the presence of God, hoping to get a handout?

When you made Jesus your Lord, He made you able to stand in the presence of the Father God as a king and a priest, not as a beggar—as the righteousness of God in Christ, not as a sinner. You have been redeemed out of the kingdom of darkness and translated into the kingdom of God's dear Son. You have been redeemed into kingship and priesthood. You are a king and a priest in Christ Jesus!

You are welcome in the throne room of Almighty God as if you had never sinned—made righteous by the redeeming blood of Jesus. The righteousness that is yours is a mighty force reserved for the sons of God, washed in His blood. Your right-standing gives you boldness and thoroughly equips you to handle every situation that comes your way. You have His ability and His strength to face anything the devil brings against you.

In the next chapter, discover your covenant rights and allow this force of righteousness to change your life!

chapter **4**

THE FORCE
OF
RIGHTEOUSNESS

by Kenneth Copeland

The Force of Righteousness

Therefore if any man be in Christ, he is a new creature: old things are passed away; behold, all things are become new. And all things are of God, who hath reconciled us to himself by Jesus Christ, and hath given to us the ministry of reconciliation; to wit, that God was in Christ, reconciling the world unto himself, not imputing their trespasses unto them; and hath committed unto us the word of reconciliation. Now then we are ambassadors for Christ, as though God did beseech you by us: we pray you in Christ's stead, be ye reconciled to God. For he hath made him to be sin for us, who knew no sin; that we might be made the righteousness of God in him (2 Corinthians 5:17-21).

Any person who is in Christ is a new creature—a new creation. He has been completely re-created. Old things are passed away, all things are new, and all things are of God—not part of God and part of Satan. Some people think a man is a schizophrenic when he becomes a Christian—that he has both the nature of God and the nature of Satan. But this is not so.

In the new birth, a man's spirit is completely reborn. It is then his responsibility to renew his mind to the Word of God and use the Word to take control of his body.

Paul wrote to the believers in Rome, who were born-again, Spirit-filled Christians, instructing them to renew their minds with the Word (Romans 12:1-2). Their faith was known throughout the world, but they had still not learned how to control their minds and bodies with the Word. He wrote to the church at Ephesus along the same lines saying, "You have put off the old man and put on the new man, so quit lying and cheating and acting ugly toward one another" (Colossians 3:9-13). All these people were believers. They had been re-created—made the righteousness of God—but most of them didn't know it!

Second Corinthians 5:21 tells us that God made Jesus, who knew no sin, to be sin for us "that we might be made the righteousness of God in him." As believers in Jesus Christ, we are the righteousness of God Himself!

What is *righteousness?* It is not a "goody-goody" way of acting or something that can be attained. Righteousness is a free gift from God, through His grace, provided by Jesus at Calvary. Now I am not referring to our own righteousness—the Bible says that in the eyes of God "all our righteousnesses are as filthy rags" (Isaiah 64:6). However, we have been given the righteousness of God in Jesus Christ.

Through our traditional thinking, we have confused *righteousness* with *holiness.* We think righteousness is the way you act, but this is not true. Holiness is your conduct. Righteousness is what you are— the nature of God.

Let me make this clearer. The word translated *righteousness* literally means "in right-standing." We have been put in right-standing with God. Jesus is the mediator between God and man.

When a man accepts Jesus, he is moved into a position of new birth. He enters into the kingdom of God as God's very own child and a joint heir with Jesus Christ. Consequently, there are certain privileges, rights, and freedoms that he has as a child of God because he is in right-standing with Him.

Accepted in the Beloved

We didn't get in right-standing with God by being good and acting right. We got there through faith in Jesus Christ and His redemptive work at Calvary. When we accepted the sacrifice of Jesus and made Him the Lord of our lives, then God accepted us. He had to! You see, God had already accepted Jesus' work on the cross. He judged it as good, glorified Jesus, and set Him at His own right hand in the heavenlies. He called Jesus "God" and inaugurated Him into the highest office in the whole universe. Therefore, the Father is obligated to accept us when we accept Jesus. Our conduct has absolutely nothing to do with it!

Let's look at 2 Corinthians 5:19 again: "To wit [or to know], that God was in Christ, reconciling the world unto himself, *not imputing their trespasses unto them....*" In other words, God does not hold our sins and trespasses against us. Very rarely has this whole gospel been preached—only pieces of it!

We have heard that God will not forgive a sinner until he confesses his sin, but this is not true. God has already provided forgiveness and is not holding our trespasses against us. This teaching about confession stems from 1 John 1:9. "If we confess our sins, he is faithful and just to forgive us...." However, this letter was written to Christians to teach them how to maintain their fellowship with God.

In 1 John 2:1 the Apostle John wrote, "My little children, these things write I unto you, that ye sin not. And if any man sin, we have an advocate with the Father, Jesus Christ the righteous: And he is the propitiation for *our* sins: and not for ours only, but also for the sins of the whole world."

John was referring to the sins of a Christian, instructing his fellow believers to partake of Jesus' advocate ministry. John 3:16 says, "For God so loved *the world,* that he gave his only begotten Son...." God loved us and Jesus gave Himself for us *while we were in sin.* God is not holding our trespasses against us. He is calling us to make Jesus our Lord, accepting us on the basis of Jesus' right-standing with Him and, in turn, putting us in right-standing with Him. The only sin then, keeping anyone out of the kingdom of God, is the sin of rejecting Jesus and what He has provided (John 16:9).

As a believer, you are a citizen of the kingdom of God and have a right to everything in the kingdom. There is a covenant between Jesus and God, signed in the blood of the Lamb (Jesus), which provides these rights for you. If Jesus is your Lord, then you are in right-standing with God—you have the righteousness of God (whether or not you partake of it). You have a right to everything God has. This is staggering to the human mind, but nevertheless, it is true. Jesus said, "Fear not, little flock; for it is your Father's good pleasure to give you the kingdom" (Luke 12:32).

Sin Consciousness

"For the law having a shadow of good things to come, and not the very image of the things, can never with those sacrifices which they offered year by year continually make the comers thereunto perfect" (Hebrews 10:1). Under Levitical Law, an animal had to be offered every 12 months to atone for the sins of the people. The word *atone* means "to cover." Actually, this word is not found in the Greek New Testament when it refers to Jesus' sacrifice.

The word we translate *atonement* really means "to remit," or to do away with. These sacrifices could not completely do away with sin, they simply covered it for a year. The blood of Jesus did not just cover sin, it remitted sin—it did away with sin completely!

With these thoughts in mind, let's read verse two. "For then would they not have ceased to be offered? because that the worshippers once purged should have had no more conscience of sins." If the blood of calves and goats had cleansed them of sin, they would have had no more sin consciousness.

Sin consciousness produces defeat and a false sense of humility. It attempts to be humble by debasing itself and pushing itself back. The Lord did not say, "Debase yourself." He said, "Think of others more highly than you think of yourself." This means even when you are standing tall as the righteousness of God, you should elevate your fellow Christian above yourself, making both of you stand tall. When you debase yourself, you make yourself lower than you are.

If you asked many Christians, "Are you righteous?" they would say,

"Me? No!" They are trying to be humble. They are afraid God wouldn't like it if they said they were righteous. Actually, they are speaking from the way they feel—from the way they have been trained—from ignorance of the Word of God concerning righteousness.

This kind of sin consciousness has caused us to focus on and preach sin, instead of righteousness. Actually, we have preached a form of condemnation on ourselves, and Romans 8:1 says, "There is therefore now no condemnation to them which are in Christ Jesus." We have carried "sin tags" with us that are stumbling blocks in the growth of a Christian.

Every time we start toward the righteousness of God, Satan will jump up in our path and say, "Remember the ugly things you've done? Don't expect God to forget all that! Who do you think you are? You're too unworthy to approach God!" But the Word says the blood of Jesus purged our sins—they no longer exist. So we should take the Name of Jesus and drive out this sin consciousness.

What do I mean by a "sin tag"? A good example is, "Well, I'm just an old sinner saved by grace." No, you *were* an old sinner—you got saved by grace! Now you are a born-again child of God!

Almost everyone is familiar with this scripture: "For all have sinned, and come short of the glory of God" (Romans 3:23). This scripture has been used untold numbers of times to preach sin. But the Apostle Paul, writing this letter to the body of believers in Rome, was instructing them about righteousness. Let's read this whole portion of scripture:

> But now the righteousness of God without the law is manifested, being witnessed by the law and the prophets; even the righteousness of God which is by faith of Jesus Christ unto all and upon all them that believe: for there is no difference: for all have sinned, and come short of the glory of God; being justified freely by his grace through the redemption that is in Christ Jesus: whom God hath set forth to be a propitiation through faith in his blood, to declare his

righteousness for the remission of sins that are past, through the forbearance of God; to declare, I say, at this time his righteousness: that he might be just, and the justifier of him which believeth in Jesus (Romans 3:21-26).

This is one sentence, constructed around the righteousness of God. Through sin consciousness, we have taken out one phrase—the only verse not referring to righteousness—and preached it with no mention of the other verses. Therefore, everyone knows about sin, but not many know about the righteousness of God. We are well aware of what we have been born out of, but have no idea what we have been born into! Colossians 1:12-13 says, "Giving thanks unto the Father...who hath delivered us from the power of darkness, and hath translated us into the kingdom of his dear Son."

Faith in Your Righteousness

You are a born-again child of the living God. It's time you began believing in the new birth and what Jesus has provided for you. Realize that the Father has invited you to come boldly (confidently, without fear) to the throne of grace with your needs and requests. The Bible says that when we pray according to His will, we know He hears us and we know we have the petitions we desired of Him (1 John 5:14-15).

When we pray in the Name of Jesus, we immediately get the ear of God. First Peter 3:12 says, "For the eyes of the Lord are over the righteous, and his ears are open unto their prayers." James wrote that "the effectual fervent prayer of a righteous man availeth much" (James 5:16).

The following is an example of prayer from this righteousness consciousness:

Father, I see in Your Word that I have been made the righteousness of God in Christ Jesus. He has provided certain rights for me, and healing is one of these rights. I receive it now in Jesus' Name, and I thank You for it. Your Word also says that You are faithful and just to forgive me of my sins when I confess them, so I take this opportunity to confess this sin and get it out of my life, in order to maintain my complete fellowship with You. I receive Your forgiveness now in the Name of Jesus. I may not feel righteous. I may not feel forgiven. But Your Word says it, so it must be true. Satan, I now put on the breastplate of righteousness and come against you with the sword of the Spirit. Healing belongs to me. My body belongs to the God of this universe. I have given my body to Him, so in the Name of Jesus Christ of Nazareth, take your sickness and disease and get out!

You have a *right* to expect your heavenly Father to answer. You have not prayed in your own name, but in the Name of Jesus. His righteousness (right-standing with God) is yours! A righteousness consciousness expects God's Word to be true and plans for success.

This kind of prayer is tough in the world of the spirit and will bring results in the physical world. After you have prayed to God and taken authority over Satan, you should take authority over your physical body. Speak to it in the Name of Jesus and command it to conform to the Word of God that says it is healed by the stripes of Jesus. I have done this and had my body to shape up immediately.

You see, *the world of the spirit controls the world of the natural.*

A Spirit created all matter. His name is Almighty God, and He is our Father! So His righteousness is now ours!

Folks, it is time to believe the Word of God. Did you know that there is no longer a sin problem? Jesus solved it! He stopped the law of sin and death at the Cross and Resurrection. When a person receives salvation, he is put into right-standing with God and re-created by the Spirit of God as if sin had *never* existed! The only problem we have is the sinner problem. It is man's choice. All we need to do is choose righteousness and walk away from the sin problem.

It is time to move in line with this revelation. You *were* a sinner—you *have been* forgiven. You are now His workmanship, created in Christ Jesus! Begin to stand on this, instead of your past life. As far as God is concerned, your past life is forgotten, Now *you* need to forget it.

Your past life died the death of the Cross. In Galatians 2:20, the Apostle Paul said it this way: "I am crucified with Christ: nevertheless I live; yet not I, but Christ liveth in me...." As I was studying the Word one day, I noticed 2 Corinthians 7:2 where the Apostle Paul was writing to the church at Corinth and said, "Receive us; we have wronged no man, we have corrupted no man, we have defrauded no man." When I read this, it startled me, and I said, "Lord, I've caught this man in a lie! I know he wronged and defrauded men. He persecuted the Christians, putting them in prison for no legal reason. He stood by and watched as Stephen was stoned to death!" But the Spirit of God spoke to my heart strongly and said, *You watch who you call a liar! The man you are talking about died on the road to Damascus!*

You see, the Apostle Paul could write to the church at Corinth with a clear conscience, and complete freedom of spirit saying, "We have wronged no man...we have defrauded no man." Paul realized the power of the gospel to raise him up when he was dead in trespasses and sins. He accepted the fact that he was a new creation in Christ Jesus—that his old spirit was dead and gone—that his past sins were forgiven and forgotten. Paul was born of God, and the power and force of righteousness was at work in his life.

Conformity With God

We have discussed the fact that Jesus was aware of His rights—His righteousness—with God. He relied on it completely during His earthly ministry and ministered freely. He did what the Father told Him to do. This is the key to the mystery: The Father was in Jesus and Jesus was in the Father—*they are One.* Jesus' will conformed completely to the will of God. They walked together and worked together in total harmony. This is how believers are to live with God—not His will *de*forming ours nor our will bucking against His, but both wills conformed to each other.

Conformity with God is a much higher form of life than just merely being in submission to Him. When you conform to God's will and do His work, you will reach a point where you will lean entirely on your right-standing with Him. Then you, like Jesus, will not hesitate to lay hands on the sick and expect God to heal them. You will freely exercise your rights in the kingdom of God as His child and as a joint heir with Jesus.

God sees you through the blood of the Lamb—the same as He sees Jesus. This is almost more than the human mind can conceive, but it's true! I will prove it to you from the prayers of Jesus Himself. Jesus knew how to pray, and if anyone on earth could get his prayers answered, Jesus could. Therefore, it would be to our advantage to examine some of the things He prayed.

In John 17:20-21, Jesus is praying to God at a vital time in His earthly ministry. It is just moments before Calvary, and He says, "Neither pray I for these alone [His disciples], but for them also which shall believe on me through their word...." This includes you and me because each of us received Jesus, either directly or indirectly, through the words of one or more of these men.

So Jesus, referring to us, prays, "That they all may be one; *as thou, Father, art in me, and I in thee.*" This is the example we are to follow in being one with each other, in conforming to one another and in conforming to Jesus. We are to be one with the Father as Jesus was one with Him. First Corinthians 6:17 says, "But he that is joined unto the Lord is one spirit." Another translation says, "He who is joined to the Lord is one spirit with Him" *(New King James Version)*.

The Holy Spirit, the life force of God, lives in the heart of a believer. We get our life from Him. As Jesus taught in John 15:5, He is the vine and we are the branches. Praise the Lord!

When you begin to operate in these things, acting on the righteousness that Jesus has given you, you will then realize that many of the differences that have separated the Body of Christ for years are actually foolish and unimportant. We have bickered and fought with one another over the most ridiculous issues.

Jesus goes on in John 17:23 and prays to the Father to show them "...that You have loved them [even] as You have loved Me" *(The Amplified Bible)*. God loves you *as much* as He loves Jesus! He sees you as equal with Jesus—there is no difference in His eyes. Begin to see yourself as God sees you and take advantage of His free gift of righteousness. Your right-standing with Him was bought with a high price...don't take it lightly. The Father's heart was hungry for a family, and Jesus freely gave Himself for this desire. What a love act!

The Gift of Righteousness

For if by one man's offence death reigned by one; much more they which receive abundance of grace and of the gift of right-eousness shall reign in life by one, Jesus Christ.... For as by one man's disobedience many were made sinners, so by the obedience of one shall many be made righteous (Romans 5:17, 19).

Here again, we have heard it preached, "There is none righteous, no, not one...." This scripture is found in Romans 3, but you must read the whole book. In the first three chapters of Romans, the Apostle Paul, by the Holy Ghost, writes a serious indictment against man in his natural state—that there is none righteous—which is absolute truth!

But as we have previously discussed, Paul explains that our righteousness does not come through the Law or through our conduct. It comes only through faith in Jesus Christ and is "unto all and upon all them that believe."

We have read in Romans 5:17 that because of one man's offense— Adam's treason—death reigned in the world. Satan became the lord over mankind and everything man did was in response to fear—of death, of accident, of failure.

Do you know of anyone who has lived two or three hundred years because there wasn't enough death to go around? Of course not! There is an abundance of death in the world, but this scripture goes on to say, "*Much more* they which receive *abundance of grace* and of the *gift of righteousness* shall reign in life by one, Jesus Christ." Praise God!

Jesus bought the free gift of righteousness, which was *much more* alive, *much more* real, and *much more* abundant than death. The fear of death is dispelled by life in Jesus Christ. As the Apostle Paul said, "O death, where is thy sting?" (1 Corinthians 15:55). The force of righteousness completely overcomes the power of sin and death like a bonfire overcomes a drop of water. We have more power over our lives as the righteousness of God in Jesus Christ than Satan had over us while we were in sin.

Romans 5:17, *The Amplified Bible* says, "Much more surely will those who receive [God's] overflowing grace (unmerited favor) and the free gift of righteousness...*reign as kings in life* through the one Man Jesus Christ (The Messiah, the Anointed One)." When you make Jesus the Lord of your life, you receive the abundance of grace and the gift of righteousness to enable you to reign in life as a king! You will be in a position to reign over your life and the circumstances surrounding you the same way a king reigns over his kingdom.

The believer must learn to lean and depend on his free gift of righteousness. This is one of the first things I found out from the

Word of God. Satan told me I didn't have any right to be healed. He said I didn't have any right to receive the infilling of the Holy Spirit and that I certainly didn't have the right to minister to the needs of other people. Well, if I happened to feel a little sinful at the time, then I would agree with him.

Actually, I didn't realize Satan was telling me all those things. I thought they were my own ideas. Then I saw in the Word that I had a right to healing, the Baptism in the Holy Spirit and to minister to the needs of others simply because Jesus gave me the right. I saw that I had been made the righteousness of God.

Do you realize what "being made the righteousness of God" really means? You have to think about it to see the full reality there. The child, or the heir, of a king has the same rights as the king himself because he is part of the king. He is born of the king and, consequently, has the same legal privileges. As the Apostle Paul wrote, even though the heir may be just a child and is still being tutored, he is nevertheless king of the land and has the authority to rule.

When you were born again, the Bible says you became bone of His bone. You have rights and privileges because you have been born of the Spirit of God. God has been reproduced on the inside of you! These rights are yours because Jesus of Nazareth paid the price for the sin problem and caused you to be reborn.

Adam was born of God. If you read Genesis, you will see that God created his body and then breathed into it the breath of life (Genesis 2:7). It was completely lifeless until God gave it life by breathing into it. Adam's life came from the inside of God, and essentially the same thing occurs in the new birth. You were dead in sins and trespasses until God re-created your spirit and gave you His life. When you accepted the sacrifice of Jesus, the Spirit of God hovered over your body and a new spirit-life that had never existed before was birthed inside you.

When you discover who you are in Jesus, your entire existence— your health, your financial life, your social life—will take on new meaning. The storms of life will be stopped as you exert pressure on them with the Word of God and the power of the Holy Spirit dwelling within you. You are to reign as a king under your Lord and Savior, Jesus Christ of Nazareth! Hallelujah!

God sees you this way. He expects you to take your rightful place and live this kind of life above the beggarly elements of the world. As a believer, He has given you the power and strength of the Holy Spirit as your comforter and Jesus Christ as your Lord and high priest to change nations and governments around the world. Begin to take the New Testament seriously. Begin to believe it and put your total trust and confidence in it. Lean hard on the righteousness that God has freely given you. You will then realize that all things are possible to you as a believer. You will say, "Without Him I can do nothing, but thank God, I have Him, and I can do all things through Christ which strengthens me" (Philippians 4:13). Your testimony will then be one of power and strength as your life is molded by the Holy Spirit.

As a born-again child of God, you are to be a superman in the eyes of the world, holding forth the word of life! When you cross the rough spots, you won't knuckle under—you'll stand tall and triumph over them. You will walk hand in hand with Jesus through the storms of life and come out victoriously!

God does not put these storms and rough spots before you—He takes you through them and delivers you from them. Satan throws these things at you to stop you from acting on the Word and exercising your righteousness in Jesus Christ. He knows these are dangerous spiritual weapons in the hands of a believer, so he is constantly trying to stop their effectiveness.

Become Righteousness-Minded

Paul said in 1 Corinthians 15:34, "Awake to righteousness, and sin not." *Awake to righteousness*. Become aware that you have been made the righteousness of God in Jesus Christ, that you have been placed in right-standing with Him through the sacrifice of Jesus at Calvary. When you do, it will stop the sin in your life. As long as Satan can convince you that you don't have any right to the things of God, he can keep you under his thumb and sin will control your life. But when you awake to righteousness, you will realize that Satan is a defeated foe and the struggle is over.

*Awake to righteousness…*become righteousness-minded! You have been thoroughly equipped to handle every situation that comes your way. You are to reign in life as a king by Jesus Christ, living in conformity with the Father. Almighty God, creator of the universe, chose to come down on your level in the form of Jesus Christ, to dwell in your heart by the Holy Spirit, and to give you His righteousness, His ability, and His strength…"greater is he that is in you, than he that is in the world" (1 John 4:4). Praise God!

Ephesians 3:20 says He is "able to do exceeding abundantly above all that we ask or think, *according to the power that worketh in us.*"

When I fully understood the significance of this scripture, I began to have some confidence in the ministry of the Holy Spirit in my life. In fact, the Lord spoke to my heart one day and said, *How much confidence are you placing in the God within you?* At that time, I had no confidence in Him whatsoever! I was praying, and *hoping* God would do something, obviously with no results. Then I grasped the reality of the indwelling of the Holy Spirit of God.

Jesus said that when the Spirit of Truth came, He would reveal the things of God to us (John 16:13-15). God, through the Holy Spirit, began to reveal to my heart the deep truths of the new birth, of the righteousness of God in Jesus Christ. He revealed the power of the Holy Spirit—God's muscle, God's mind, God's everything—and showed me how this part of the Godhead was living inside every born-again, Spirit-filled believer! These truths then became deeply rooted in my spirit, and I began to become righteousness-minded.

How do you become righteousness-minded? Romans 8:5 says,

"For they that are after the flesh do mind the things of the flesh." We have occupied ourselves much of the time with fleshly things. Proverbs 4:20 instructs us to attend to the Word of God. In the past we have not done this. We have thought *sickness* instead of *healing...weakness* instead of *strength...trouble* instead of *victory...poverty* instead of *prosperity...sin* instead of *righteousness*. We have attended to these other things, almost completely ignoring the power of the Word of God to deliver us from the flesh.

Hebrews 5:13 tells us, "For every one that useth milk is unskilful in the *word of righteousness:* for he is a babe." He doesn't know how to use the Bible—how to believe it or how to fight Satan with it. Verse 14 says, "But strong meat belongeth to them that are of full age, even those who by reason of use have their senses exercised to discern both good and evil."

Only by feeding on the Word will we grow and be able to overcome the things of the flesh and function in line with God. I can speak from experience here because I was overweight and hooked on cigarettes. For several years, I fought against my body with little success. But when I grew in the Word of God and began to walk in the spirit, I no longer fulfilled the lusts of the flesh. When I learned that I could control my physical body, my weight came down to normal and the smoking habit was broken!

Success in Righteousness

A person who thinks *righteousness* instead of *sin* is valuable to God, to himself, and to the people around him. He will always be there when you need him. This is not true of the sin-minded, defeat-minded Christian. There is a very deceitful area here that most people have fallen into at some time in their lives without realizing it. I have heard this many times and have been guilty of saying it myself: "Well, we're praying about this situation, and if the doors are open, then it's God's will for us to go. But if they're not, then it must not be God's will."

Folks, if an "open door" is evidence of the will of God, then the Apostle Paul was never in God's will! He faced obstacles and barriers throughout his ministry, but he took the Word of God and knocked the doors open in order to get the job done! Even when he was thrown in prison, he prayed his way out. He did his job despite the obstacles.

Sin consciousness will look for a way *out* of a situation: "We might not have enough money to go...I might not be able to take off work." But a righteousness consciousness always finds a way *in*. When I was preaching in Jamaica, there was a man who had quit a good job in order to attend our meetings and hear the Word. He would walk six miles twice each day just to be in the meetings, and when I questioned him about it, he said, "Brother Copeland, I fasted and prayed for a year that God would send someone to teach us the Word, and I'm not going to miss out on any of it! With what I'm learning about faith from the Word, I can get a better job!"

You see, this man was looking for a way in! He wanted more of the things of God. He knew that Jesus had said, "But seek ye first the kingdom of God, and his righteousness; and all these things shall be added unto you" (Matthew 6:33).

Another area in which many people have been deceived, is in "putting out a fleece." The person who uses a fleece is depending on a *physical* sign of God's will in a situation, and if he's not watchful, *he'll get fleeced.*

Now Gideon used a fleece, but let's analyze his situation for a moment. In the first place, Gideon was not a reborn man. Consequently, he was forced to rely on physical evidence. He had no knowledge of God whatsoever because his entire family was following Baal. Second, there was no prophet in the land to give him the Word of God, and in those days the prophet was the only source of revelation knowledge. Third, Gideon was dealing with an angel—something completely foreign to him. Therefore, in his position, he had no choice but to put out a fleece—get a physical sign showing him what to do.

As believers, you and I are not in Gideon's position. We have been born again and are led by the Spirit of God. We have access to the Holy Spirit and the written Word of God to use as a guide in finding God's will for our lives. If you don't know what to do in a particular situation, go to the Word of God, spend some time in prayer, meditate in the Word, and the Lord will begin to lead you. He said, "My sheep hear my voice" (John 10:27).

You will know what to do by the leadership of the Holy Spirit. We don't have to depend on a sign from the natural, physical world to lead us. We are not blind. We have spiritual eyes, and we are to use them. Also, when you put out a fleece in the natural world, you give Satan a chance to foul up the operation since the physical world is his field of operation.

Here is a three-step formula that will cause success in every area of your life. Nothing can stop it. Every Christian endeavor, no matter what it is, will succeed when it is backed with this kind of prayer and dedication because God is behind it.

> 1. *Find the will of God in your situation by prayer and meditation in the Word.*
>
> 2. *Once you have found the will of God, confer no longer with flesh and blood.* Don't ask other people what to do. I may discuss a situation with my wife or my staff, but once we have prayed and I know the will of God, then it doesn't matter what they think or say about it.
>
> 3. *Get your job done at all costs.* Don't allow anything or anyone to stand in the way of God's will.

To live in this kind of successful life, the believer must come to the realization that he has complete access to the ministry of Jesus. Jesus said in John 16:13-15, "Howbeit when he, the Spirit of truth, is come…he shall receive of mine, and shall show it unto you. All things that the Father hath are mine: therefore said I, that he shall take of mine, and shall show it unto you." What a statement! This is almost more than the human mind can comprehend.

The Spirit of God has been sent into an earthly ministry just as legal and real as Jesus' earthly ministry. Jesus came *to provide* the way for us, and the Holy Spirit has come *to teach* us the way. Jesus came to fulfill the Abrahamic Covenant. The Holy Spirit has come to see that the Christian covenant is fulfilled.

The Spirit of God did not take the place of Jesus—He is God the Holy Spirit, and He is fulfilling His own ministry as God the Father directed Him.

The Word of God and the Name of Jesus have taken Jesus' place here on earth. He said, "As long as I am in the world, I am the light of the world" (John 9:5), and "Believe in the light, that ye may be the children of light" (John 12:36). As a new creation in Christ, you have the Name of Jesus, the Word of God, and the Spirit of God to enable you to stand and minister in the place of Jesus.

Benefits of Righteousness

As a believer, you have total access to the ministry of Jesus, the ministry of the Holy Spirit and to all the Father has. To receive from Him, all you have to do is go to His Word! The only reason we have been such easy targets for Satan is because we have not known our rights and privileges in Jesus Christ. Therefore, he could easily usurp authority over us. But the Bible says we have authority to tread on serpents and scorpions and over all the power of the enemy.

We must find out what the Word has to say about the things of life and walk in line with it. We must renew our minds and put the force of righteousness to work in our lives.

If you are led by what you see or how you feel, you will fail. When you lean on your righteousness in Jesus Christ, you'll know what belongs to you and you'll not lie down under sickness or any other attack of Satan. You will go to the Word concerning healing, receive it for yourself, and walk in it because it is the Word of your Father.

Almighty God is your very own Father! You are bone of His bone, spirit of His Spirit, a joint heir with Jesus Christ, and living in the kingdom of God. As you realize these things you become God-inside-minded. You no longer think of God as being a million miles away. He is residing inside you!

Righteousness then becomes a force in the life of a believer that undergirds his faith. The reality of righteousness enables a believer to do the impossible. Jesus approached the tomb of Lazarus and said, "Roll away the stone." He never wavered in His faith. Actually, throughout His entire ministry, He showed neither a lack of faith nor an abundance of faith. He simply knew who He was and took advantage of the authority that was His. You might say, "Yes, of course He did—He was the Son of God!" Well, who are you? Romans 8:14 says, "For as many as are led by the Spirit of God, they are the sons of God." I have heard it argued that we will not receive our rights as sons of God until we get to heaven. However, Philippians 2:15-16 says, "That ye may be blameless and harmless, the sons of God, without rebuke, in the midst of a crooked and perverse nation, among whom ye shine as lights in the world; holding forth the word of life." There is no crooked and perverse generation in heaven. The only crooked and perverse generation is here on earth where we are to be the sons of God and hold forth the Word.

We are told, "Let this mind be in you, which was also in Christ Jesus" (Philippians 2:5). Jesus never stopped to think whether He had enough faith. He merely acted according to His rights in the kingdom of God. He stepped to the mouth of Lazarus' tomb with a divine assurance, illustrating His awareness of His right-standing with God—His righteousness consciousness. Jesus revealed what righteousness really is.

Is it reasonable? No. Is it real? Yes, regardless of what the natural mind says, and it will work in the life of a Christian.

Look at the apostles after the Day of Pentecost. They had a right-standing relationship with God, and it was working in their lives. Peter stood and preached the Word, ministering boldly in the Name of Jesus. After all his failures, he realized that God loved him and that his past had been wiped away. He was filled with the Spirit of God and doing the things Joel had prophesied would be done.

The righteousness of God in Jesus Christ is the driving force behind our faith, causing us to triumph in His Name. Jesus triumphed over Satan in three areas. First, during His earthly ministry, He spoke to Satan and said, "It is written…," and Satan had to obey the Word of God. Second, at the cross and resurrection, Jesus stripped Satan of his power and took the keys of hell and death. However, the third and most important area of Jesus' triumph over Satan is His victory in the new birth. This is real victory! It was impossible in Satan's thinking for God to turn a man of sin into righteousness, give him the armor of God and enable him to triumph as Jesus did. This is victory of the highest order! Sin turned into *righteousness! Death* turned into *life!*

Righteousness triumphs in the face of Satan and the whole world. No devil in hell is big enough to stop it, and it is available to "whosoever will." All are the same in the eyes of God. All need the power of God in their lives. When they cry out to God in the Name of Jesus, He receives them with open arms, re-creates them, gives them His righteousness, and makes them virtual powerhouses of faith! It is happening today all over the world to people in all walks of life!

God sees the believer as *righteousness.* In 2 Corinthians 6:14 Paul wrote, "Be ye not unequally yoked together with unbelievers: for what fellowship hath righteousness with unrighteousness? and what communion hath light with darkness?" Here the Word refers to the believer as *righteousness* and *light* and to the unbelievers as *unrighteousness* and *darkness.* We are the light of the world. Praise God!

As believers, we have His righteousness. We are the crowning creation of God! A reborn man is the greatest creation in the universe! Man in his natural, sinful state was headed straight to hell. By all laws, he deserved to be condemned forever, but God intervened and legally changed the laws. He beat Satan at his own game, and life became ruler over death! Jesus became the Lord and the champion of our salvation, the bishop over our souls in the new birth. He gave us His righteousness—the ability to triumph in His Name—and we have peace with God. He who knew no sin, was made to be sin. He was made to be our sinfulness so that we could be made His righteousness. We have been made to sit with Him in heavenly places in Christ Jesus, victorious in Him! This is real victory! You don't just bow a subservient knee to God—you join your faith with His, giving Him the opportunity to do a miracle in your heart and turn you into the righteousness of Almighty God! You can then approach the throne of grace boldly, without a sense of fear or condemnation, and receive from your Father all that is yours as a new creation in Christ.

Because you are re-created in His righteousness, you are born of His love. God is love. First John 4:7-8 says, "Beloved, let us love one another: for love is of God; and every one that loveth is born of God, and knoweth God… for God is love." God, the Father of love, sent the Son of His love so you could become part of His great love family.

His love nature is in you, so He has commanded you to love others and go into all the world in the power of that love as His ambassador. Love is the answer to every problem because it never fails. God *has* faith, but He *is* love.

As you read the next chapter, remember that as a new creature, re-created in Him, you are a child of His love. Therefore love is the secret to your success!

chapter 5

LOVE—THE SECRET TO YOUR SUCCESS

by Gloria Copeland

Love—The Secret
to Your Success

Love. You hear a lot about it. But, the truth is, few people really know what love is.

For most, it's an emotional phantom that appears—then vanishes—without warning. Illusive. Undefinable. Forever sought but rarely found.

Even believers seem to be confused about it at times: But they don't need to be. The Word of God reveals clearly what love truly is.

Look at 2 John 6: "And what this love consists in is this: that we live and walk in accordance with and guided by His commandments (His orders, ordinances, precepts, teaching). This is the commandment, as you have heard from the beginning, that you continue to walk in love [guided by it and following it]" *(The Amplified Bible).*

Quite simply, God says love is keeping His commandments. That brings love out of the indefinite into something explicit. But God has done even more than define love for you. He's given you instructions so that you can know how to love as He loves. By giving you His Word, God has given you His love manual in black and white! All you have to do is follow it, and you'll be walking in love.

If you've made Jesus Christ the Lord of your life, you've already taken the first step of obedience. The love of God has been born within you. But unless you take action, that love will remain hidden within you. Love works in much the same way as the force of faith. Faith is born into you when you are begotten of God, but until you begin to act on God's Word, that powerful force lies dormant. The same thing is true concerning the love of God. You can have the love of God abiding within you and still be unable to allow that love to work through you to reach other people. Like faith, love becomes active through knowledge of the Word.

That's why the Apostle Paul wrote to the church at Philippi

saying, "And this I pray, that your love may abound yet more and more in knowledge and in all judgment" (Philippians 1:9).

The love of God is released in your life by acting on the knowledge of God's Word. Without revelation knowledge followed by action, love lies undeveloped and selfishness continues to reign supreme in you—even though you are a new creature.

"But whoso keepeth his word, in him verily is the love of God perfected: hereby know we that we are in him. He that saith he abideth in him ought himself also so to walk, even as he walked" (1 John 2:5-6).

As you act on God's Word, the love of God will be perfected in you. That's when love will begin to flow from you to others.

There is nothing—absolutely nothing—more important than learning to love. In fact, how accurately you perfect the love walk will determine how much of the perfect will of God you accomplish. That's because every other spiritual force derives its action from love. For example, the Bible teaches us that faith works by love. And answered prayer is almost impossible when a believer steps outside of love and refuses to forgive or is in strife with his brother.

In the beginning of the love chapter, 1 Corinthians 13, the Word says that tongues is just noise if there is no love. If a person has the gift of prophecy, understands all knowledge, and has enough faith to move mountains, without love he is nothing. If he gives all that he has to the poor and even sacrifices his life, without the love of God he gains nothing.

Without love, your giving will not work. Tongues and prophecy will not work. Faith fails and knowledge is unfruitful. All the truths you have learned from God's Word work by love. They will profit you little unless you live the love of God.

First Corinthians 13:4-8 paints a perfect picture of how love behaves:

Love endures long and is patient and kind; love never is envious nor boils over with jealousy, is not boastful or vainglorious, does not display itself haughtily. It is not conceited (arrogant and inflated with pride); it is not rude (unmannerly) and does not act unbecomingly. Love (God's love in us) does not insist on its own rights or its own way, for it is not self-seeking; it is not touchy or fretful or resentful; it takes no account of the evil done to it [it pays no attention to a suffered wrong]. It does not rejoice at injustice and unrighteousness, but rejoices when right and truth prevail. Love bears up under anything and everything that comes, is ever ready to believe the best of every person, its hopes are fadeless under all circumstances, and it endures everything [without weakening]. Love never fails [never fades out or becomes obsolete or comes to an end] *(The Amplified Bible).*

That may sound like a tough set of requirements—but you can meet them. You are a love creature. God has re-created your spirit in the image of love. And He has sent His love Spirit to live in you and teach you how to love as He loves. You *can* live the love life!

Become love conscious by confessing and acting on God's Word concerning this love. As you meditate on these scriptures, see yourself living the love life.

You are the one who must make the decision to perfect the love of God in your life. No one else can do it for you. So, make the decision in faith and commit yourself to obey God's Word about love.

Let me warn you, though. There will be times when you would rather do anything than allow love to rule. (It will seem as though it is taking off a pound of flesh!) There will be times when it would be much easier to go ahead and get mad, to seek your own and retaliate.

Love is directly opposed to the senses. The senses have been trained to put themselves and their desires above anything else—to selfishly seek their own way. But love, the Word says, does not seek its own rights or its own way. And to walk in love, you must demand that your senses (flesh) be subject to the Word.

Without a definite decision, you will not continue in the love of God. So commit yourself to agape—God's love—now. And when temptation comes, you'll remember your decision and obey love.

Once you've made the decision, the most powerful thing you can do in perfecting the love walk is to continually confess that you are the love of God. Base your confession on 1 Corinthians 13:4-8. This God kind of love will begin to influence all you say and do. If someone says something unkind to you, love will say, "That's OK. I am not touchy, fretful or resentful. I take no account of that." And you go free!

Learn to believe in love. It is the most powerful force in the universe. Walk in love by faith in the Word. Walking in love is walking in the spirit. It is walking as Jesus walked.

Love never fails. Nothing works without it, and there can be no failure with it. When you live by love, you cannot fail.

It takes faith to believe that love's way will not fail. The natural mind cannot understand that because the natural man and his world are ruled by selfishness. He believes if you don't look out for number one (himself), no one else will. And in a sense, he is right. No one else *can* look out for him. His selfishness shuts the door to the love of God, and he winds up on his own.

But when you practice love by faith and refuse to seek your own, you put the Father into action on your behalf. He will allow no man to do you wrong (1 Chronicles 16:22). As long as you stay in love, God the Father seeks your own. He sees to it that love never fails. Walking in love is to your great advantage!

Agape love is a new kind of power. It makes you the master of every situation. As long as you walk in love, you cannot be hurt and you cannot fail. No weapon that is formed against you will prosper. No one even has the power to hurt your feelings because you are not ruled by feelings but by God's love. You are loving as He loves.

E.W. Kenyon accurately tagged this agape love "a new kind of selfishness." You no longer seek your own success, yet your success is guaranteed!

This love is revolutionary. If we fully understood the great return from living God's love, we'd probably be competing with each other, each of us trying to love the other more. And without a doubt, everyone would emerge from that competition a winner! For love is truly the only sure secret to our success.

Prayer for Salvation and Baptism in the Holy Spirit

Heavenly Father, I come to You in the Name of Jesus. Your Word says, "Whosoever shall call on the name of the Lord shall be saved" (Acts 2:21). I am calling on You. I pray and ask Jesus to come into my heart and be Lord over my life according to Romans 10:9-10: "If thou shalt confess with thy mouth the Lord Jesus, and shalt believe in thine heart that God hath raised him from the dead, thou shalt be saved. For with the heart man believeth unto righteousness; and with the mouth confession is made unto salvation." I do that now. I confess that Jesus is Lord, and I believe in my heart that God raised Him from the dead.

I am now reborn! I am a Christian—a child of Almighty God! I am saved! You also said in Your Word, "If ye then, being evil, know how to give good gifts unto your children: HOW MUCH MORE shall your heavenly Father give the Holy Spirit to them that ask him?" (Luke 11:13). I'm also asking You to fill me with the Holy Spirit. Holy Spirit, rise up within me as I praise God. I fully expect to speak with other tongues as You give me the utterance (Acts 2:4). In Jesus' Name. Amen!

Begin to praise God for filling you with the Holy Spirit. Speak those words and syllables you receive—not in your own language, but the language given to you by the Holy Spirit. You have to use your own voice. God will not force you to speak. Don't be concerned with how it sounds. It is a heavenly language!

Continue with the blessing God has given you and pray in the spirit every day.

You are a born-again, Spirit-filled believer. You'll never be the same!

Find a good church that boldly preaches God's Word and obeys it. Become part of a church family who will love and care for you as you love and care for them.

We need to be connected to each other. It increases our strength in God. It's God's plan for us.

Make it a habit to watch the *Believer's Voice of Victory* television broadcast and become a doer of the Word, who is blessed in his doing (James 1:22-25).

About the Authors

Kenneth and Gloria Copeland are the best-selling authors of more than 60 books. They have also co-authored numerous books including *Family Promises* and *From Faith to Faith—A Daily Guide to Victory*. As founders of Kenneth Copeland Ministries in Fort Worth, Texas, Kenneth and Gloria are in their 43rd year of circling the globe with the uncompromised Word of God, preaching and teaching a lifestyle of victory for every Christian.

Their daily and Sunday *Believer's Voice of Victory* television broadcasts now air on more than 500 stations around the world, and their *Believer's Voice of Victory* magazine is distributed to more than 1 million believers worldwide. Their international prison ministry reaches an average of 60,000 new inmates every year and receives more than 17,000 pieces of correspondence each month. Their teaching materials can also be found on the World Wide Web. With offices and staff in the United States, Canada, England, Australia, South Africa and Ukraine, Kenneth and Gloria's teaching materials—books, magazines, audios and videos—have been translated into at least 22 languages to reach the world with the love of God.

Learn more about Kenneth Copeland Ministries
by visiting our website at **www.kcm.org**

Books Available From
Kenneth Copeland Ministries

by Kenneth Copeland

*   A Ceremony of Marriage
    A Matter of Choice
    Blessed to Be a Blessing
    Covenant of Blood
    Faith and Patience—The Power Twins
*   Freedom From Fear
    Giving and Receiving
    Honor—Walking in Honesty, Truth and Integrity
    How to Conquer Strife
    How to Discipline Your Flesh
    How to Receive Communion
    In Love There Is No Fear
    Know Your Enemy
    Living at the End of Time—A Time of Supernatural Increase
    Love Letters From Heaven
    Love Never Fails
*   Mercy—The Divine Rescue of the Human Race
*   Now Are We in Christ Jesus
    One Nation Under God (gift book with CD enclosed)
*   Our Covenant With God
    Partnership—Sharing the Vision, Sharing the Grace
*   Prayer—Your Foundation for Success
*   Prosperity: The Choice Is Yours
    Rumors of War
*   Sensitivity of Heart
*   Six Steps to Excellence in Ministry
*   Sorrow Not! Winning Over Grief and Sorrow
*   The Decision Is Yours
*   The Force of Faith
*   The Force of Righteousness
    The Image of God in You
    The Laws of Prosperity
    The Outpouring of the Spirit—The Result of Prayer
*   The Power of the Tongue
    The Power to Be Forever Free
*   The Winning Attitude
    Turn Your Hurts Into Harvests
    Walking in the Realm of the Miraculous

* Welcome to the Family
* You Are Healed!
  Your Right-Standing With God

by Gloria Copeland

* And Jesus Healed Them All
  Are You Listening?
  Are You Ready?
  Be a Vessel of Honor
  Blessed Beyond Measure
  Build Your Financial Foundation
  Connecting With God's Master Plan for Your Life (DVD/CD curriculum)
  Fight On!
  God Has Your Miracle on His Mind
  God's Master Plan for Your Life (New York Times best-seller)
  God's Prescription for Divine Health
  God's Success Formula
  God's Will for You
  God's Will for Your Healing
  God's Will Is Prosperity
* God's Will Is the Holy Spirit
  Go With the Flow
* Harvest of Health
* Hearing From Heaven
  Hidden Treasures
  Live Long, Finish Strong
  Living in Heaven's Blessings Now
  Looking for a Receiver
* Love—The Secret to Your Success
  No Deposit—No Return
  Pleasing the Father
  Pressing In—It's Worth It All
  Shine On!
  The Grace That Makes Us Holy
  The Power to Live a New Life
  The Protection of Angels
  There Is No High Like the Most High
  The Secret Place of God's Protection (gift book with CD enclosed)
  The Unbeatable Spirit of Faith
  This Same Jesus
  To Know Him
  True Prosperity
  Walk With God

*Available in Spanish

Well Worth the Wait
Words That Heal (gift book with CD enclosed)
Your Promise of Protection—The Power of the 91st Psalm

Books Co-Authored by Kenneth and Gloria Copeland

Family Promises
Healing Promises
Prosperity Promises
Protection Promises

* From Faith to Faith—A Daily Guide to Victory
From Faith to Faith—A Perpetual Calendar
He Did It All for You
LifeLine Series: Practical Tools for Everyday Needs
• Healing & Wellness: Your 10-Day Spiritual Action Plan
• Your 10-Day Spiritual Action Plan for Complete
   Financial Breakthrough
• Your 10-Day Spiritual Action Plan for Building
   Relationships That Last
One Word From God Can Change Your Life

One Word From God Series:
• One Word From God Can Change Your Destiny
• One Word From God Can Change Your Family
• One Word From God Can Change Your Finances
• One Word From God Can Change Your Formula for Success
• One Word From God Can Change Your Health
• One Word From God Can Change Your Nation
• One Word From God Can Change Your Prayer Life
• One Word From God Can Change Your Relationships

Load Up—A Youth Devotional
Over the Edge—A Youth Devotional
Pursuit of His Presence—A Daily Devotional
Pursuit of His Presence—A Perpetual Calendar
Raising Children Without Fear

Other Books Published by KCP

Hello. My Name Is God. by Jeremy Pearsons
John G. Lake—His Life, His Sermons, His Boldness of Faith
Protecting Your Family in Dangerous Times by Kellie Copeland Swisher
The Holiest of All by Andrew Murray

The New Testament in Modern Speech by Richard Francis Weymouth
The Rabbi From Burbank by Isidor Zwirn and Bob Owen
Unchained! by Mac Gober

Products Designed for Today's Children and Youth

And Jesus Healed Them All (confession book and CD gift package)
Baby Praise Board Book
Baby Praise Christmas Board Book
Noah's Ark Coloring Book
The Best of *Shout!* Adventure Comics
The *Shout!* Giant Flip Coloring Book
The *Shout!* Joke Book
The *Shout!* Super-Activity Book
Wichita Slim's Campfire Stories

*Commander Kellie and the Superkids*_{SM} Books:

Superkid Academy Children's Church Curriculum (DVD/CD curriculum)
- Volume 1—My Father Loves Me!
- Volume 2—The Fruit of the Spirit in You
- Volume 3—The Sweet Life
- Volume 4—Living in THE BLESSING

The SWORD Adventure Book
*Commander Kellie and the Superkids*_{SM}
   Solve-It-Yourself Mysteries
*Commander Kellie and the Superkids*_{SM} Adventure Series:
   Middle Grade Novels by Christopher P.N. Maselli:

#1 The Mysterious Presence
#2 The Quest for the Second Half
#3 Escape From Jungle Island
#4 In Pursuit of the Enemy
#5 Caged Rivalry
#6 Mystery of the Missing Junk
#7 Out of Breath
#8 The Year Mashela Stole Christmas
#9 False Identity
#10 The Runaway Mission
#11 The Knight-Time Rescue of Commander Kellie

*Available in Spanish

World Offices
Kenneth Copeland Ministries

For more information about KCM and our products,
please write to the office nearest you:

Kenneth Copeland Ministries
Fort Worth, TX 76192-0001

Kenneth Copeland
Locked Bag 2600
Mansfield Delivery Centre
QUEENSLAND 4122
AUSTRALIA

Kenneth Copeland
Post Office Box 15
BATH
BA1 3XN
U.K.

Kenneth Copeland
Private Bag X 909
FONTAINEBLEAU
2032
REPUBLIC OF
SOUTH AFRICA

Kenneth Copeland
PO Box 3111 STN LCD 1
Langley BC V3A 4R3
CANADA

Kenneth Copeland Ministries
Post Office Box 84
L'VIV 79000
UKRAINE

We're Here for You!

Believer's Voice of Victory Television Broadcast

Join Kenneth and Gloria Copeland and the *Believer's Voice of Victory* broadcasts Monday through Friday and on Sunday each week, and learn how faith in God's Word can take your life from ordinary to extraordinary. This teaching from God's Word is designed to get you where you want to be—*on top!*

You can catch the *Believer's Voice of Victory* broadcast on your local, cable or satellite channels.* Also available 24 hours on webcast at BVOV.TV.

 * Check your local listings for times and stations in your area.

Believer's Voice of Victory Magazine

Enjoy inspired teaching and encouragement from Kenneth and Gloria Copeland and guest ministers each month in the *Believer's Voice of Victory* magazine. Also included are real-life testimonies of God's miraculous power and divine intervention in the lives of people just like you!

It's more than just a magazine—it's a ministry.

To receive a FREE subscription to
Believer's Voice of Victory, write to:

Kenneth Copeland Ministries
Fort Worth, TX 76192-0001
Or call:
800-600-7395
(7 a.m.-5 p.m. CT)
Or visit our website at:
www.kcm.org

If you are writing from outside the U.S., please contact the KCM office nearest you. Addresses for all Kenneth Copeland Ministries offices are listed on the previous pages.